P9-DNV-881

A Complete

Guide

to Learning

and

Loving Jazz

New York

Printed in the United States of America. For information address: Hyperion, 77 W. 66th Street, New York, New York 10023-6298.

Library of Congress Cataloging-in-Publication Data

Szwed, John F.
Jazz 101 : a complete guide to learning and loving jazz / John Szwed.
p. cm.
Includes bibliographical references and index.
ISBN 0-7868-8496-7
1. Jazz—Analysis, appreciation.
MT146 .S94 2000
781.65—dc21 00-035055

Book design by Ruth Lee

FIRST EDITION

10 9 8 7 6 5 4 3 2 1

To

Robert G. O'Meally

Contents

Part 3

Part 4

Part 5

Preface

J*azz 101,* a basic book about jazz, but not a book for idiots or dummies. Jazz made simple, but not for simpletons. Better to think of it as an introductory book for an interested reader which takes a look back over the first century of the music. There's music history to be found here, tips on what to hear and read and see, and suggestions about how to think about this music and the ways in which it has shaped American and world culture. Though this is not a scholarly book, criticism of the conventional critical and historical approaches to jazz are found here, as well as discussion of alternative ways of thinking about key issues that have surfaced in recent years. But there are limits: not every important name in jazz appears here; the stylistic periods of the music are de-emphasized; jazz history is shown to be a bit less continuous and coherent than it is often claimed to be; and there are fewer definitions, flow charts, and summaries than one usually encounters in this sort of book. Partisanship and various forms of favoritism are also evident, both in the space given to some underdiscussed subjects and in the choices of recommended recordings. We are a long way from the sixteenth century when Giorgio Vasari could shamelessly declare his favorite artists' work as "divine" and get away with it. Nevertheless, no attempt has been made here to conceal personal enthusiasms.

That's the plan. But even the best-intentioned books that aim to summarize, condense, or introduce complex subjects, inevitably pass on received ideas that should have been challenged or give weight to opinions on issues that are far from settled. Maybe worse, such books take on an omniscient tone, and jazz is now far too complex for any one person to know it all. Apologies and claims made, therefore, and warnings and promises issued.

New York City
February 2000

Acknowledgments

Books such as this one rest on the lessons learned from countless people. My debt is to the musicians first and foremost, but also to the producers and the fans. Especially important to me on musicological matters were the writings of Max Harrison and Gunther Schuller. On history and discography, I learned from Dan Morgenstern. Joe McPhee and Anthony Braxton have been exemplary teachers on living the music. My students at Yale University deserve my thanks for putting up with my efforts to learn about this music along with them. I owe a great deal to Amiri Baraka, Gary Giddens, Francis Davis, Howard Mandel, and Greg Tate for offering wonderful examples of jazz writing. For what is readable in this book, much is owed to

Anne Cole, Adrian C. James, Erin Clermont, Rita Putnam, and David Yaffe. David Cashion first asked for this book, for which I remain eternally thankful. And as usual, my thanks to Sarah Lazin, Marilyn Sue Szwed, and Matthew Szwed.

PART 1

1 Introduction

Jazz has often been called America's only original art form, its classical music, the twentieth-century music par excellence. Yet despite such acclamation, the music typically receives only superficial and uninformed discussion from the popular media or even from most music scholars. Knowledge of jazz has always lagged behind the music's development, but in the last thirty or so years the gap has widened even more drastically. In part, this disparity is the consequence of a series of social and aesthetic factors that resulted in jazz undergoing changes experienced by no other music in so short a time: from its beginnings as an ethnic music it moved to the center of the culture, becoming *the* popular music of America, heard on every radio station and jukebox, only to next become avant-garde, a minority music once again, sustained by a mix of intellectuals, hipsters, and people from every part of the world, all this in less than half a century. Now, near the end of its first hundred years, jazz has splintered into many things for many people, an avant-garde or alternative music for some, a traditional music for others, its audience deepened if not widened. For most people today, jazz is seen as the music of Duke Ellington, Count Basie, Dizzy Gillespie, and Charlie Parker; in other words, as swing and bebop, music now well over fifty years old, played by artists no longer alive. Many seem unaware that there have been major changes over the last half century, or even that there are new, young players of a variety of styles developing apace. Over the last twenty years articles in the *New York Times* and *Newsweek* expressed astonishment on discovering that jazz musicians exist who are in their teens or early twenties. Similarly, when the sales manager of one of the nation's leading record chain stores was asked why classical and jazz records were being displayed together in the same section of his stores, he answered that "classical music is music played by old white men and jazz is music played by old black men."

But jazz did not stop developing in the 1950s. In fact, the music that followed was extraordinarily original and varied. By 1959 it was evident that there was a permanent shift in the air. The music of Ornette Coleman, Cecil Taylor, John Coltrane, and others had become the avant-garde, and as it turned out, the last acknowledged avant-garde music of the twentieth century. This is not to say that nothing new or different has happened since—quite the contrary. But it is still necessary to speak of much that has come since as "post-Coleman." In the 1960s jazz established its "new," which would stay new for years. At the same time, bebop moved to become the center of jazz, and swing underwent a late revival. It was the beginning of permanent diversity in jazz.

Throughout the 1960s there were continuous changes in jazz, especially in the form of musical mergers and alliances: links were made with folk, popular, and classical musics of all types, including those from beyond the West. New musical resources and techniques never called on before were put to use in jazz. And the musicians in parts of Europe, Africa, Japan, and Latin America saw in these American musical developments new possibilities for using their own native resources as the basis of a distinctive jazz or improvised music.

Right on the heels of this artistic fomentation, many jazz musicians of various persuasions began an intense reevaluation of the works of their predecessors. Avant-gardists like Muhal Richard Abrams and neo-traditionalists like Wynton Marsalis became proselytizers for access to the treasures of earlier jazz. It was a reminder that great periods of artistic achievement are often followed by great periods of criticism. But in this case, most of the critical reevaluation took place inside musicians' circles, since the influence of journalists and scholars had lost much of its force during the previous thirty years.

Jazz now finds itself caught between what critic Gary Giddins called the institutionalized classical music elite and the populist centrists: it is excluded on one side as merely "pop music" and on the other as being no longer popular; neglected because of its lack of pedigree and ignored commercially because it doesn't sell enough records. Despite the expansion of leisure and arts activities in recent years, radical shifts in taste and changes in the allocation and distribution of cultural resources have severely limited Americans' access to jazz. Jazz in nightclubs is now a rarity in any but a few of the nation's largest cities, and in any case, many of the new musical forms and styles are unsuitable for clubs, as they are, strictly speaking, no longer "entertainment." Radio stations that play jazz are similarly confined to the biggest cities and some college towns, and television is virtually closed to the music. It is quite possible to grow up in America now without ever having heard a musician play jazz. This is especially odd, given that the breadth and variety of jazz is now probably great enough that everyone could find some form of jazz to their liking.

Yet there is more to jazz than music, and it is there, paradoxically, that its influence is profound. Jazz is also a loosely connected set of ideas: it has a history and a tradition of thought, an imagery and a vocabulary that have given it reality and presence. It has its own hagiography, even if a rather democratic one, with its saints from time to time being voted in and out of beatification (Louis Armstrong, for example, who was up for years, then down, is now back on top again). And it has a mythic geography as finely detailed as those imagined by mythologists like Italo Calvino or Jorge Luis Borges: Just at the moment when classical music began to abandon programmatic composition under the influence of neoclassicism, jazz arrived, sprinkling its titles and lyrics with the street names, railroads, junctions, rivers, deltas, coasts, and cities that make up Jazz America. Soon whole countries and even continents also surfaced in this music through borrowed and imagined melodies and rhythms.

Jazz has been represented in a striking number of ways

and by a variety of means. "Jazz" (as we might now call this larger area of discussion) has outgrown its original means, moving beyond the music to become what some would call a discourse, a system of influences, a point at which a number of texts converge and where a number of symbolic codes are created. "Jazz" has a history of interaction with other art forms, its authority reaching far beyond the music through a variety of representations—on recordings, on film, in art, literature, advertising, clothing, speech, food and drink, even in other musics. The photographs of jazz musicians, for example, have recently become models of a lifestyle, popping up in chic ads or flavoring the walls of the apartments of hip characters in films; and ever since Louis Malle used Miles Davis for the 1958 soundtrack of *Ascenseur pour l'echafaud* (a.k.a. *Frantic*) jazz has been the music of choice for films noir. In short, the talk jazz generates is far greater than its audience, and now has a life of its own largely independent of the music.

Yet all of this should not seem that new. Since jazz was born under the sign of race, it is impossible to think of jazz apart from the history of African-American people, a history which is also the history of America, and a part of the psyche of every American. This idea of the universality of the black experience is a common theme in American literature, a subtext of writers like Mark Twain, Herman Melville, and William Faulkner. Other writers—such as W.E.B. Du Bois, those of the Harlem Renaissance, Norman Mailer—have told us that part of the power of this experience is its ability to be communicated without language through images of the body, music, and dance. In Europe in the late nineteenth and early twentieth centuries artists who sought an escape from industrialization and the rising middle class found an appeal in blackness. A literature developed that was ambivalent at best, slumming at worst, around writers like Arthur Rimbaud and Andre Gide, or artists like Picasso and Modigliani. The life and look of the black jazz musician offered a double attraction, that of the alienations of both artist and color. Whatever jazz might have been as an actual occupation, the jazz musician offered one of the first truly nonmechanical metaphors for the twentieth century. Not since the English Gentleman, with his modality of poise, authority, and how-one-should-be, has such an image dominated the world. Some abstraction or other of the lives of jazz performers and their followers now gives shape to the mores and moves of street people and media executives alike; it informs the muscles of professional dancers as well as the cadence and timing of stand-up comics; and it feeds the languages of fashion designers, basketball players, soldiers, and countless other characters of the American landscape. Now, whether one has heard of Charlie Parker or not, we inherit a notion of cool, an idea of well-etched individuality, a certain angle of descent.

Jazz was perhaps the first art to challenge the definition of high European culture as *the* culture, the first to challenge the cultural canon, the idea of the classics as "time-honored" and "serious." This challenge did not pass unnoticed. In 1917, the year the Original Dixieland Jazz Band of New Orleans made the first jazz recording, an article in the *New Orleans Picayune* disavowed the music, asserting that any music strong in rhythm and weak in harmonic and melodic content could only appeal to lower sensibilities. Eleven years later the *New York Times*, in assessing the state of American civilization, would list the "jazz mode of thought and action" along with lawlessness, boasting, intolerance, and jealousy on the deficit side of a literal ledger. Even jazz's defenders among the high arts found it vaguely threatening. When it first reached Paris during World War I, the response of the cognoscenti to jazz registered as shock: the music was not simply musical, they said—it was physical, visual, social, and emotional as well. And everyone noticed that this was a black music, even if it was sometimes played by whites.

Whether or not all this talk of jazz as metaphor and symbol is good for jazz the music is another question. Once the music is unsnapped from its origins and practice, and set free as a kind of discourse, "jazz" may have peculiar and unpredictable consequences. To paraphrase musician Don Byron, today everybody wants to dress jazz, drink jazz, talk jazz, even be jazz—but nobody wants to listen to jazz. He might have added that today everybody wants to study jazz. And why not? The hybrid, synthesizing, and combinatory nature of jazz has become an appealing model for modern culture, and shows no sign of fading as a paradigm for the new century. Jazz was postmodern before we knew what that was, shamelessly borrowing anything not fastened down, ignoring origins and cultural status; mocking hierarchies and pomposity, relishing contradiction and absurdity. High art was casually examined and remodeled by jazz musicians from the very beginnings (whether by Phil Specht and the Astor Orchestra's 1922 recording of a portion of *Lucia di Lammermoor,* John Kirby's energized "Beethoven Riffs On" of 1941, or Larry Clinton's 1956 "Bolero in Blue"—a 4/4 ballroom treatment of Ravel's "Bolero"), at the same time as they revised and updated folk, minstrel, and vaudeville songs (such as Tim Brymn's 1921 "Boll Weevil Blues," the Casa Loma Orchestra's "My Bonnie Lies Over the Ocean" of 1938, or Jimmie Lunceford's 1940 "I Ain't Gonna Study War No More").

At the end of its first century jazz is at a critical juncture, its borders shifting, its name coming loose from its moorings. Some might say that this first multicultural and postmodern art form has become a victim of its own success. Though the actual sale of jazz recordings suggests that it remains a minority art, its influence strangely seems to be growing. Jazz continues to define and give shape to American culture, even as it is becoming more popular elsewhere in the world.

Today there are some who urge that popularity should not be of concern, and that it is time that jazz be given respect by academics, concert halls, the media, and governmental agencies, something which is long overdue. In many respects, this is the way much of jazz has been headed for some time, or at least ever since critics and historians of the music began seeking redress for the slighting of the music, and began revising its history along the lines of that of European classical music—by developing a history based on a doctrine of progress, marking out its growth in terms of fixed stylistic periods, defining a tradition and a "classical" body of works, and enshrining it through the creation of the kind of repertory orchestras that play classical music in respectful surroundings. The beginnings of this revision lie in the 1950s, a period in which the rise of bebop led critics to treat it either as essentially different from other forms of jazz and therefore a break in the tradition (Charlie Parker, after all, once said that bebop had nothing to do with jazz) or, on the other hand, as the latest and most intense manifestation of jazz. The 1950s was also the period in which the long-playing record was developed, reissues of jazz recordings from every era became available, and it became necessary to connect all the parts and give the music shape.

By the same token, there are some today who want to purify jazz of what they perceive as its weaknesses, its evolutionary wrong turns, its departures from the tradition. To those who hold this view, jazz, like America itself, has drifted away from its accomplishments and has abandoned its greatness: what must be done now is to stand up for values and defend the best that has ever been thought and played in this country. The apex of this aesthetic activism is the jazz wing at Lincoln Center in New York City, where Wynton Marsalis, Rob Gibson, Stanley Crouch, and others have created an unprecedented multileveled educational and performance program designed to put jazz on display and to shape its development.

Others—often fans of avant-garde jazz of the 1960s and 1970s or other more recent jazz developments—have decried such views as the kind of elitism that deadened classical music and froze it in its tracks, discouraging innovation and narrowing perspectives. There are still others who embrace another kind of purism in jazz, one which sees music as free from function, tradition, ethnic origin, and the like. For them, lines crossed in music are natural, not artificial or arbitrary, for music knows no boundaries. Although this later group does not frame its argument with traditionalists quite this way, they might argue that just as jazz has, at one time or another, claimed all of the world's music as source material for its own, the world has now come to claim jazz as its own. Jazz can now be heard played by musicians of great accomplishment in places like Sicily, Archangelsk (above the Arctic Circle in Russia), South Africa, India, Japan, Nigeria, the Faroe Islands, Jamaica, Cuba, Azerbaijan, Brazil, Argentina, Indonesia, Lapland . . . all with local inflections, but still recognizably part of the family.

Jazz is at a critical juncture. But then, when has it not been?

2 Recordings and Performance

There are different ways to come to know jazz. At various moments in the history of this music different media were dominant, and the means through which the music was heard shaped its reception and understanding. In the earliest years, it was only listened to at live dances. Later—in the 1920s—many first heard it on phonograph records, as well as at dances. In the 1930s, '40s, and '50s, radio, records, movies, or dances were the main sources. Today, with new media available, the audience for jazz is even more divided. Some find it through live performances at clubs, bars, or concerts. Others may see it occasionally performed in films. Still others hear it on radio, behind ads on TV, in a music class, or played by friends and family at home. And a few still discover jazz through dancing. But at the beginning of the twenty-first century, recordings are the main sources of jazz knowledge, so while keeping each of these ways of coming to jazz in mind, records will have to be our main concern, and at least some listening will have to be assumed of the reader.

Records are the textbooks of jazz, Max Roach once said, and though musicians sometimes complain about recordings being merely frozen moments in time and unrepresentative of an essentially live music, they nevertheless remain our touchstones, our ultimate points of reference, our literature. Unlike classical music, there are no scores to be examined for much of jazz, and even when they are available, the performances of them are often quite different. And in any case, solo improvisations do not appear on scores.

Without recordings, the history of jazz would have been written quite differently, if it could have been written at all. The good news is that recordings have existed throughout most of the history of jazz, and all forms of jazz are there to be heard, played by most of the key jazz musicians who ever lived. And since reissues of jazz recordings are more available than ever, we are living in something of a golden age for listening. Besides, changes in technology and the economics of performance have recently altered the way even musicians look upon recordings: they now talk of the need to document their music, to record and preserve the development of their aesthetic.

The only bad news about records is that when we *talk* about recordings we are two steps away from the original performance; no words can substitute for music, and no amount of lists or summary statements will communicate what happens in a performance. It is also true that no matter how fine the recording and the playback system, recordings will never approximate the experience of live music. This is true of all recorded musical performances, of course, but jazz is especially handicapped when it is restricted to the auditory dimension. It is a visceral, corporeal music, dependent on the interaction of performers and audience, and driven by rhythm instruments that are difficult to record (especially the cymbals). And, with the surprises of improvisation and the expectation that each performance will be different, a recording fixed in time is a very different experience.

The relationship between live performances and recordings is complex, and never completely resolved. For the first forty or so years, the technology of recording was such that records were limited to three minutes, give or take. For some performances this was time enough—a song could be sung, interspersed with an instrumental solo or two. For others—like Count Basie's 1930s arrangements which played live could go on for 30 minutes or more—the recordings were only pale shadows of the excitement generated from the stage. Still, the basic musical form of the live performances remained intact on the records, with only the solos truncated. Occasionally the time constraints of records could even serve as incitement for tighter, more refined performances than those heard live at dances or concerts. With the development of long-playing records in the late 1940s it became possible to record performances of 40 to 50 minutes, but there are only a few examples of single performances that fill an entire record . . . and fewer still after the CD expanded the length of potential recordings to over 75 minutes.

When 78 rpm records ruled (from almost the beginnings of recording to the late 1940s), most jazz recording sessions produced two single records with one song on each side. But the sessions actually often resulted in more than four pieces, in what are called alternate takes, or multiple versions of the same pieces recorded either to attempt to improve on what they had already done or as a backup in case of accidents. For many years these other versions—the rejected takes—have fueled reissues of records aimed at collectors eager to compare and contrast their favorites. Every 78 rpm record was given several numbers: 1) a matrix number, which was scratched onto the surface on both sides; 2) a take number, such as A or B, which follows the matrix number of the record surfaces; and 3) a catalog number, which is found on the record's label and identifies the record in company catalogs. This kind of marking system continued into long-playing and 45 rpm recordings. When there were several takes of a single piece on records, it was hard to know what the definitive version was, the classic version, and debates on such matters have kept collectors busy for years. With the coming of multitrack tape recording, the take number ceased to be so important, since the components of the music were now on separate tracks and tapes. Now, there was no longer any single master recording as such, just a group of tapes. (CDs now are normally marked with only their catalog number.)

No one will ever live long enough to hear everything on record, of course, but anyone serious about this music ought to at least sample some of the key recordings of every era. In that spirit, a number of records have been singled out in this book for special attention. These recordings may or may not be easily available by the time this book is read, but given the history of this music on record, there is every reason to believe that they can be found somewhere, or that they will be available again soon. Wherever possible, selections have been made from CD collections such as *The Smithsonian Collection of Classic Jazz, Visions of Jazz: A Musical Journey*, and *Lost Chords: White Musicians and Their Contribution to Jazz*, because of the range of music they contain and their availability. Most of the selections discussed are regarded as among the very best that the music has to offer. Nonetheless, they should not necessarily be looked at as constituting a "best of" list, for some have been included because they make a particular point especially well, or because they are representative of an era, or because they are personal favorites.

The technology of recording has steadily improved through the century, but the thin and rough sound of early recordings will test even the most serious of fans. Some fine restoration of early sound recording has been recently done, and wherever practical, the best editions have been referred to in this book. But even beyond the sonic limitations, some of this music may sound hopelessly of its own time: it may seem rhythmically simple, out of tune, and crude. And in many cases it may be. But we should never be fooled into thinking that badly recorded music cannot be great music. Close listening to these scratchy old records will usually reward the listener with an understanding of the principles that organized the music . . . and three minutes' listening time is not much to ask.

3 Defining Jazz

To a question asking him what jazz was, Louis Armstrong's famous reply was supposed to have been, "If you've got to ask, you'll never know." Whatever else he meant, Armstrong was at least implying that jazz is knowable, though not necessarily explainable in words. And true enough, jazz resists definition like no other music. Even the word *jazz* has escaped identification: five or six languages have laid claim to it, but so far no one has been able to persuasively locate its linguistic source.

Created from materials derived from widely disparate sources, homegrown, a minority music initially developed for the most part beyond the hand of commerce, its early history partly obscured by having preceded phonographic documentation, it has been inclusive by nature and relatively free from constraint. (Sometimes it seems that one or another form of music has been included under jazz only because it has been excluded from classical and pop.) Consider the usual definitions: jazz is said to be an African-American music, originated by black people for black people; an improvised music; a music characterized by a rhythmic feel called swing; and a music influenced by the blues. But race and ethnicity are not as clear and solid as American mythology would imply. Throughout the history of jazz there have been people of other races and ethnicities—whites of several nationalities, Cubans, Mexicans, Native Americans, Haitians, and, overseas, Europeans of all sorts involved to some extent in its creation. And further confusing the matter, throughout the second half of this century jazz has ceased to be especially popular among people of African-American descent, much as it has for most Americans.

Is it an improvised music? But much of jazz is only partially improvised, some not at all; and even if it were largely improvised, many other musics of the world involve improvisation to varying degrees. The blues? The presence of some elements of the blues in much of jazz would seem undeniable. But what *is* the blues? A kind of scale? A harmonic form? A poetic form? A way of articulating tones? A set of verbal sentiments similar to those used in folk blues songs? A feeling? Any of these may be what is meant by the blues, for no agreed-upon definition exists. Or what is meant may be racial, metaphorical, a reference to attitude, or even a shared history. But in any case the blues may be a necessary but not a sufficient characteristic to define jazz: not every jazz musician plays the blues well, and some—like pianist Bill Evans—avoid playing it most of the time. And whatever definition of the blues is intended, many of its elements can also be found in other forms of music such as country, gospel, and pop music.

If the blues is difficult to define, swing is even less well understood, and has become the most metaphysical term in jazz. Swing is said to be a way of feeling rhythm, an attitude toward rhythm that has been described as syncopated, or more specifically as off-beat accentuation, or playing with "swing eighth notes" (eighth notes played with variable values or lengths). But syncopation is so hopelessly general as to fit much if not all of the world's music; off-beat accentuation—putting emphasis just before or after an expected beat, or emphasizing an unexpected beat—is also not specific to jazz; and swing eighth notes can be found in all sorts of music, including pop, country, and classical (in "Happy Trails," or Steve Reich's "Music for 18 Musicians," for instance). Aside from definitional problems, few people agree on what constitutes swing. Instead, the term is used more often to exclude or chastise ("he can't swing"). And it is worth remembering that figures as central to the music as John Coltrane and Duke Ellington have from time to time wondered about even the necessity of swing.

In an effort to define jazz, some writers make a list of features (such as vocalized tone, the importance of a unique, individualized sound), or the use of certain forms (ballads, blues, Afro-Cuban rhythms). Yet it is never clear what role these features play, or whether they are merely a part of a configuration that is distinct, if difficult to describe. The first jazz writers defined by contrast, stressing the differences between classical music and jazz, thus avoiding the overlap of their definitions with other forms of non-classical music;

but as the history of jazz unfolded, they found themselves having already defined the next development out of the music. What's left? By implication, some have settled for the idea that jazz is simply a tradition—originally and chiefly an African-American one, but one that is still under construction.

Any of these definitions look workable until someone insists that, say, Kenny G. is a jazz musician, and then the arguments begin. In fact, Mr. G. is an acoustic musician who plays the soprano saxophone, the instrument identified with Sidney Bechet and John Coltrane, two of the icons of jazz history. He has a distinct sound, uses swing eighth notes, arguably has at least *some* blues "feeling," came up on the edge of jazz tradition (beginning his career by playing rhythm and blues as part of Barry White's orchestra), plays ballads, etc. The definitional exercise quickly grows tiresome. In fact, today many writers wisely avoid definitions altogether, and only by what they exclude and what they prize is it possible to know what they mean by jazz. This book will follow a similar course, but will also at times allude to a body of musical work that only loosely falls within the circle of jazz.

THE ARRAY of musics we call jazz is the result of North and South America having inherited and gathered together many of the world's musical resources, creating an aggregate possibly greater than that of any part of the world. All the components, methods, and styles of these musics brought to the Americas are available to every musician or singer, and they form what critic Max Harrison has called a matrix of elements, a matrix that has incredible persistence, allowing for various permutations and combinations of elements over a great period of time. This matrix is the basis of the America's fabled hybrid or creole forms of music.

But hybridization and creolization do not guarantee openness, change, or flexibility, as witnessed in hybrid musics like flamenco, which, at least until recently, has been characterized by conservatism and resistance to change. The North American matrix of musical elements allowed for change by means of creolization, the process of cultural development in which historically unrelated traditions may merge and produce totally new, historically unpredictable forms. The elements of the American musical matrix are stored and maintained in many places—such as marching band music, children's game songs, popular dance music, and, notably for jazz, the African-American church.

A startling variety of musical styles has formed over the last century. American classical composers such as Charles Ives drew on the matrix, as did thousands of pop song writers, but the imaginative combination of these elements seems to have been more fully realized in jazz. Because of the persistence of these elements, styles of jazz have emerged or been reinvented more than once under different names. In nineteenth-century New Orleans Louis Moreau Gottschalk wrote piano pieces with elements of ragtime thirty-five years before ragtime itself appeared. Cool jazz of the late 1940s and 1950s—with its low vibrato, understated drama, and quiet rhythm sections—had its prototype as early as the 1920s, and reemerged in the 1990s in some versions of Downtown New York City music. Intensely vocalized playing and collective improvisation were part of earliest 1920s jazz, but then resurfaced with a vengeance among free jazz players in the 1960s and 1970s. Whatever else may happen to them, musical styles do not die. The stability of the matrix helps to assure that all of these past styles remain, still being played beyond their apparent historical moment despite America's thirst for novelty. In New York City on any given night you can hear Dixieland, bebop, ragtime, swing, the blues, third stream, free jazz—virtually any form of music produced in the history of jazz. (It is the persistence of these styles that makes them available for recorded documentation and study, and one of the reasons that jazz might well be the best documented art in the history of the world.)

Parallel forms of musical creolization and the development of matrices of elements were at work in the Caribbean and Latin America as well, where such forms as calypso, samba, the son, danzon, merengue, rumba, and tango developed. There are many similarities between these musics and North America's, and in some cases, such as the use of riffs (repeated short melodic and rhythmic background figures) in jazz and in Cuban music, they seem to have developed at the same time. There is great diversity in African-American music in different parts of the Americas, but there are also similarities which in spite of innovation and cultural influences are still recognizable. These similarities make parallel developments possible between different musics, and also allow different musics to periodically reunite and converge. Such developments often appear to be innovations, but they might be better understood as cultural homecomings.

Understanding the way in which such combinatory musical elements develop is not easy. With several cultures contributing to them, how can we date and specify their origins? Do they begin in a single place and time, or in several? Unfortunately, the histories of music that have been written for the Americas do not consider these problems seriously, and most of them are almost invariably single-sourced and limited by short time perspectives.

4 Elements

Instruments

There are no musical instruments that are alien to jazz: virtually every one has been used by jazz musicians at one time or another, including all of the instruments of the European classical ensembles. Some instruments, once in favor, have gone out of style—the banjo is one, largely replaced by the guitar in the 1930s, where a smoother, quieter form of chordal rhythm was required. Other instruments have virtually disappeared only to come back later with a different role to play. Such is the case with the tuba, which began as a rhythm instrument and was replaced by the string bass at the end of the 1920s, but returned in the late 1940s and again in the 1970s as a melodic instrument. Others, like the clarinet, once one of the most popular of instruments, faded, and have never made a complete return.

The most popular instruments, however, have remained

the saxophone, trumpet, trombone, bass, drums, piano, and guitar—instruments for which the pattern of use was set early in the beginnings of jazz. They have all been used in big band configuration, with each group of wind instruments forming a different section (as in marching bands); and even in small bands, where each different horn served as a mini-section in itself. The piano, drum, bass, and guitar are designated as a rhythm section. (Piano trios—with bass and drums—or their equivalent in organ trios, represent the rhythm section pulled out of the larger band formation.) Electrical instruments and electrically amplified instruments have in many cases been pioneered and introduced by jazz musicians, yet most jazz instruments remain accoustic, and even when played electric, are kept at an accoustic level of volume.

Harmony and Melody

The easiest thing to say about melody—the tune, the song—is that there is nothing especially unique about this element of the music, because jazz has freely used virtually anything as a melody at one time or another. So pop songs, children's tunes, folk songs, classical works, music from beyond the West, almost everything has functioned as a vehicle for jazz playing. Therefore an equally large variety of harmonic structure has been used in jazz, for every note used in a melody can imply a different chord or chords: the groups of notes that trace the movement of the melody and that form a configuration in relation to a scale or key.

Rhythm

The history of the rhythm section in jazz is part of the history of empire, born out of a convergence of different conceptions of rhythm instrument groupings—especially the African and the European. It's not always easy to separate these historical influences. By the 1920s, for example, even European symphony orchestras were displaying the influence of African and Afro-Latin percussion in playing the compositions of Stravinsky and Shostakovich. It is clear that in the jazz context, the bass functions as a chordal instrument in the European sense, but in a real break from European tradition, also as a percussive instrument. The early bass players like Pop Foster can be heard snapping the strings of their instruments on many recordings, and though such percussive playing went out of fashion in the late 1920s, it returned again in funk played on electric basses in the 1970s.

Another case is the development of the drum kit, the bundling together of various percussive instruments played by a single drummer. This was an American invention, and though the date of its development is not clear, it is no older than the twentieth century. Once the essentials were in place—bass drum, snare, tom-tom, and cymbals—older percussion instruments were added to the kit, along with new inventions that appeared rapidly to accommodate the versatility of a single drummer: foot pedals, varieties of cymbals, brushes (originally portable fly swatters), mallets, etc. These drum sets were themselves illustrations of the musical matrix: cymbals and triangles from Turkey, tom-toms from

China, snare drums from Europe, and cowbells and woodblocks from Africa. But more important than the instruments' sources are the way these instruments are used in performance. There the African side of the equation is foremost: the various drums of the set are used for different tones (either by tuning or using the hand, foot, or elbow to control pitch), reflecting their origins in African cultures where pitch carries distinct meaning in language, and tuned drums are used to send messages or to "talk" to dancers; drummers' hands and feet were called on to be independent of each other (the hands even distinguished by gender, as is common in West Africa, calling right-hand strokes "Ma-Ma" and left-hand strokes "Pa-Pa"). With this tonal variation and independence of articulation it became possible for one person to play polymetrically—that is, in more than one rhythm at once—replacing the drum corps of three or four drummers common in much of West and Central Africa.

Though polymeter can sometimes be difficult to hear on the earliest jazz recordings, drummers often played a "Charleston" beat on the cymbal or snare against a two-beat on the bass drum, creating an additive rhythm, a variation of the common drum patterns of West and Central Africa. The earliest drummers played these beats on the metal rims of their snare drums, later on the metal stands, then finally on the ride cymbal, the large cymbal now used for playing timekeeping patterns.

A FEW distinctions and some terminology about rhythm might be helpful here. *Tempo* is the speed at which the music is moving. The *beat* is a heard or felt pulse of a piece of music. The *meter* is a grouping of beats based on their repeating pattern. (A *bar* or a *measure* is a grouping of beats, which also tells us something about the meter of a particular piece of music.) Beats in sequence are distinguished by some being louder or longer or having different tonal qualities than others, and these differences are heard as accents.

Certain beats are "strong" and others "weak," depending on where the accents are placed. In much Western music the *downbeat* (the first beat of every bar) has often been the strongest, the third beat the next strongest, and the second and fourth the weakest. In early jazz, especially, the first and the third beats of the bar were emphasized (particularly by the bass), often leaving the second and the fourth beats silent, with a resulting "boom-chick" feel. This form of rhythm organization is known as *two-beat*, or playing in two. When the second and fourth beats are strongly emphasized it is often called a *backbeat*. By the swing era, all four beats were relatively equalized in a rhythm known as *four-beat*, playing in four. But neither form of rhythm accentuation was ever exclusive to any period. Four-beat could be heard in early jazz, and often both two- and four-beat alternated in the same piece (Jelly Roll Morton's music often contains both rhythms). During the swing era, two-beat was also sometimes used, and some bands—like Jimmy Lunceford's—were famous for their flowing use of two. Even in the bebop and post-bebop eras, two-beat remained, where it was mixed with four, especially in ballads (Miles Davis used two- and four-beat in most of his ballad playing in the 1950s and early 1960s).

More complicated still, beats can be subdivided, and some argue that in much of jazz a single beat is felt as having three somewhat uneven parts. A soloist can think in these terms, and will place emphasis just "behind" or "ahead" of the beat, or play it short or long, over a rhythm section which is itself varying the beat in interaction with the soloist. Time in music is a highly subjective matter, and jazz often makes a virtue of what others might see as a problem. Different drummers, for example, play tempi differently, even while they are playing at the same speed.

Drummers from the beginnings of jazz settled on a repertoire of rhythm devices. *Double-time*, for example, means a doubling of tempo in the melody while the accompanying instruments continue at the same speed, or a doubling of tempo in the accompanying instruments while the melody remains at the slower tempo, or perhaps all of the instruments doubling the tempo together. This is a standard device in ballad or slow tempo playing that allows the soloist to display a range of abilities and express different responses to the original melody. Or it can be a simple means of further upping the excitement of an already fast tune. *Half-time*, less common in jazz, reverses the process, and can make it appear that the soloist is floating inside of a faster tempo. The *break*—which Jelly Roll Morton said was essential to jazz—is a short suspension of the accompaniment while the soloist or melody instruments continue playing. The effect it creates is one of tension release, but when the rhythm returns it can also suggest that the whole piece seems to accelerate. *Stop-time*, another rhythm device, has the accompanying instruments playing the rhythm with especially sharp accents, exaggerating the rhythm which, despite its name, does not stop. The "Charleston" rhythm is the most famous of stop-time figures.

Ragtime drummers followed the rhythm of the melody (say, in the "Charleston"), playing on one rhythm instrument at a time. Later, New Orleans drummers like Warren "Baby" Dodds played mostly on the suspended cymbal, rims, and wood blocks, creating an independent line behind the band, working on different parts of the kit in different ways behind each of the soloists. Gene Krupa, a flamboyant, loud drummer (critic Whitney Balliett once remarked that the public thought Krupa looked like what a drummer should sound like) played in this older pattern, adjusting it to a swing beat. It took Jo Jones of the Count Basie band to pioneer a lighter, more flowing swing beat, articulating the bass drum rhythm sparingly, using it independently, like a snare drum, and allowing the string bass to function like a drum.

The idea of a section implies a unity, an internal interaction that operates somewhat apart from the rest of the instruments of the band. In the earliest jazz bands the rhythm instruments were used redundantly, each of them stressing the same beats and doubling functions (as when the piano and bass play the same bass line, or the bass snaps its strings on the same beats with the drummer). Some swing bands, most notably Count Basie's, created a new division of labor, with the drummer using the bass drum not to keep every beat, but to punctuate the rhythm being kept by the ride cymbal, and the pianist abandoning the left-hand bass line, thus leaving the bass player (and possibly the guitarist) to maintain the pulse. And even where the rhythm instruments played on the same beat, a certain variability and flexibility of approach was built in; again, in Basie's band, the beat was felt differently by the bass and rhythm guitar, the guitar beginning the downstroke on the chord slightly ahead of the bass.

Bebop extended this kind of rhythmic specialization, freeing the piano and drums to play around and even against the beat, which was now being kept by the bass alone. The even-four beats of swing were increasingly treated less evenly, the weaker beats irregularly accented, sometimes with the sense that eight beats were being felt (although not sounded), since accents were being placed in between.

Post-bebop rhythm sections have extended this line of specialization, drummers playing more loudly, aggressively, encircling the soloists with rhythm, snapping the high hat cymbals closed on the second and the fourth beats (sometimes with even stronger emphasis on the fourth), and drawing on Latin rhythms, at times using conga or bongo drums to fill in and activate the spaces.

By the 1960s the drift toward equality of drummers with soloists became more obvious. Cymbals were played more independently from the beat, setting up a boiling and churning rhythm; bassists varied their playing by moving from beat-keeping to freer playing; pianists began to interact more directly with the bassists, their pianos becoming increasingly percussive and drumlike. Bassists became melodic, strumming and arpeggiating, or using the bow to play sustained lines; drummers sometimes played melodically, or played around the beat, toying with it, commenting on it. With no one directly responsible for the beat, the pulse was often felt rather than stated. But having gone that far, with the development of jazz-rock and the subsequent return to older styles, many rhythm sections returned to the redundancy of roles, but even so retained a certain flexibility, allowing the entire section to slow or accelerate, or shift rhythms at once.

Every beat can be played on the felt pulse, or slightly before or behind. It can be articulated loudly or softly, played to sound short or long, and it can be pitched high or low. Every member of the rhythm section has the independence to do the same, so enormous flexibility is built into their syntax. And since they all play in response to the soloist and the collective, variability is introduced into the mix. This interaction with a rhythm section is so strong that even when jazz musicians play solo, they operate as if a rhythm section is implied.

Further Listening:

Anthology of Jazz Drumming, Vol. 1: 1904–1928 and *Vol. 2: 1928–1935*, Masters of Jazz MJCD 804 and MJCD 805, provides a survey of early jazz drumming. For an overview of drummers up until the 1950s there is *The Engine Room: A History of Jazz Drumming From Storyville to 52nd Street*, Proper Records Properbox 2 (4-CD set).

Ornette Coleman once said that when the band is playing with the drummer, it's rock and roll, but when the drummer is playing with the band, it's jazz. This is not a bad rule of thumb, but jazz rhythm sections are by no means the only ones that play interactively, shifting with the musical events around them. The best funk bands—like the Meters on their 1974 recording *Rejuvenation* or James Brown's in 1969–1970—are remarkable in their interplay. Latin bands such as Tito Puente's have rhythm sections whose instruments virtually talk among themselves and to the band; similarly, great reggae rhythm groups such as those anchored by Sly Dunbar and Robbie Shakespeare regularly make subtle rhythm shifts around singers; a few rock bands—Frank Zappa's, with drummer Vinnie Coliauta, for example—have also played interactively and free of a fixed beat.

5 Forms

The most common type of improvisation in jazz is one in which the melody and/or harmony of an existing song is varied. Though there are many thousands of compositions used as a basis for improvisation, most of them can be divided into a very few types or forms. The forms most fundamental to the history of jazz are pop songs and blues (though in earlier years hymns and spirituals, marches, rags, and other older forms were also used). But jazz musicians have also felt free to make changes in these conventional forms. During the swing era, for example, pop songs and blues were the common forms to be varied and developed by solos and riff sections. But many swing arrangements simply faded out (through drops in volume), with nothing left to vary or develop, with no particular dramatic conclusion, and nowhere to go but repetition. Bebop in the 1940s was sensitive to the limitations of the pop and blues forms and often rewrote the melodies, retaining their harmonies only as a basis for providing a string of solos. The revised melody was then simply restated at the end of the piece in order to signal the ending. In the 1960s modal jazz—jazz written or improvised on a scale or chord or two—also frequently followed pop song forms, though radically simplifying their harmonic conventions. On the other hand, free jazz and jazz-rock tended to depart from pop song forms, and even where a melody opened and closed the performance, the improvisations played might not directly relate to it.

A conventional means by which musicians change the usual forms is by breaking them up into solo units of eight bars, four bars, two—or, if they're especially daring, even one. This is called "trading eights" (or fours, etc.) and means that soloists will take turns improvising for the length of time it takes to play these bars, and then another musician will take up the solo. At its best, one musician's line connects to another's, but more often than not these units are played as if they stood alone. Although the practice is not as common as it was in the 1940s and 1950, when beboppers pushed it to new heights, drummers still are given space to trade with soloists or with the ensemble itself.

There have also been innovations in form, and many of the greatest jazz musicians have developed distinctive means of shaping music: Duke Ellington, Sun Ra, George Russell, John Coltrane, Miles Davis, Charles Mingus, Cecil Taylor, and Anthony Braxton are some of the most distinguished at creating their own forms.

Pop Song

The American popular song derived from a complex history of European folk song, theater music, and light opera, and was modified in turn by American music, especially Broadway musicals, African-American folk song, and the blues. The history of the pop song form is one of devolution, growing shorter and simpler over time. In the earlier years of the twentieth century the range of subject matter was so great that there seemed to be nothing that the pop song could not address, from a child's birthday (Johnny Mercer's "Mandy Is Two") to bucolic meditation ("Lazy Afternoon"), drunken reverie ("One for My Baby" or "Lush Life"), suicide ("Gloomy Sunday"), and lynching ("Strange Fruit"). It contained an endless variety of human emotions and situations. Today, however, pop songs are most exclusively concerned with couples—either in love or falling out of love. The structure of pop songs has become simpler as well. Songs of the early 1900s were mini-dramas, divided into two parts—a *verse*, whose words set the scene for what was to come and whose melody was freer and nonrepetitive, and a *refrain*, whose words and melody were usually repeated with small variations with every chorus (every complete statement of a theme and its variation is called a *chorus*). By the late 1920s the verse had begun to be dropped in performance, and by the 1940s often not even written as part of the song, turning songs into vignettes whose titles were often repeated as a hook ("Blue Moon," for example, or "It Might as Well Be Spring"), leaving only the refrain, a 16- or 32-bar theme, divided into four- or eight-bar phrases grouped into patterns such as AABA or ABAC. The B section in these songs is referred to as the *bridge* or the *release*, and its words, melody, and harmony contrast it to the A sections. The most common pop songs played by jazz improvisers are of the AABA 32-bar type, such as "The Man I Love" or "I Got Rhythm," or of the 64-bar type, like "Cherokee." But there are many other varieties of the form, like "Embraceable You" (ABAC) or "Night and Day" (ABABCB), and varieties of length as well, such as "I Dream Too Much" (80 bars) or "Gee, Baby, Ain't I Good to You" (16 bars). The poetry, melody, and harmonic structure of these small songs all function together to continually recycle back to the beginning to repeat again. They are perpetual motion machines, seemingly capable of repeating forever.

Blues

If pop songs derive from European prototypes that became modified by African-American practice, the blues are an African-American form (or forms), modified from songs possibly from the central Sudanic area of Africa (Mali, northern Ghana, northern Nigeria, and central Cameroon), and adapted first to African-American and ultimately to Euro-American musical tastes. Though the African sources of the blues have been debated for years, increasing musicological evidence points to the Sudan as one of the likely points of origin. Whatever the specific locations, this is no longer a Euro-American or African-American conclusion: now African musicians such as Ali Farka Toure or Toumani

Diabate claim the blues as a distant relative and have recorded with American blues musicians.

The story of the adaptation of the blues has also been one of devolution, the blues growing simpler and shorter over the years, and in the process jettisoning much of their length, varied structure, rhetorical power, and rhythmic complexity. Some commentators on the blues, unfamiliar with the enormous body of country and folk blues or resistant to their achievement, speak of a "refinement" in the later blues of the city and vaudeville, a development that might more accurately be described as standardization and simplification. In older rural blues the form was far more flexible and irregular, even open-ended, and came in many forms such as chantlike repetitions, elongated cries, and talking blues, all of which varied in bar length. The melodies of blues were characterized by "blue notes," which are not so much fixed pitches in a scale, but areas around pitches that could be flatted or sharpened, or passed through on the way to a particular pitch. The rhythms of the early blues ranged from a single unified rhythm to multiple, interlocked rhythms. Mississippi singer Charlie Patton, for example, might sing in one meter, pick the guitar in another, and tap his foot in a third.

Within jazz, musicians for some years have accepted a 12-bar form of the blues (with three phrases of four bars each) as standard for their needs. When sung, the first two phrases pose a question or offer a statement that is repeated, then answered or responded to in the last phrase. The blues form thus continues the call-and-response of older African-American music. The 12-bar blues form can also be recognized by its harmonic structure. Though it's often played with some variation, blues as played in jazz in its simplest form uses the I, IV, and V chords. This means, for instance, that in the key of C (as in the example below), the chords are built on the first, fourth, and fifth steps of the scale:

C7
Why do people believe in some old sign?

F7 C7
Why do people believe in some old sign?

G7 C7
You hear a dog howl, someone is surely dyin'.

What is striking is that each level of blues structure reinforces the other, so (again, in this example) the moment of greatest harmonic tension (when the dominant seventh or G7 is heard) occurs just after the question has been posed twice, and just as the answer is begun. Once the answer is completed, it resolves back into the tonic (C) with which it began. The highest note of the vocal line is also likely to occur at this same point of tension and then move back down to the note on which the singer began. A musical "solution" or commentary is thus matched by a verbal one.

Some musicians speak of a "blues scale," with a blue or flatted third step of the scale, a blue fifth step, and perhaps a seventh, implying that the blues scale is a major scale that has been altered. But it might be better to think of blue notes as being tones that are bent or changed to increase the expressivity of the music, not to merely alter an existing scale. Miles Davis once said that musicians who think in terms of blues scales "sound like they had to learn to play the blues." The blues, in his terms, are a matter of feelings, of attitude, not a point of music theory.

Despite its name, the blues do not have to be sad, even though some of the finest examples of tragedy in Western music have been in blues form. Needless to say, all sad songs are not blues: "Stormy Weather" may be "bluesy," but it is in pop song form. Also many songs titled blue—like "Blues in the Night"—are pop songs. The blues can be either in a major or minor key, and they can be spirited, light, or even driving (as in the hands of Count Basie). They can even be played as a march (Glenn Miller's "St. Louis Blues March" and Art Blakey's "Blues March" being classic examples).

The Jam Session

The jam session, or jamming, is the most informal means of using musical forms, and one that depends solely on the shared knowledge of jazz traditions among the players. It was once a common practice, often occurring after hours, in clubs or spaces set aside for musicians and their friends to be entertained and to learn their trade. A body of tunes was held in common, along with agreed-upon tempos, a sense of how solos could be accompanied by riffs, countermelodies, and collective accompaniment, as well as a view of how to end a solo so as to present the next soloist in the best light (or not). The 1940s were the golden age of jamming, a period in which it could be packaged and put onstage by Norman Granz's Jazz at the Philharmonic and taken around the world. The 1940s were also the last time musicians from every era of jazz could be heard together on some of the key records of the period. But beginning in the 1950s, the ability of musicians to jam together comfortably was rapidly waning. Styles were fragmenting, and some traditions were becoming exclusive. Today, the number of tunes shared by musicians is small, the opportunities for jamming limited, and the practice has become more the exception than the rule.

6 Improvisation, Composition, and Arranging

Improvisation—the art of composing in the moment, while performing, without a written score—has long been seen as the hallmark that sets jazz apart from other musics, even though many musical cultures of the world do improvise to one degree or another. It may or may not be true that no other music counts so much on instant creativity, expecting every musician to rise to a certain level of creativity, but jazz musicians talk and act as though it is. They speak of going beyond the limitations of the precomposed, beyond the simply interpretive, to a more deeply inspired and more instantaneous level of creativity; a level that may put the improviser in touch with his or her conscious and unconscious states.

To say that jazz musicians improvise does not mean that they play without thought, or "naturally," or that there are no constraints, arrangements, or plans for what will be played. Even where the arrangements are minimal and not written down—as in a jam session—there are nonetheless agreed-upon principles as to what might be invented and how it relates to the whole, and at least some standards that determine whether the improvisation will be successful or not. These standards are shared to varying degrees by the audience as well.

The burden that improvisation puts on musicians can be daunting. Audiences for jazz expect that what they are hearing live on a particular occasion is different from what any other musician would play, and—unlike pop audiences—different from what they have heard even on the performer's recordings.

If the same piece is played again later in the evening it, too, is expected to sound new. (The applause given each jazz solo—rather than just the tune itself, as in pop music—rewards the fulfillment of this expectation, even if only as a formality.) The level of creativity demanded here is incredibly high, as well as unrealistic: musicians are asked to sound different from all others, but also different from themselves as well. Asked to be completely unique, some performers resist the influence of other powerful soloists by studying only their own playing and recordings, thus in effect influencing themselves; others seem to be so remarkably focused on their own projects that they avoid listening to jazz altogether. For a musician who performs several times a night for six nights a week for thirty years, the problem of constantly coming up with new ideas that nonetheless still sound like one's own poses a near-impossible task. In reality, even the most distinctive and creative of improvisers (a

Charlie Parker or a Sonny Rollins) play with repeated personal stylistic elements (or "licks") which makes them susceptible to imitators. And even for these master players, there is always a fear of falling prey to self-imitation, which can turn into self-parody over time.

The distinction between improvisation and composition (the improviser working within a group of musicians versus the solitary composer toiling alone) is not as clear-cut as it might seem. Both are forms of composition, and both are involved to varying degrees with performance. Some composers are able to communicate their compositions (which may or not be written in a score) by singing them or playing them for the musicians who will perform them. And some compositions have always been developed through and during rehearsal. Now, since the dawning of the tape recorder and other means of electronic storage and retrieval, distinctions such as this make less and less sense.

It is also possible for a musician to play written music so that it *sounds* improvised, even play it physically so it *looks* improvised; and it is equally possible for a composer to write music that sounds improvised. Some of jazz's most dedicated composers—Jelly Roll Morton, Duke Ellington, Gil Evans, George Russell, and Anthony Braxton—have done just that.

The role of the composer in the beginnings of jazz was determined partly by technological limitations—the three-minute single record—and the location of jazz in the realm of commercial music. Though compositions could sometimes be as complex as Jelly Roll Morton's "Black Bottom Stomp," with its four different themes, most jazz compositions were made up of one or two themes, with variations by soloists and the ensemble. But even after the development of the long-playing record, with its potential for extending a composition for up to forty minutes, few jazz composers attempted truly extended works. Even Duke Ellington, jazz's greatest composer, either kept his compositions to approximately fifteen minutes or else used the suite form—a series of short, related pieces. Some have seen the lack of long works as the failed result of the problem of integrating improvisers and compositions over long stretches of time. But this seems to be a red herring. The length of a musical work appears, rather, to be an artifact of a particular music's history, and it is difficult to demonstrate that there is anything inherently superior about longer works (especially when so many short jazz compositions are gems of balance, detail, and shape, and are completely realized within a few minutes). Besides, there *have* been enough longer compositions in jazz—John Lewis's "Comedy," George Russell's "All About Rosie," Charles Mingus's "Epitaph," Ornette Coleman's "Free Jazz," and John Coltrane's "Ascension," some tilting either toward improvisation or composition—to show us that it is possible to achieve. And in the last twenty-five years the German-based Globe Unity Orchestra, Barry Guy's London Improvisers Orchestra, and Anthony Braxton have all created compositions that call for the entire orchestra to improvise collectively over long stretches of time.

A further complication in the composer-improviser distinction is the importance of the arranger. An arrangement is a plan that musicians agree to abide by before they play, intended to give shape to their performance beyond the melody and the harmony. An arrangement, then, may be as simple as an agreement to play the melody at a certain point, to solo in a certain order, and to stop at a particular moment. Arrangements can be agreed upon just before the music begins or even take shape as they are played: "head arrangements" are often developed in the playing, made up night after night, with some parts being added as they go along, and others dropped. In small groups, an arrangement may provide riffs to be played behind a soloist, countermelodies to be used against the melody, or any number of small variations in routine. In larger groups the arranger emerges as a more prominent figure, creating distinctive voicings for the harmony, changing the harmonics, recomposing the existing melody with small variations, or writing full variations of the melody. The best arrangers in jazz find ways to fit soloists into the orchestral frame, balancing the single voice against the whole. Duke Ellington, Gil Evans, and George Russell, for example, made the groups they wrote for into distinctive forces. As with great soloists, the arranger's style is always recognizable, regardless of what material is being arranged. And in the best arrangements, those that are organic and unified, it's sometimes difficult for the listener to separate the arranged parts from the composed and the improvised.

Jazz, then, breaks with Western conventional thinking, denying the distinctions between composer and performer, creator and interpreter, composer and arranger, soloist and accompanist, artist and entertainer, even soloist and group. In jazz, it is the activity itself that is as important as the result. It is a music that is learned in the doing, in collective play: it is a social music, with some of the features of early African-American social organization still evident in its execution. As such, it is a way of being as well as a way of doing. It is an emergent form, a social form, and as much an ethic as it is an aesthetic. No wonder, then, that many jazz musicians speak of their music in metaphysical or spiritual terms, or justify the music in terms of personal and collective survival.

HOW SPONTANEOUS is improvisation? How unplanned? Sometimes even the greatest musicians rehearse and plan a solo, playing the same solos year after year, making only small changes over time. One of Louis Armstrong's finest improvisations, his solo on his 1926 recording of "Cornet Chop Suey," had been worked out and written down at least two years before it was recorded. And in every recorded version of Charlie Parker's "Embraceable You" it is possible to hear some of the same elements played, especially at the ends of phrases and in the last few bars of each chorus. Otherwise each solo is remarkably fresh, so much so that in some performances he sounds like a different player. A few jazz composers did not trust their musicians to get everything the way they wanted it, so some of the most interesting breaks and solos on Jelly Roll Morton's records were written out for the band. At the other extreme, some musicians have gone to extraordinary lengths to resist playing the same way twice. Saxophonist Ornette Coleman, for one, seems to have taken up other instruments in order to disrupt the conventional or formulaic figures he developed in his improvising; and in fact he manages to sound very different on violin and trumpet.

How do musicians go about improvising? Is it possible to improvise melodies from scratch, working with nothing more than emotional and intellectual resources? Yes, it is, but more often than not jazz musicians choose to improvise "off" something or "against" something—a preexisting melody, something all members of the musical group know from memory—or they may read from a *lead sheet,* a musical outline that contains the melody line, the harmonic structure (indicated by alphabetical or numerical symbols for the chords), and perhaps the words of a song. They may alter the original melody in whole or in part, changing the phrasing, the rhythm of the melody, the intervals (the distances between the pitches of notes) in various ways—by recombining, subtracting, adding, transposing, inverting, or playing it backwards. For some improvisers it is enough to change only the phrasing of the melody, much as one would change the phrasing of speech, so that the internal organization of the melody is changed, with different points of emphasis or tension. Others prefer to paraphrase the original melody or ornament the existing theme. This can be as simple a gesture as changing only a few notes, or as complex as recomposing the whole melody. Still others may think in smaller units, by playing only a few notes, varying those, then varying the ones just played and continuing varying them in sequence. Some take a small fragment or motive of the original and vary it throughout the solo; and some may bring their own personal stock of formulas or clichés to the solo and link them together in creative ways. Whatever they play, improvisers strive not to give in to what is called noodling—aimless, shapeless playing.

SOME MUSICIANS commonly build their own melodies on the harmonic structure of a preexisting song, possibly never even paraphrasing the original melody. Or they may paraphrase or quote from another melody where it fits the existing harmonic structure. Players like Dexter Gordon or Nat "King" Cole were expert at quotation and could often construct witty narratives from parts of different songs. (Cole's 1944 piano solo at the Jazz at the Philharmonic on "Body and Soul," for example, is built entirely of bits of other songs, from "Grand Canyon Suite" to "Humoresque.") Or they may play what is called modal jazz—using only a scale or two for improvisation. Some minimalist improvisers even choose to play on single chords, or single tones, drones, or repeated figures called vamps.

But this is only the beginning of the sources of improvisation: some musicians are drawn to improvise on songs with particularly interesting conjunctions between lyrics and melody, such as Jerome Kern's "The Song Is You," where the melody modulates upward just at the point where the lyrics ask a series of questions. The soloist is sent soaring upward by both a harmonic rise and the upturned pitch of the questions to a new place where the horn—like a voice—can sing. Some modern musicians look for new or older forms to play on; others improvise from images, paintings, even colors and shapes. Still others make sheer virtuosity the basis of solo performance, using instruments in new ways, or using newer techniques such as circular breathing (storing air in the cheeks so that abnormally long phrases can be played) and multiphonics (playing more than one note at a time on a horn by manipulating the breath stream). Throughout, the source of improvisation can be intellectual, physical, emotional, or it can be spurred by "the spirit"—whether by trance associated with religious belief or in the subconscious spirit of Surrealism and Dadaism.

Jazz musicians have justified their preoccupation with improvisation as a means of escaping the limitations of what can be composed and written. There are, of course, limits to what can be improvised, but in many cases they are the same limits of formal composition: the degree of complexity of the form, the length a piece can be played, and the amount of time an audience can remain attentive. Nonetheless, early jazz musicians (as well as the free-jazz musicians of the 1960s and 1970s) developed remarkably complex collectively improvised polyphony (multiple lines of melody played at the same time). And the speed at which some players improvise is much faster than composers can compose: Charlie Parker's 1945 recording of "Koko," for example, generally agreed to be one of the greatest improvisations, is played at ten notes a second, meaning that Parker moved from idea to finger motion to key action, and breath to mouth and lips at least ten times a second. Nor does length of improvisation seem a limitation: John Coltrane was capable of sustained improvisations of forty-five minutes to an hour (the length of a symphony), and saxophonist Evan Parker once gave a 24-hour concert of continuous improvised music.

But what of mistakes? (Perhaps "mistakes" is too strong a word, since improvisers aim at innovation, and it's not always clear to an audience what was intended.) Errors do get made in improvisations—notes are missed, musicians run out of breath (or, worse, out of ideas), or lose the beat (though accomplished improvisers know how to turn mistakes into fresh ideas). But within the conventions of improvisation some degree of error is allowed and treated as part of the performance, especially when a musician is breaking new ground. Among the cognoscenti, mistakes may even be relished, as they offer access to the soloist's mental processes. The greater problem for the improviser is not to repeat him or herself, or to become comfortable with a certain level of expression.

7 Sources

The history of jazz has by and large been written by amateurs, most of them musically untrained. Who else would have written it, since jazz had to struggle—still has to struggle—to find any recognition among the arts? Amateurs have that mixture of obsession and zeal that leads them to scrounge for old records, collect dusty magazines, pester musicians for their memories, and hang out on the scene. The results of their efforts are often astonishing: detailed maps of the entertainment zones of New Orleans and Chicago, portraits of daily life in America's cities, intimate interviews with legendary figures, biographies of obscure musicians known only to a handful of other musicians, huge collections of photographs, and the most complete and detailed discographies of any music ever recorded. But jazz historians have not been musicologists, and when they turn to questions of the music's sources, they begin to falter, either exposing their prejudices (though not always predictable ones—as when early French writers lionized black musicians exclusively) or turning to generalizations based on the slimmest of evidence. And nowhere is this more apparent than on the question of the African and European contributions to the music.

Africa and Europe

No person serious about jazz today would doubt that this music is the product of the merger and transformation of musics rooted in Africa and Europe. Even in the earliest years of jazz, commentators understood this fact, and made it clear in no uncertain terms, whether in attacks on the music as degrading and dangerous or in celebration of its freshness and vitality. Although neither in Africa nor in Europe can musical parallels to jazz be found, both places exhibit many musical characteristics that also emerge in jazz. The European contribution has been well documented (overdocumented, some would say): diatonic melodies, certain forms of harmonic structure and rhythm, many of the instruments, and some of the musical forms used. But the African contribution is less often commented upon, and when it is, it's usually misunderstood or underestimated. Assumptions like the following are offered up as if they were self-evident: Africa is too complex to allow us to speak of an "African" style of music; African music does not sound like jazz; slavery destroyed whatever cultural elements might have been brought to the Americas; "European" culture is the only shared culture in the United States. Such comments are what one would expect from those who have only studied European culture. But over the last sixty years, research in ethnomusicology, history, anthropology, and African-American studies have proven such statements to be so grossly inaccurate that it's embarrassing even to have to bring them up again.

Suffice it to say here that the contributions of African music to jazz are extensive and critical to its history. A few of the African elements include: 1) rhythm patterns played on the ride cymbal, which serve as a means of organizing and directing musicians and dancers—an equivalent to the kind of time line rhythm instruments played in much of Africa, such as the Yoruba *agogo*, the double bell which can also be heard in the United States in Latin bands and even in dance club music; 2) drum rhythms constructed on an additive principle (such as 3+3+2, for example), rather than a divisive principle (2+2+2)—such rhythms can be heard in the stop-time of the Charleston beat, in the New Orleans second line beat, or in older rhythm and blues; 3) overlapping call-and-response—not just antiphony with one part being answered by another, but with one line continuing as the response begins, the two (or more) lines overlapping—such a pattern can be seen in Louis Armstrong's early playing, where he begins his solos before the ensemble has finished playing; 4) vocalized timbre and articulation, the instrument imitating the voice with speech-inflected tones, or horns "talking"; 5) voice/instrument interchange, with the voice imitating the instrument, as in scat singing; 6) staggered entry—beginning a performance or single piece of music as a solo and adding one instrument at a time until they are layered both polyphonically and polymetrically; 7) percussion tonality, tactility, and enrichment: damping and altering the drum head with a foot, hand, or elbow; rim shots; playing the metal cymbal stands; rivets or chains on the ride cymbal to extend the sound; the use of sandpaper, brushes, popped bass strings, and the like.

Some, maybe all, of these can be found elsewhere in the world, but as a group of features clustered together, they can be found nowhere other than Africa. Africa is a huge continent, with an incredible diversity of musical styles, but these features are common in the areas from which African Americans' ancestors came. It would be interesting to know in great detail where each of these features is found in Africa, but that is no more necessary for understanding how they came to be part of America's musical matrix than it is to know the exact origin of every European style feature. In any case, more significant than instruments, melody, rhythm, harmony, and special features, is the way these characteristics come together to form a distinctive musical social organization in performance. Jazz musicians play *against* as well as *with* other jazz musicians, working one rhythm or melody against another competitively but also reciprocally. It's what Ralph Ellison called the cruel contradiction implicit in the music, the individual finding personal identity against and within the group. Individual musicians assert themselves in solos, but other musicians may enter into each other's solos, not so much as an interruption but as a gesture of support and attentiveness. Jazz at its most complex—say, during collectively improvised playing—calls on the musicians to play with unique voices, to sound like no one else, and yet at the same time to cohere as one, with a single goal. There is simply no model for social or political groupings like this in the West.

ONE REASON that rhythm has always received emphasis in talk about jazz is because it is there that its differences from European music are most pronounced. Though it would be unreasonable to expect to find all, or even many, of the rhythms and use of rhythm found in many parts of Africa, jazz has always valued at least an implied use of polymeter, and this, as much as any other feature of jazz, points toward the contributions of West and Central African music. In polymeter, multiple rhythms are used simultaneously, and when put together, emerge as a beat structure different from any one of the rhythms being played, often giving the impression that all the contributing rhythms are changing. This is most likely to occur in short bursts, as when a soloist plays in a different rhythm from the rest of the group. Louis Armstrong, for example, sings twelve bars in 3/4 time over nine bars of guitar accompaniment in 4/4 time on his 1927 recording of "Hotter Than That." Or it can be heard when a Charlie Parker or an Ornette Coleman momentarily emphasizes one rhythm over another in the rhythm section. (Miles Davis said that when he played with Charlie Parker, drummer Max Roach would yell to pianist Duke Jordan not to follow Parker's rhythms but to stay where he was; otherwise Jordan risked "turning the beat around" for good—that is, making the irregularly phrased accents to be heard as regular accents, and therefore completely realigning rhythmic expectations, instead of hearing them as a moment of tension.) Jazz does not use polymeter to the same degree as in Africa (or even Latin America), where polymeter results in cross-rhythms (a kind of musical conversation between rhythm lines, which can produce a kind of collective melody in the rhythm); still, there are brief moments in early bebop and free jazz rhythm sections where such rhythms are strongly suggested.

THESE ELEMENTS of African music had profound influence on the development of jazz, and are one reason why African Americans have most often been the pioneers and originators in the music. Yet, the nature of this cultural merger and its transformation is generally misunderstood, and many jazz scholars have twisted and turned history in order to escape this conclusion. Art historian Barry Ulanov, for example, saw no African influence in jazz and assumed that it was more Gypsy than African. The ragtime historians (and art critics) Rudy Blesh and Harriet Janis thought African rhythms were communicated to African Americans of Southside Chicago by a Dahomean drummer at the Chicago World's Fair of 1893. The conclusions were large; the facts supporting them were slim.

Even today such unsupported generalities persist among jazz writers in statements such as "Africa provided the rhythms and Europe contributed the melody and harmony," or "The blues are the results of the imposition of a European scale over an African scale, with the resulting scale being a deviant form." To be blunt, there is simply no one alive who knows all of the musics of Europe and Africa well enough to make such claims. But the best writing on African music should force us to recognize that much of what we think we know about this music is either wrong or stereotypical. For example, as striking as some African rhythms may be to Western ears, drums and rhythm instruments do not appear to be the dominant instruments of that continent; instead, horns and wind instruments are more widespread and important to music all over Africa. And even the slightest familiarity with African rhythm (or Latin American rhythm for that matter) reveals that where there is rhythm there is melody. In any case, more needs to be known before conclusions are drawn, and there is reason to doubt most of what we think we know about African music and its relation to the history of American music.

Recently, some who celebrate jazz have argued that Africa contributed very little to it; and others have been so bold as to claim that the blues may have originated in England. Still others, in the name of justice and equity, call any efforts to characterize and historicize jazz in cultural terms racist. Similarly, many of those who point to the cultural complexity of Africa and argue that it is impossible to generalize about the enormous variety of African musics often quickly turn and generalize about the enormously complex nature of Europe, and not surprisingly wind up claiming European dominance. Some others stress the essential Americanness of jazz and view it as a totally new product. In other words, whatever the material contributed from the old countries, the transformations that have taken place have made its origins moot. But surely these writers overstate their case. Consider that many elements of jazz are also found in African-American church music: call-and-response, polymetrics, breaks, clapping patterns, subdivided beats, and staggered entry. And vice versa: when early jazz bands portrayed funeral parades (Jelly Roll Morton's 1926 "Dead Man Blues") or church services (Jimmy Lunceford's 1930 "In Dat Mornin' ") what they play is too close to the original to be seen as unqualified parody.

8 Listening to Jazz

With some knowledge of the elements and sources of jazz in place, it's reasonable next to ask how one should go about listening. It should by now be apparent, however, that jazz is a term that covers such an enormous variety of music that any attempt to offer blanket rules or even modest suggestions for understanding these styles is asking for trouble. Some may hear it bodily, finding pleasure at the physical level of response, and for this jazz can offer a great deal. On a good night, a jazz group that plays together regularly can work its way up to incredibly intense moments that will have an audience riding the wave with them, jumping up from their seats, and shouting out spontaneously. The language often used to describe great jazz solos is important here: "testifying," "storytelling," "telling it like it is," "shouting," and "preaching." And the cries of response to such a performance are equally telling: "Go on," "Talk to me," "Uh-huh," "Yeah," "Have mercy," and that ultimate urge to deepen the effort, "Work!" It's a language that signifies church, and all the seriousness, joy, comfort, and maybe even redemption that is available there. A few players—Sonny Rollins, for example—can get such a response even without other instruments, by playing with such sheer melodic inventiveness and rhythmic force that their energy leaps out at the audience, creating an almost spiritual aura of community around the musicians, if only for a set. Jazz record companies pioneered live recording in the 1940s, and some records of the period, such as *Jazz at the Philharmonic: Best of the 1940s Concerts*, Verve 557534—preserve the kind of audience excitement that jazz could evoke. As opposed to today's collective audi-

Sonny Rollins, "Autumn Nocturne." *Don't Stop the Carnival*. Milestone M-55005.

Rollins is a man whose art thrives on an audience's reaction, and this recording from the Great American Music Hall in San Francisco in 1978 is especially inspired. "Autumn Nocturne," a song seldom sung because of the difficulty of its angular melody, is here taken at full tilt, beginning with a long obligato introduction (which takes up over half of the six and a half minutes of the record). He throws everything he knows into it, quoting rhythm and blues licks, nineteenth-century salon favorites, and pop songs. When he finally begins the melody he's been withholding and the rhythm section joins him, he doubles and triples the time, skating past the song, drifting back to it, then breaking loose from it again, as if there were something unbearably difficult about facing it head on. Close to free jazz, close to barroom rhythm and blues, this is Rollins spreading fire through an audience. And if it's not his most coherent and compositional solo, it is certainly one of his most exciting, and gives us a snapshot of a man racing to keep up with his ideas.

ence shouts and whoops, in the 1940s, such cries, pleas, and even imprecations were often personal, discrete, and easily distinguishable on record.

But jazz can also be listened to with different degrees and modalities of intellectual activity—say, as a kind of auditory architecture or visual structure, while hearing melodies built note by note, forming figures against a ground of rhythm and harmony; or by listening to music as scrims, as textures of sound woven tightly or loosely. Or the music can be experienced simply by following the musicians much as one would professional athletes—through interaction with other fans, keeping score, compiling lists of names, tracking trends, and guessing at outcomes. And where and how one encounters jazz—whether in a concert or on record, in the background at a restaurant or while dancing, as a score to a film or in a small club—greatly determines what one hears and how one should or will react to it at the moment.

Still, there are a few basic things one might point to in any encounter with jazz. One is the importance of rhythm, and more specifically the rhythm section (if there is one). Rhythm is found in all music, of course, but in jazz it is fundamental, and elevated to an equal (or even higher) status with melody and harmony. In virtually every jazz group, it is the rhythm section that centers and drives the music. While it is possible to play great jazz without a great rhythm section, it's usually fair to say that it is great in spite of this absence. (On the other hand, while it is tempting to say that a great drummer makes a poor jazz band sound great, the truth is that a great drummer can make a poor band sound even worse, as they flounder against a strong beat.) Fans may argue that so-and-so doesn't swing, can't keep time, has no rhythm, but all musicians in the jazz tradition, even those at the margins, play with a strong rhythmic sense, even when—maybe especially when—they play against the beat, or play with what could be called conceptual rhythm.

Many of the arguments about what jazz is or what it should be in the future spin around rhythm. In its simplest terms, the question is something like this: must jazz always display a complete commitment to the sense of rhythm (or swing) that can be heard in Bud Powell's (or some other totemic figure's) playing? Or can jazz be played with other, more subtle, diffuse, or even oblique, rhythmic sensibilities? Think of the range of pianists now playing—Keith Jarrett, Matthew Shipp, Randy Weston, Borah Bergman, John Lewis, McCoy Tyner, Myra Melford, Andrew Hill, Jessica Williams, Cecil Taylor, Joanne Brackeen, Dave Brubeck, Geri Allen—must they all be judged against Powell, or is there room for innovation and revision? Just how fundamental *is* rhythm? This is, of course, simplistically put, but such arguments are equally simplistic.

Another element to attend to is variation. Most jazz solos and even ensembles vary what has come before, recomposing the melody again and again, forming fresh links to it, whether it be the original melody, a recording of that melody by another musician done years ago, the soloist who just finished playing, or even the chorus that one has just completed. Pop fans hearing jazz wonder what happened to the melody, since variation is not especially important in pop song. Classical fans may also wonder about jazz melody, but they should know better, as variation underlies their music as well. So, during a jazz performance of, say, "Body and Soul," one might hear a player varying the original melody as written by Johnny Green, or creating a variation on the previous player's solo, or even a variation of Coleman Hawkins's 1938 recording of "Body and Soul," a classic among saxophonists.

A third thing to listen for is interaction—the response of one musician to another in the midst of a performance. Though this is not understood as improvisation per se, shifts made in response to what another has played is basic to jazz, and a form of collective improvisation. The chords chosen by an accompanying keyboardist, the placement of the chords, or for that matter the choice of playing nothing—the use of silence as a musical device—all in response to a soloist who is also responding to the keyboardist's choices is the kind of interaction in jazz that is fundamental and always present. But it is more complex than that. The independent choices made by the bassist and the drummer at the same

Coleman Hawkins, "Body and Soul." *The Smithsonian Collection of Classic Jazz.* Also on *Body and Soul.* Bluebird ND 85717.

"Body and Soul" is a remarkable recording for many reasons, not the least being that in 1939 it made its way up the pop charts and echoed across the country on jukeboxes, where it would be heard for many years after. It was extraordinary for a pop hit, too, in that it never completely states the original song's melody. It was a report on the state-of-the-art tenor saxophone playing of the time, an exceptionally coherent, composerly, and satisfying improvisation. It is Hawkins's all the way, beginning softly, at the bottom of the horn, with rounded, almost leisurely notes. But as the solo unfolds over two choruses, he slowly moves his improvisation higher, louder, faster, and, toward the end, his notes stabbed out, his vibrato rich and emotional, he arrives at a properly dramatic conclusion. Hawkins was to record this piece again several times, including once unaccompanied, but never with the force and cohesion that this original recording offered.

time are also part of the mix of interplay. Groups like the Miles Davis quintets of the mid-1960s or Bill Evans's Trio with Scott La Faro and Paul Motian are examples of interactive play at its best.

Bill Evans, "Witchcraft." *Portrait in Jazz.* Original Jazz Classics OJCCD088-2.

Piano trios before Bill Evans's have usually been less a trio than a pianist accompanied by drums and bass. Evans had just recorded *Kind of Blue* with Miles Davis shortly before he took bassist Scott La Faro and drummer Paul Motian into the studio in 1959. As rewarding as his piano had been on the Davis recording, Evans triumphed with this new rhythm section. He played with what some call a floating pulse, by deemphasizing the beat, avoiding the usual vocal phrases of songs, and phrasing so as not to start and stop at points that highlight the rhythm of the tune. His touch tended toward the legato, a soft bluring of notes, his left hand often locked together with the right, embedding the melody within harmony. Such impressionistic piano lines needed sympathetic resonance, and he found it in Motian's understated pulse and concern with texture, and especially with La Faro's melodic bass. Playing free of the timekeeping role, La Faro tossed out arpeggios and guitarlike flourishes, swirled around the piano's lines, sometimes stated the melody before Evans could play it, sometimes chased after him with echoes of what had just been played on the piano. Evans left a lot of room for a bass to maneuver, and since he did not observe the beat closely, La Faro did not have to state it and frequently played somewhat free of time. This was a new kind of trio playing, where the beat was often felt rather than heard, so when La Faro does apply himself to the beat, as he does on the bridge, it comes as something of shock and sends the group hurtling forward. A recording like this one invites us to refocus our listening habits, so as to hear the piano, not so much as a storyteller but as only one part of an inspired group of narrators out of which the story will emerge.

9 The Clubs

Jazz grew up in a variety of venues as diverse as America itself—in taverns, ballrooms, music halls, theaters, gambling clubs, concert halls, brothels, apartments, back rooms, riverboats, hotels, amusement parks, gardens, festivals, wherever there was space and enough demand. But the music really first took hold (and still grows) in nightclubs, those small retreats where smokes and drinks have prevailed (with whatever else the traffic has allowed); those dens which were often run on shoestrings by local entrepreneurs, or franchises, or even mob money. Musicians will tell you that the club owners and audiences are disrespectful to their music, that the atmosphere is noisy and poisonous to their health, that the money is never good, and that they dream of playing the great concert halls of the world. Yet it is those little clubs with their tiny audiences where the music flourished. (It is sobering to listen to the live recordings of John Coltrane and Sonny Rollins—some of the greatest jazz ever recorded—and hear how few people were present those nights.) Funky and disreputable as many were, and are, they provided the chamberlike setting that was perfect for acoustic music, and an unfocused, relaxed atmosphere that allowed for movement, dancing, even a kind of conversational badinage between musicians and audience. Sitting close to the band, listening to music without amplification is the way this music was heard for many years, and it can still be rewarding to the listener. The cymbals—the basic timekeeper in many forms of jazz—never record or amplify well, but sitting close to them you can hear the sizzle caused by the chains or the rivets that many drummers use to keep their ride cymbals buzzing, the dry click of stick on closed high-hat cymbals, and the swish and spin of brushes on the snare drum. The deep, wooden sound of the acoustic bass (always lost in amplification), the depth and natural volume of the piano, its percussive feel, the mix of air and sound emerging from the horns—all this is best heard as close to the bandstand as possible.

But these little clubs are more than showplaces for bands. They are the sites at which all jazz musicians came to maturity, schoolrooms where mistakes are made, triumphs observed, and careers launched or ended. These are the spots where musicians hang out, where they come to hear their colleagues, and sometimes to challenge them, climbing up on the stand to sit in, either to experience some of the new music, to learn from it, or even to show that the music that's being played is nothing new at all. Many musicians spent the larger part of their adult lives in clubs, drank there, ate there, avoided the draft, found lovers and mates, confronted enemies, and met their ends—by acclaim, triumph, gunshot, drugs, whatever. Stories and legends attach themselves to these places and are called up long after they cease to exist. They are truly lost shrines in the history of the music.

Think of Slug's Saloon, located on East 3rd Street, between Avenues C and D on Manhattan's Lower East Side from the mid-1960s until 1972. A former Ukrainian bar and restaurant, it was far off the beaten track of New York nightlife, distant from the subways, too dangerous for even the cabs to venture near. But it was perfectly situated for the community of artists growing up around it at the time. When it first opened, Slug's was a nightly meeting place for local drug dealers, each arriving with their own bodyguards, there to talk over business as the night's work began. In order to get rid of them, the owner invited in the new neighbors—musicians who were playing the "new thing": Sun Ra's Arkestra, roaring and screaming in almost total darkness except for the tiny lights on their headdresses. It was an instant scene, as they said, and soon poets were coming, then painters, followed by celebrities (Salvador Dali turned up one night, surrounded by his acolytes carrying candles). Only a carved sign and door (artfully hung so as to squeak on entry) set the building apart from the squalid neighborhood in which it sat. But it was the kind of place where one night you might see Sonny Rollins enter the bar playing, and leave, walking home, still playing; or hear Ornette Coleman play his white plastic saxophone; or, on one fateful night, witness trumpeter Lee Morgan's common-law wife shoot and kill him on the bandstand.

Slug's was barely a blip on the screen of American popular culture, and in its first six years only one review of what went on there reached the public, and that in the infamously underground magazine, *The Evergreen Review*. But that was what it was, the center of a newly emerging underground, the shrine of a new form of music and the basis of what America years later would think of as *la vie des artistes*. Many of the clubs have this kind of aura, and so they live on, not so much in the histories of jazz as in the stories that fans and musicians tell about the music. Sometimes it is an especially well-etched character who takes center stage, like Pee Wee Marquette, the tiny MC and doorman (or woman, as that was part of the mystique) at the old Birdland in New York City who insulted musicians and customers alike; or it could be merely a one-liner, such as the one about the anonymous hipster who sat at the bar in Birdland the night someone ran in crying, "Chano Pozo's dead!" (announcing the murder of Dizzy Gillespie's great Cuban conga player across town) and answered in the Zen mode of the moment, "Never mind that! How was his last set?" Or it might be a place so identified with one kind of music—like the Lighthouse at Hermosa Beach, California, stronghold of West Coast jazz—that it takes on the character of a shrine of creation.

Though there were always moderate-sized nightspots in the biggest cities which favored jazz, some of the most important clubs were those that grew up in African-American communities and served a population barred from white places of entertainment. And in cities with well-delineated neighborhoods, local nightclubs were everywhere—places like the Aqua Lounge or Watt's Zanzibar in Philadelphia, Newark's Hi-De-Ho and the Silver Saddle, or the Red Keg and Henri's in Indianapolis. There was the Jungle Inn or the Bohemian Caverns in Washington, D.C.; in San Antonio, the Black Orchid, or the Nip and Sip; or the Reno in Kansas City. In Cleveland, it was the Rose Room and Gleason's Musical Bar. In Brooklyn it was the Putnam Central and the Blue Coronet, and it was Blainell's or the Club Alabam in Los Angeles. These were some of the most vital of the black institutions built on the lines of a segregated society; but by the 1960s they had largely vanished, victims of desegregation, urban blight, the ravages of urban renewal, changes in taste, and the fragmentation of audiences along age lines.

Some clubs, such as the fabled Cotton Club of New York City, though located in the black areas of the cities, were nonetheless racially segregated, serving the needs of white customers looking for adventures in race without actual social contact with African Americans. As odd as such an arrangement was, the musicians often made the best of it. In the case of Duke Ellington's lengthy stay as the house band at the Cotton Club from 1927 to 1930, writing for a great variety of dancers, singers, and entertainers allowed the Duke to expand his compositional skills and to move jazz outside of the narrow range of social music.

If nightspots like the Cotton Club seemed to guard the status quo, other clubs within the black community became part of the vanguard of racial integration. Starting in the 1930s, these "black and tan" clubs welcomed both white and black customers on an equal footing. In Chicago, the Club DeLisa operated from the 1930s to the 1950s as a state-of-the-art establishment. Faced with glazed white bricks and lit inside with red fluorescent bulbs, it had a dance floor that was hydraulically raised up to the bandstand when their elaborate floor shows began. It held over a thousand people and ran four shows a night, while another crowd gambled downstairs in the basement casino. It was the kind of place where you could find showbiz folks like Bob Hope, Paul Robeson, Gene Autry, Joe Louis, George Raft, Mae West, and Louis Armstrong when they were in town. John Barrymore was often seen there with his regular drinking partner, blues singer Chippie Hill. In Cleveland, the favorite black and tans were the Cedar Gardens and Val's in the Alley, and it was the Eastwood Country Club in San Antonio. In New York City it was Cafe Society, the Greenwich Village nightery that answered the Cotton Club's exclusivity and exoticism with WPA artists' murals that mocked Uptown high society. Other spots were less famous for "race mixing," but were open nonetheless (the music director of Monroe's Uptown House, one of the sites of the birth of bebop in New York City, recalled that one night the entire Woolworth family turned up at the club after hours).

New York City—the fiery center of jazz activity—is of course a special case. Black jazz musicians in New York have always to some degree been part of the mainstream, whether it was James Reese Europe providing music for the Castles' pre-World War I chic dance salons, James P. Johnson or Noble Sissle who wrote and played for Broadway shows, or the dance halls and clubs like the Savoy Ballroom, Small's Paradise, and the Park Palace (home of Latin jazz in the late 1940s), all of which were open to black and white audiences. Beginning in the 1930s, the integration of jazz in New York City was completed when its center moved downtown to 52nd Street, the most famous strip of clubs in jazz history, containing places like The Three Deuces and the Onyx, as well as the spillover of clubs around the corner that included Birdland. "The Street" was desegregated, but a mixture of high prices and the chill that many black folks felt when they went downtown meant that jazz had taken a fateful, permanent turn. African Americans would ultimately lose control not only over the economics of the music but also over the critical commentary and literature on jazz, weakening what the writer Albert Murray called the black patrimony of the music, the ethnic authority that lay behind its performance (and for some, its mystique as well).

As jazz continued its slow march downtown in New York City, every major shift in the music found new clubs rising to embrace it. In the 1950s, the Five Spot, which had been the center of bebop and the location of Thelonious Monk's famous extended residency, became the principal location of performances by Ornette Coleman, Cecil Taylor, Charles Mingus, and Eric Dolphy. Greenwich Village was awash in music in the early 1960s. "The British Invasion" had sent a shiver through the complacency of early rock and roll, and the folk revival was booming. New clubs and coffeehouses like the Café Wha?, the Cafe A Go Go, and the Dom were drawing together programs that would include the Blues Project one night, Cecil Taylor the next, and Jimi Hendrix the third. Much of this music happened beyond the eyes of the media, so the musicians were free to borrow from each other across the usual lines, and eclectic groups of all kinds were springing up.

The new jazz of the 1960s arrived on the margins, in coffeehouses, rented halls, and basements and other out-of-the-way venues. One solution still remaining to musicians was the model provided by the painters who occupied abandoned factory lofts. They could live there cheaply, though illegally, and at the same time turn them into mini-performance areas where shared meals, ideals, and a sense of community could thrive. As the scene developed, loft concerts seemed less like club events and more like church picnics or political rallies. Out-of-town squatters like Anthony Braxton, David Murray, and Anthony Davis first found their places on the New York scene in the lofts, as did Stanley Crouch, as drummer, critic, and club programmer. There had always been some loft activity for musicians, but between 1969 and 1979, downtown New York was markedly changed by the rise of new venues in the Houston Street area—places such as Sam Rivers's Studio Rivbea, Rashied Ali's Ali's Alley, and John Fischer's Environ. The new dwellers on the fringes of the Village—the Lower East Side and SoHo—who attended the lofts were distancing themselves from the glitz, booze, and tourists of the traditional jazz clubs. Lofts operated on almost no money, with no advertising, but the word got out. Joseph Papp opened the Public Theater to the new music and new musicians, and record labels like India Navigation sprang up to record them. The clubs finally got the message, though often grudgingly. The then new jazz club Sweet Basil sponsored loft festivals, and radio station WBAI opened its studios to the new music.

But what at first looked to the musicians like a promising means for taking hold of the music was done in by gentrification and new city laws that drove the artists and musicians out. It was also a dry period for jazz, and only the oldest and most stable of the clubs survived. There would be other waves of clubs coming along, but at the end of the century most of the new ones were either supper clubs modeled on an old-time idea of social class, tourist sites aimed specifically at foreign clientele (and sometimes owned by foreign money), or eclectic new takes on '60s-styled loft clubs like the Knitting Factory, booking everything imaginable.

PART 2

10 Jazz Styles

Following the tradition of the histories of other arts, jazz has been divided into styles and periods, each of them associated with players and composers who epitomize the historical moment. A typical chronology might show the following styles flourishing in these approximate time periods:

Pre-jazz (ragtime, vaudeville)	ca. 1875–1915
Early jazz (New Orleans jazz)	1910–1927
Swing	1928–1945
Bebop	1945–1953
Cool jazz/West Coast jazz	1949–1958
Hard bop	1954–1965
Soul/funk jazz	1957–1959
Modal jazz	1958–1964

Third-stream jazz	1957–1963
Free jazz	1959–1974
Fusion and jazz-rock	1969–1979
Neo-traditionalism	1980–

But things are more complicated than such a table would suggest. If we had books that kept track of recordings according to the year rather than the artist, it would be possible to see that at any given time records were being made in many different overlapping styles. In the face of this complexity, however, many writers and merchandisers prefer to construct a kind of evolutionary or dialectic model of musical change, where one style opposes another, until a new one is generated and the old ones die. But music styles do not die: they persist and change, often at different rates, rubbing up against each other as they go. During the heydays of bebop, for example, Latin music spread in New York City and became a part of the jazz scene, with groups such as Machito's hiring jazz musicians such as Charlie Parker. The most common mistake made with jazz styles is to focus on the differences between them instead of seeing what they share in common, and this is where a definition of jazz—if one is possible—is likely to be found.

A second problem with organizing jazz history by styles lies in the tendency to see them as forming a single line of historical development toward some projected goal or state of complexity. This kind of theory of progress can lead to overvaluing the present merely because it is an evolutionary result; overvaluing the past as the authentic, the pure, the original; omitting some styles from history because of personal preferences; or constraining the contributions of individual musicians whose evolution fails to fit an approved model of jazz history. Thus, great figures are said to go wrong and fall from grace, and music history becomes a kind of tragedy, or a ritual in which new kings and queens are enthroned to replace the fallen. (Those who guard the borders and create these ritual dramas are sometimes referred to as the "jazz police.")

A third complication arises from the number of stylistic revivals that have occurred throughout the existence of jazz, though jazz histories are often silent on them. For example, there was a Dixieland revival at the beginning of the 1940s in which many younger musicians played in the older style; but it was also a moment that created opportunities for older musicians, especially those from New Orleans (which was then being enshrined as the birthplace of jazz) to be heard again, or for a few famous figures such as Bunk Johnson and George Lewis to be heard for the first time. There were two more revivals of this same music yet to come, one in the late 1940s and another in the 1960s, each drawing on the music of the previous revivals. During the 1940s there was also a revival of boogie-woogie in both its piano and orchestral forms (its first wave of popularity was between 1927 and 1938, though boogie-woogie is usually marginalized altogether by jazz history).

It's important to remember that styles are more often singled out and named by the fans and journalists than by the musicians. The term "West Coast jazz," for instance, was part of an attempt by writers and record companies to distinguish a certain form of music from cool and bebop—

styles associated with the East Coast—at the same time that it was an effort to package California as a style and an attitude. Similarly, in the 1980s bebop and hard bop were highlighted by the media amid the appearance of a new wave of younger musicians, a tendency that continues.

It is within this existing paradigm of jazz history that bebop, third-stream, free jazz, fusion, and jazz-rock become problems. Granted that every new style has been greeted as decadent or a wrong turn by some, when bebop appeared many thought it to be such a radical break in the jazz tradition that it was treated as 1) non-jazz; or 2) the apogee of where jazz had been heading all along; or 3) a new beginning that was itself authentic and pure. On the other hand, third-stream jazz (a classical-jazz fusion) appeared to some to be a wrong turn toward Europe, or a pretentious, attention-grabbing search for dignity. Free jazz and jazz-rock were sometimes dismissed as the refuges of incompetents or vulgarians.

In recent years it has become popular to suggest that we have reached the end of the development of jazz styles because we have entered the era of postmodernism, where everything has already been done. In the 1950s and 1960s jazz journalists used to ask "What is the future of jazz?"; now they ask "Is jazz dead?" (It is tempting to answer the latter question the way the always-prescient Sun Ra did: "Jazz is not dead. Jazz will never die. It's the musicians who are dead . . . they've been dead for the last ten years.") One now also hears that jazz is on the verge of death, because the avant-garde jazz of the '60s and '70s failed to generate new styles and audiences, and instead stopped the progress of jazz, becoming its permanent avant-garde by default, until revisionists and traditionalists arrived to attempt to return the music to the principles that underlay older styles. This is a strange argument, if for no other reason than it assumes some kind of single-stranded progress in jazz, and purports to understand the destructiveness of those who stray too far from . . . what? African musical principles? swing? bebop? When we look back from one era to the previous one, we can see that not only did these musics coexist in the same time period, but that the players formed a cohesive whole, shared many of the same principles, and sometimes played each other's music. More to the point, it becomes possible to see that the greatest musicians of an era not only embody in their playing all of the music that exists, but also anticipate music yet to come. Louis Armstrong, for example, not only used elements of ragtime and New Orleans collective playing but played with a rhythmic and melodic style that made him seem comfortable in the early swing era. Beboppers like Charlie Parker knew the blues and even Dixieland elements so well that they could incorporate them into their own playing, even as they could sometimes play free of the new conventions which they had helped create.

The matter of jazz styles urgently needs rethinking. Composer/saxophonist Anthony Braxton has suggested that the changes that occur in jazz (though he includes all music in this conception, and perhaps all art, culture, and technology) can be seen in terms of what he calls restructuralists, stylists, and traditionalists. Restructuralists are musicians who change music to the extent that the structural properties of the music change—change to the point that they may literally threaten the musical and even the social order. Stylists, on the other hand, take the music created by restructuralists and recode it and render it publicly acceptable. They are the technocrats of the music, Braxton says, and confirm the existing reality. If Charlie Parker was a restructuralist, Phil Woods is a stylist; ditto the relationship between John Coltrane and Charles Lloyd. (Critic Martin Williams once dryly remarked that Charles Lloyd's effort was one of making Coltrane safe for democracy.) Traditionalists are those who live in complete awareness of what came before and reproduce the past by adjusting it for contemporary reality. Using Braxton's ideas, we can look at the music conventionally grouped under the heading of bebop and see it as being a restructuralist music in the 1940s and early 1950s, a stylistic music in the later 1950s, and a traditionalist form ever since.

One can quibble about who fits under what heading, but an analysis like Braxton's would complicate the way we think about styles and offer some correction to the oversimplifications of jazz history. It is also interesting to follow his conclusion that all three of these tendencies should be present in a healthy musical culture. Restructuralism gives music a sense of development and direction, but if there were no other forces at work, it would produce novelty rather than culture, one change following another forever. Stylists alone would put an end to forward motion in music by slowing or ending innovation (this is the tendency in music most favored by nightclubs, schools, and public institutions). Traditionalism, if carried to its logical conclusion, would stop change altogether and expend its efforts attempting to adapt another era to our own under a nostalgic rejection of the current cultural situation. (Such a condition now exists in opera where the "classics" have closed out all but the occasional new work.)

SINCE 1980 it has been difficult in jazz (as in other arts) to single out distinct stylistic developments. But while this has often been described as a postmodern phenomenon, it may always have been the case for jazz, where one style blends into another. What *is* different is that the music now lacks strong journalistic and recording company support to help underline new styles as they develop. In addition, much of the artistic foment of the last twenty-five or thirty years has involved musicians of one style of music being influenced by those of another, especially since they have been free to adopt elements of other musics without interference from tastemakers.

While the concept of style has its uses in grouping together musicians and musical directions, it is often used so rigidly that it boxes the music in, minimizing the achievements of some who go beyond that framework and overvaluing others of limited means who are nonetheless seen as exemplifying a style or era. Styles will be referred to in this book, but the reader might keep in mind that the ideas of styles we have received may not always offer the best way to hear this music, and are sometimes the products of nostalgia or limited listening. The invention of a style is always the result of someone's theory of aesthetics, someone's idea of how music should sound, even if that idea is never completely articulated (even in the minds of its theorists).

Likewise, while styles will be referred to in this book as

coming into being in given decades of the twentieth century, it should be borne in mind that even while they flourish in a given period they may also continue to develop, often into something quite different in a later period when some other style may dominate. By the same token, many players who seem to fall into the stylistic cracks, or who challenge the very existence of styles, will be emphasized here.

11 The Beginnings of Jazz

The first problem in writing a history of a music whose roots lie entangled among so many different cultures is how to go about determining sources and origins. The beginnings of jazz have usually been conceived of in terms of musicians who came from the tradition of marching bands, and the heroes of early jazz history have thus been trumpeters first and reed players a distant second. Pianists have always taken a backseat in this vision of early history, and so ragtime, which is said to have preceded jazz, has been pushed out of the story altogether. Ragtime has also been dismissed from jazz as too pianistic, too rhythmically stiff, and perhaps too European, and has instead been left hanging ambiguously as one form of jazz prehistory. To confuse things further, the word jazz was not widely used to describe the music for some years, and many of the earliest musicians said that what they played was ragtime.

If the history of jazz was rewritten to fully include ragtime as part of its origins, new progenitors would appear. Names like Scott Joplin and Joseph Lamb would move to the front of the list. The dates of the first recordings would be pushed back to the 1890s, and the date of the first recording by a black jazz artist would be 1915 (Lionel Balasco's recording of "Junk Man Rag" in Trinidad); composition would taken on new importance; the careers of key figures who began in ragtime, such as Duke Ellington and Benny Moten, could be seen as more coherent; the list of venues in which the music first flourished would be expanded; the piano would move to the front; and there would be new respect for the role of women pianists like Lovie Austin and Lil Armstrong.

It's sobering to realize that the sidetracking of ragtime is exclusively a product of the critics and writers: modern musicians like Don Pullen, Sun Ra, Henry Threadgill, Anthony Braxton, and Marcus Roberts have incorporated ragtime into their repertoires and transformed it as they would any other style of jazz.

Ragtime, Stride, Boogie-Woogie, and the Beginnings of Jazz Piano

Long before the golden age of ragtime, raglike rhythms and melodies could be heard in banjo tunes, quadrilles, minstrel songs, and marches. "Ragged rhythm" was how they described this common kind of dance music. If pushed back even further, rag rhythms could be related to dances like the cake-walk, the beguine in Martinique, the *danzón* in Cuba, or the *maxixe* in Brazil, and found in the piano works of classical composers like New Orleans' Louis Moreau Gottschalk or the Brazilian Ernesto Nazereth. But it is a mistake to think of ragtime as primarily European. There is a strong line connecting black country dance music to urban rags, and the influence also carried back across the ocean, from African American to Euro-American to European.

What we now think of as classic ragtime was first published in the form of sheet music late in the last decade of the nineteenth century, but its sudden appearance and rapid spread tells us that rags must already have circulated widely before then. But once they were in print, pieces like William Krell's "The Mississippi Rag" (1897) or Scott Joplin's "Maple Leaf Rag" (1899) created America's first twentieth-century dance and music craze. It was the French settlements of Sedalia and St. Louis in Missouri that were the creative centers of rag, but ragtime compositions turned up on sheet music all across America, and within ten years had become staples for concert bands like Arthur Pryor's and the U.S. Marine Band. In less than twenty years, rag became the basis for European classical works like Igor Stravinsky's "Ragtime" and Eric Satie's "Ragtime." But the clearest sign that ragtime was a true force and not just a craze was the way it was quickly appropriated by pop music. Even songs with little or no rag content gestured toward the originals, and some—such as Irving Berlin's "Alexander's Ragtime Band" and "Hello My Baby, Hello My Ragtime Gal"—became huge sellers. With the rise of other styles of jazz and popular music, rags quickly began to date, but not before they had changed popular musical rhythm and dance permanently, and provided an early model for how jazz improvisation could be formally organized. Rags and the influence of rags could still be heard years later in the guitar playing of blues street singers like Blind Gary Davis in the 1960s, as well as in the country music of Merle Travis or the bluegrass of Earl Scruggs. Ragtime was also briefly revived in the 1970s following the use of Joplin's music for the soundtrack of *The Sting*.

Rags began as piano compositions (though they were full and "orchestral" enough to be translated easily for bands) typically made up of four different melodies of 16 or 32 bars each, with an introduction, short connecting vamps, and a coda, most often played in two-beat. A fixed bass line of single notes in the left hand moved at half the tempo of a syncopated melody in the right hand: strongly accented notes were placed against the regular emphases of the bass, resulting in what we hear today as a mild

Scott Joplin, "Maple Leaf Rag." *The Smithsonian Collection of Classic Jazz.*

This is the one that set off the craze for rags, published in 1899 and cut as a piano roll in 1916 with the composer allegedly at the piano. "Maple Leaf Rag," like many rags, borrows its form from that of contemporary marches with its four themes arranged in AABBACCDD form, with its C or trio theme in a different key (offering contrast to what came before and setting up the last theme for a rousing finish). But it differs from marches in the repeat of theme A before the beginning of theme C, and—like all rags—in being rhythmically more flexible, with the left and right hands set against each other in syncopated tension.

This is classic ragtime, the kind that is best known, but hearing some of the more unusual rag forms is also rewarding. Joplin's "Solace: A Mexican Serenade," for example, provides a rather delicate link to the tango and what Jelly Roll Morton called "the Spanish tinge."

Further Listening: Various Artists, *Classic Ragtime: Roots and Offshoots.* RCA 63206.

rhythmic clash, but what must once have been genuinely startling. Today, rags are often played very fast, either to show off the player's technical ability or to accommodate contemporary listeners' notions of how older music was played, but most rags were originally marked to be played slowly. To add to the confusion, ragtime piano rolls were often edited, with elaborate flourishes placed in the compositions' empty spaces.

As ragtime spread across the country it flourished, especially in the New York City area, Atlantic City, Baltimore, and New Orleans. Its popularity on the East Coast was so great that it eventually affected all the music of America. In the music of player-composers like Lucky Roberts, James P. Johnson, or Eubie Blake, a distinct form of ragtime developed called stride, which became associated with new African-American dances that were springing up. In a reversal of the usual flow of popular culture, many of these dances were first communicated not to the masses, but to an influential and wealthy white audience through Broadway shows like *Shuffle Along* or through the society dancers and trendsetters Vernon and Irene Castle and their salon orchestra led by James Reece Europe. East Coast stride was played faster, full of flash and filigree, and often involved some improvisation, departing both melodically and rhythmically from the published music. It continued the left-hand bass pattern of ragtime, only with a more complex figure in which the hand strides from two notes in the bass—often an octave apart—up to a chord in the middle register, while the right hand improvises more freely. Stride, like rag, was often orchestral in form and easily transferred to arrangements for bands; in fact, Fletcher Henderson, Duke Ellington, and Count Basie, three of the greatest swing band arrangers and leaders, were stride pianists. Others, like Fats Waller and Eubie Blake, carried stride over into pop music. Off to the side was another school of stride, that of the enormously popular "novelty jazz" piano composers such as Zez Confrey ("Kitten on the Keys" or "Parade of the Jumping Beans") and Roy Bargy ("Pianoflage"), who emphasized speed and "finger busting" melodies. Years later, stride was still influential in popular music (Mike Stoller, half of the songwriting team of Lieber and Stoller, who dominated pop songs in the late 1950s and early 1960s, was a student of James P. Johnson's in New York City).

Yet another piano style—boogie-woogie—closed in on the ragtime-stride tradition in the late 1930s and rose and fell in popularity well into the late 1940s. Appearing first in the

James P. Johnson, "Carolina Shout." *The Smithsonian Collection of Classic Jazz.*

Johnson was a pianist-composer who spent his life as a working jazz player, pop song writer ("If I Could Be With You One Hour Tonight"), and composer for Broadway musicals and classical orchestras alike, becoming a model and informal teacher for Duke Ellington and Fats Waller. Though raised in New Jersey and New York City and well trained as a pianist, he got to know the rural peoples of coastal South Carolina who migrated north to work on the docks, and his music often alludes to their folk songs, set dances, and shouts. "Carolina Shout" (1921), in spite of being a sophisticated and virtuosic composition that every serious stride pianist of the time took on, was based partly on the shout, a shuffle circle dance, which was a favorite of South Carolina folks for both religious and secular occasions. It is a set of eight variations on a 16-bar theme, and at several points Johnson introduces musical material close to the call-and-response of folk shouts. And though in 4/4 time, near the beginning Johnson's left hand divides up the beat into a 3-3-2 pattern that suggests the polymeter of those dances.

Southwest in the 1920s, where it was called by several names including "fast western," boogie-woogie was a quasi-folk form, derived in part from the interlocked rhythms of two-guitar country dance bands. Boogie came in a variety of styles, from a languid tangolike slow drag, to a fast-walking, rocking music played in a 12-bar blues pattern, filled with crashing cross-rhythms. Unlike rag and stride, boogie was the music of largely untrained pianists who treated the piano primarily as a percussion instrument (the players sometimes even "prepared" their hammers—well before John Cage and the classical avant-garde—with carpet tacks which cracked loudly against the metal strings). As boogie-woogie grew in popularity, every swing band had at least one boogie arrangement, and some—like Will Bradley's—became famous as boogie

Meade Lux Lewis, "Honky-Tonk Train Blues." *The Smithsonian Collection of Classic Jazz.*

Lewis first recorded this piece in 1927, and it was its rediscovery that in large part set off the boogie revival in the late 1930s. This 1937 rendition is Lewis's third. The music is programmatic, referring to the funky, low-fare trains that carried working-class folks on summer excursions and included pianos onboard for dancing in cars without seats. Boogie was not so much about writing multiple themes and inventing new material as it was about developing the rhythmic possibilities of a single theme. Here Lewis is a veritable rhythm machine, churning up momentum, testing how far he can pull one hand out of phase with the other, turning the piano into a one-person rhythm section. No wonder that Lewis was one of the pianists that Piet Mondrian listened to while he painted his famous "Broadway Boogie Woogie," finding in the piano's cross-rhythms and sprinkled accents an audio analogue to New York's grid-patterned street rhythms.

Further Listening: Various Artists, *Boogie Woogie Stomp!* ASV Records CD AJA 5101.

big bands. As with rags and stride, published piano arrangements of boogie-woogie were rhythmically simplified and regularized to make them playable, and this was the pattern that big band boogie followed as well. An even simpler form of boogie appeared in the late 1940s and early 1950s as honky-tonk (as on Bill Doggett's huge 1956 hit, "Honky-Tonk") or rhythm and blues. It was this kind of revisionist boogie that played a large role in shaping early rock and roll through records such as Joe Turner's "Shake, Rattle and Roll" (where he is accompanied by boogie great Pete Johnson).

A HISTORY of jazz might be written to begin this way, a story that recognizes the piano as the central instrument of the tradition, treating it as the focal point for the convergence of salon music, rural string bands, marching bands, and classical piano literature. It would be a very different history from the one we have received, which consecrates New Orleans as the point of origin. True enough, New Orleans was and is America's most exotic city, the bottom of the United States and the top of Latin America, a nexus of cultural development, and in many ways the Athens of the New World. True also that New Orleans was the gathering point (if not the birthplace) of many different musics: jazz historians point to the African songs and dances of Congo Square, the presence of opera, military bands, dance bands, singing street vendors, balls and parades. But other cities also had a vibrant musical mix. Philadelphia, for example, was a place where African music and dance could be heard and seen in Washington Square near Independence Hall (then a slave burial ground) in the late 1700s. It, too, was a city with singing vendors, funeral parades, black opera, and the world famous Frank Johnson Orchestra, which played everything from folk tunes and train songs to European classics, along with their cornetist-conductor's multithemed quadrilles and rondos. Lack of research about other cities, especially in the South and the Midwest, make it difficult to say with certainty that New Orleans should be known as the exclusive birthplace of jazz. New Orleans jazz has been portrayed as more distinctive and focused than the musics of other cities and as a music that matured more rapidly and in turn had greater influence on the rest of the country. This may turn out to be correct. But in order to hold this conception in place, the origins, characteristics, and uniqueness of New Orleans jazz have often been oversimplified and idealized.

12

1900–1925: New Orleans

Jazz is usually said to be a music that developed in New Orleans within the spaces opened up between the marching bands in the streets and the dance bands in the bawdy houses of the Storyville section, and between the working-class African Americans in the uptown district and the Creoles of color downtown. The idealized New Orleans jazz band supposedly included a trumpet (or cornet), a clarinet (usually the French Albert model, an instrument with a unique sound and fingering), trombone and rhythm section (piano, banjo or guitar, drums, and tuba, and, later on, string bass), a perfectly reduced version of a marching band, but with the three melody instruments improvising a collective polyphony, the clarinet and trombone decorating the trumpet's lead melody, all of the horns weaving together over a two-beat rhythm. In this idealized history, these bands are the ur-forms of jazz, and the trumpet players were the stars. But surely the picture was more complex than this.

The African-American bands of New Orleans played for a wide variety of functions, including picnics, parties, and dances. The musicians were flexible enough to make these orchestras work inside the halls or outside in the streets of semitropical Louisiana, since they had experienced the double pull (if not counterpull) of two kinds of social musics and adjusted to their demands. This flexibility was shared with the musicians elsewhere in the Americas, in Cuba, Brazil, and Martinique. As with the bands in those other countries, much of their musical activity was shaped by social clubs, parades and funerals, and the festivals demanded by the ritual calendar of the Roman Catholic Church.

The New Orleans bands existed in greater variety than just the three-horn front line that has been canonized as classic: cornetist Buddy Bolden—who, although never recorded, is said to be the first jazz musician of importance—first played in a salon group, a string and horn band like the *charangas francescas* of turn-of-the-century Cuba. Nick LaRocca, the trumpeter with the Original Dixieland Jazz Band, also began his career in such a group. Many New Orleans bands had saxophones in them, as well as violins, with the three-horn front line, and many also played in four-beat or alternated four-beat with two-beat within the same pieces. At their most creative, interlocking polyphonic melodies were improvised, though based on routines that had been worked up and conventionalized from many elements. In addition to polyphony, New Orleans ensembles used a form of heterophony, a simultaneous but minimal improvisation on the melody by each horn that seems closer to unison playing than polyphony. This form of ensemble playing is usually dismissed as sloppy by outsiders to the tradition, but it is a practice that recurs in different forms throughout jazz history (even in the Miles Davis Quintet of the mid-1960s). One of the insights of New Orleans music seems to be that no one should ever play in unison in the European sense of the term.

New Orleans bands drew their melodies from almost everywhere: pop tunes, hymns, marches, vaudeville songs, blues, and rags. But it was the dance melodies that were strung together to play for set dances or quadrilles (lengthy suites made up of mazurkas, waltzes, polkas, schottisches, and the like, performed with callers whose rhymed dance directions anticipated rap) that provided musicians with a model for adding on music as new dances developed—such as the slow drag, the two-step, and the foxtrot—and also enabled them to knit together different melodies in different keys into single pieces.

Jelly Roll Morton

In the Northeast, pianists like James P. Johnson or Willie "The Lion" Smith were writing suitelike compositions based on dancers' requirements, but it remained for New Orleans' Jelly Roll Morton to refine these dance set forms and unify them so that they became something other than medleys of incongruous songs. More than those of any other jazz musician, Morton's pieces were balanced—structurally, rhythmically, and melodically. His works for his Red Hot Peppers, such as "Black Bottom Stomp" and "Grandpa's Spells," were wonders of contrasting texture and form—multithematic works in which every repetition of a theme was varied in instrumentation, rhythm, and dynamics. Morton took the forms of ragtime and quadrille and went beyond them to find a way to set up sectional contrasts within single compositions. His piano pieces were thoroughly orchestral, virtual arrangements with the various instruments' parts clearly audible in the playing, just waiting to be transferred to a band.

Morton also brought the blues and ragtime together, giving new flexibility to the existing form of ragtime. The blues and ragtime had grown up side by side, each creating its own craze, so their merger in Morton's music was something quite sensational. His melodies were often borrowed from other sources as well: Creole folk songs, marches, operatic arias, Mexican pop songs, Cuban *sones*, music hall melodies, and

Jelly Roll Morton. "Tiger Rag." *Kansas City Stomp: The Library of Congress Recordings, Vol. 1.* Rounder CD 1091.

Between May 23 and June 7, 1938, Jelly Roll Morton sat before a recording machine with folklorist Alan Lomax in Coolidge Auditorium at the Library of Congress recounting his life, punctuating his story with chords from the piano. From time to time he played whole compositions to illustrate his points. With "Tiger Rag," he wanted to show how he had transformed some French dance songs used in a well-known quadrille into what was to become one of the most popular hot jazz compositions of the first half of the twentieth century. The quadrille he drew on had an introduction (during which dancers found partners) and four themes, each in a different meter (such as the waltz or the mazurka). All of these elements, he said, were transformed into "Tiger Rag." Morton was widely regarded in his time as a braggart and a spinner of colorful tales, and here he was rather casually reclaiming authorship of "Tiger Rag" from the Original Dixieland Jazz Band, who had always said it was theirs. But the confidence with which Morton explains and performs this piece seems genuine enough, and offers us a rare chance to hear one of the founders of jazz discuss his compositional methods, and then play with a force and excitement that would seem fresh for years.

French tunes. But these appropriations were not the sign of a lack of originality, but rather a part of the tradition of borrowing in order to create long dance suites within the quadrilles and set dances.

Morton's intention was always to "jazz up" these borrowed melodies, not merely to arrange them in new settings, and it is clear that a certain degree of familiarity with the original melodies was required of the dancers so that the variations would be easily understood. Morton summarized his method simply: "Jazz is a style that can be applied to any type of music."

The often-told sad story about Morton is that he had the bad fortune of recording his finest work just at the point at which the fashion in music was changing from multistrained, complex forms to 32-bar pop songs. The biggest names in jazz were now improvising on these simpler forms. Morton resisted the trend for a long time, but it cost him an audience and dated him before his time. Only in retrospect do we recognize that he was jazz's first great composer.

It becomes increasingly clear that dance suites, ragtime, and early jazz are all historically related. But there is no reason to see them as an evolutionary sequence, with each form replacing the last. For half of its existence, jazz remained a music for dancing; and in New Orleans, brass bands are still playing multithematic musical compositions, not just as remnants of an evolutionary step toward a later musical development, but as a thriving, ongoing tradition of its own.

Nor have we seen the end of the dance suite's influence on jazz. The late Dennis Charles (drummer with avant-gardists such as Cecil Taylor and Steve Lacy) was born and raised in St. Croix, the Virgin Islands, in a family that performed West Indian quadrille music. Once asked about his unique approach to playing the cymbal, he allowed:

> Years ago in the West Indies these guys used to play and they had a guy who played triangle. The triangle is the kind of beat I try to get, ting-a-ling ting-a-ling, it's the same three you play on the cymbal, but it's that feeling I try to capture.

In other parts of the Americas the first stages of the creation of jazz also seem to have been reached at roughly the same moment as in the United States. In Martinique, for example, the beguine was being played

Jelly Roll Morton, "Black Bottom Stomp." *The Smithsonian Collection of Classic Jazz.*

This is a much-heralded Morton recording, and rightly so, for it's one of the first masterpieces of jazz composition and a wonderfully performed piece. Morton manages to incorporate the "Spanish tinge," stomps, breaks, stop-time, dynamics of volume, all the elements of jazz as he understood it. "Black Bottom Stomp" from 1926 is divided into two parts, the first having three themes (although all are based on the same chord sequence), with all three written out. (The solo trumpet passages that alternate with the whole band in the second theme were written out, though they sound improvised, as does the clarinet solo in the third theme.) After a brief interlude and a change of key, a second theme appears, which is then varied by soloists and the full group six more times. The constant shifting of rhythms and rhythmic devices gives each theme and its variation a lively feel. Every chorus seems fresh and inspired, with a new combination of instruments appearing each time (there are six different instrumental combinations used, though there are only seven instruments in the band).

Before it's over, we hear stop-time, backbeat, two-beat, four-beat, and a complete suspension of the rhythm section during the piano solo. Especially striking is the contrast in the last two choruses. In the first of these the whole band comes together but drops the volume to a whisper; and when they reach the last chorus they erupt in a musical shout, with the drummer shifting to a backbeat. All of this happens within approximately three minutes, and yet it seems organic, every note leading to the next, with drive and spirit and inevitability.

Further Listening: Jelly Roll Morton. *Birth of the Hot*. Bluebird 66641-2.

at the turn of the century by bands in which clarinet and trombone wove polyphonic melodies together over a rhythm very similar to one played by the Creole bands in New Orleans (for example, on Kid Ory's "Blanche Touquatoux" from 1960, or at the beginning of Paul Barbarin's 1955 recording of "Eh, La Bas"). Although there was a connection by boat between Martinique and New Orleans in the late nineteenth century, a volcanic eruption in Martinique's biggest city in 1903 put an end to it, so these two musics must have developed independently but in parallel after that date. Something similar can be heard with the *choros* (literally, the "weepers") of Brazil, instrumental groups made up of flute, clarinet, and guitar that began in the late nineteenth century and by the 1920s and 1930s were collectively improvising their counterpoint, and through which great improvisers like the flutist Pixinguinha became legends. In Cuba, salon bands who played *sones* had a similar approach to orchestral form and melody. But in Martinique, Brazil, and Cuba each of these musics evolved into very different forms of music from jazz, or else stayed close to the same original form.

• • •

IT WOULD be nice if we were able to give a firm date to the origins of jazz, but dependent as we are on recordings, we are often driven back to 1917, the year the Original Dixieland Jazz Band from New Orleans first recorded what we have come to call jazz. Most of the best-known early figures of jazz did not record until some years later. Bands that were given the name "jazz" (or "jass") at the beginning of the century may have played something we can recognize today, or they may have merely been raucous vaudeville or novelty stage bands, or even "pep" bands, smaller spin-offs from marching bands.

Another problem rests with the word *jazz* itself, which was not used by many musicians for many years. Jazz, much like the music itself, is a word whose origins are shrouded in ambiguity and counterclaims, having been identified at one time or another as originating from French, Ki-Kongo, French Creole, American slang, or just from a press agent's imagination. Again, many of these musicians called what they were playing ragtime, and indeed they often played rag compositions or other tunes with rag phrasing.

If we can't give jazz an exact birthdate and birthplace, we can at least acknowledge that it was most likely being played in a number of places in the United States at roughly the same time. Whatever else it was, jazz was for some years a dance music, and it reflected the changes in social dances during the late nineteenth century and early twentieth century. Group dances were becoming couple dances, and complex patterns that took upwards of an hour to dance were succumbing to shorter, easier-to-learn steps like the two-step, and to the various "animal" dances like the turkey trot. And many of the most innovative features of early jazz—such as breaks and stop-time—were developed to accommodate dancers' moves.

The spread of early jazz across America is also problematic, since it is difficult to determine what kinds of music were being played everywhere at any given time. For example, that first recording by the Original Dixieland Jazz Band was not made in New Orleans, but in New York City, when they were playing in 1917. It was not until 1922 that the next New Orleans musicians recorded, this time in Los Angeles. Recording activity in New Orleans was sparse at first, so a few key musicians in that city never recorded at all. The situation in other cities was not much better, and where there was some recording, as in the records made of musicians like Fate Marable and Charlie Creath in St. Louis in the 1920s, the allegiance was primarily to ragtime. In fact, rag rhythm continued to dominate in some areas for many years: as late as 1928 in Kansas City, Bennie Moten (whose band was later

Further Listening:

Ragtime to Jazz 1: 1912–1919. Timeless CBC 1035.

Jazz in Texas: 1924–1930. Timeless CBC 1033.

Jazz in California: 1923–1930. Timeless CBC 1034.

Jazz in St. Louis: 1924–1927. Timeless CBC 1036.

New Orleans in the '20s. Timeless CBC 1014.

Jazz From Atlanta: 1923–1929. Timeless CBC 1038.

The Chicago Hot Bands: 1924–1928. Timeless CBC 1041.

Jazz Is Where You Find It: 1924–1930. Timeless CBC 1040.

Brunswick/Vocalion Odds & Bits: 1926–1930. Timeless CBC 1055.

transformed into the Count Basie Orchestra) was still recording music that shows elements of ragtime persisting into early swing; Bessie Smith's blue tonality sometimes clashed with her pianists (especially Fletcher Henderson, whose own band hung on to ragtime fundamentals for some time); even Duke Ellington was still playing ragtime piano in the late 1920s. All of this suggests that fitting together the elements of jazz from the matrix was not always easy.

The Original Dixieland Jazz Band

Precisely because historians have decided that the Original Dixieland Jazz Band was the first to record jazz, the ODJB will be forever mired in controversy. Having declared them as white imitators performing an inferior version of the real thing, the writers of jazz history were unhappy to see them be the first to record. The Original Dixieland Jazz Band appeared to the nation just as the first shots were fired in the war in Europe, and so fortuitously became part of the Great War's history and its attendant manic mobilizations and postwar disillusionment. To early twentieth century ears this was a rough, wild sound: barnyard noises, rude smears and snickers of sound, accelerating tempos, a Bronx cheer in the dance hall. But the ODJB also put on a visual show. The drummer juggled his sticks, the soloists stood up from their chairs holding their instruments at bizarre angles. It was a crazed cross between a concert and a ballet. Those not excited by these innovations thought them vulgar, much as modern listeners do, though for different reasons.

The ODJB's repertory was filled with compositions inspired by marches, hymns, and rags. Solos were not so common, partly because these pieces were difficult to squeeze on to three-minute records, and/or because the players were not all strong as soloists. Though they proudly proclaimed they were untrained musicians and that everything they did was improvised, their records suggest that they counted far more on prepared routines. In fact, their polyphonic ensemble playing was standardized to such a degree that it suggests there were probably already rules for such playing in place for some time before them.

This is not easy music to listen to today, but most of the compositions they recorded became jazz standards (such as "Royal Garden Blues," "Tiger Rag," "Clarinet Marmalade," and "Fidgety Feet"). They were also blessed with an exceptional drummer in Tony Sbarbaro, who kept them in high gear, and whose innovation of playing on a different percussion instrument behind

The Original Dixieland Jazz Band, "I've Lost My Heart in Dixieland." Various Artists, *Lost Chords: White Musicians and Their Contribution to Jazz*. Retrieval RTR 79018.

Between 1919 and 1920 the ODJB toured England and recorded a number of 12-inch singles that allowed them to play arrangements which were a minute or so longer than the 10-inch records they had made in the United States in 1917, and also far less frantic and brittle. Though music at this stage of development (and marginal recording quality) is not likely to win many converts, it represents a baseline level from which to consider the history of jazz. But there is also a certain charm in the details that it would be churlish to deny: the delicate interplay of soloist and background polyphony, the surprising but pleasing rise and fall of volume throughout, and a youthful optimism about what they are attempting. This was avant-garde music in the early 1900s, and if it no longer has the potential to shock us as does Picasso's *Demoiselles D'Avignon* or Duchamp's *Large Glass*, it is evidence of how much more effectively jazz has already changed us.

each soloist and ensemble part enriched the dynamics and texture of the band and opened up new possibilities for drummers to come.

King Oliver and the Creole Jazz Band

Because he recorded more than most, and because the young Louis Armstrong was second trumpet in his band, King Oliver and the Creole Jazz Band are the most widely discussed of all the early jazz groups. Their music was a juncture of styles and forms, bringing together and reconciling the different directions of the historical moment. They played rags and marches ("Snake Rag" and "High Society") and other three-themed pieces, along with pop songs and blues ("Riverside Blues" and "Dippermouth Blues"). Their variety of melodic and rhythmic devices became basic to jazz, most notably breaks or stop-time passages with the two trumpets playing written or

King Oliver, "Dippermouth Blues." *The Smithsonian Collection of Classic Jazz.*

"Dippermouth" was King Oliver's nightly feature, his big "hit," and his solo on this first recording of it (April 1923) was striking. Listening to it now is musical archeology, and it takes some discipline to hear through the murk of the acoustic recording. What you find when you do is the two trumpets of Oliver and Armstrong playing the melody, while clarinetist Johnny Dodds winds around them, gracing their lines. It is Dodds who solos first, with two dark variations on the blues, using lines he most likely worked out in advance. The ensemble returns (this time with Armstrong playing the lead) to set up Oliver's solo of three choruses. ("Solo" might not be quite right, as the band can be heard playing softly behind him.) This is the feature that had audiences at the Lincoln Gardens in Chicago shouting to a trumpet solo that literally preached to the audience (Oliver's one hand holding the trumpet and fingering the valves, the other working a small mute to get a talking effect). It is also one of the first examples on record of a coherent, well-built, powerfully improvised solo, with each of the three choruses relating to the others in a systematic, thoughtful manner. It was a solo heard by trumpet players around the world, and was copied note for note for years, later even arranged for whole trumpet sections of swing bands to play in harmony.

Further Listening: *Louis Armstrong and King Oliver*. Milestone MCD-47017-2.

Johnny Dodds [The New Orleans Wanderers], "Perdido Street Blues." *Johnny Dodds 1926*. Classics 589.

The primary task of a New Orleans clarinetist was to decorate the trumpet's lead lines from above, so it's interesting when we get a chance instead to hear one of the best of the early clarinetists in the role of leader. In this 1926 recording with George Mitchell's trumpet and Kid Ory's trombone we have the opportunity to hear Dodds playing in two distinct styles: the bravura, throbbing lead voice that could cut through any number of horns, and the deep, slightly-on-the-flat-side vibrato he used to get the proper feeling that New Orleans music expected of clarinetists playing the blues. Trumpets may have been kings, but it is this kind of clarinet sound that haunts the serious listener of New Orleans music. And it was a sound you could also hear soaring over big bands such as Duke Ellington's for the next fifty years, long after New Orleans–style jazz became passé.

improvised lines in harmony. Solos were brief and pointed, each person playing distinctively, though their improvisations were often only slight paraphrases of the melody. As the band developed, their older multithemed melodies were replaced by single-theme pieces much like today's pop songs. And although their rhythm section can seem unexciting, even plodding, their stop-time breaks and some of Lil Hardin's accompanying piano figures connected them to Latin and African polymetric traditions. Revolutionary though they were in American music, they were also conservative, as Gunther Schuller suggests in his book *Early Jazz*, because they were distilling much of the best of American music and creating a standard for a tradition to come.

Louis Armstrong

Louis Armstrong is arguably the most important musician that the United States has ever produced. His influence was so profound, so far-reaching, that it tests the credulity of anyone who has not seriously considered his work. To begin with, after leaving King Oliver's group he recorded extensively, especially with blues singers throughout the late 1920s but also with any number of other musicians and singers; and whether it was Hawaiian music, hillbilly, gospel, or the shallowest pop tune, in the few seconds he could be heard he managed to transform almost every recording into an event. He was as well known in radio and motion pictures as he was on recordings and live performances, and later, during the Cold War, he toured for the State Department and became a spokesperson for the United States. Such a range of musical performance is usually reserved for the superstars who underwrite their fame by side-trips into other entertainment media, keeping their names before the public. But Armstrong began that way, and never stopped, and before he was through he had performed everywhere and with everyone, internationalizing jazz and spreading American influence.

Though the first thing that strikes the new listener to Armstrong today is his vocal growl and his casual, almost languid approach to a melody, in his day what gripped audiences was his incredible virtuosity on the trumpet. He was simply louder, wider-ranging, and more articulate on his horn that anyone else. There was a brilliance to his sound that was not always captured on record (though "Chantez Les Bas" on *Louis Armstrong Plays W.C. Handy* gets very close) but could easily be

Louis Armstrong, "West End Blues." *The Smithsonian Collection of Classic Jazz.*

For the first half of his life everything Armstrong did was copied as fast as he recorded it, but this 1928 recording of a 12-bar blues was especially riveting for trumpet players, who struggled with it for years. From the very first, Armstrong announces that no matter how new what he's playing is, he will play it with complete confidence and poise. His opening, out-of-tempo unaccompanied solo sets a pattern for what's to come: starting with four simple quarter notes, which by all rights should not sound syncopated but do, he moves through eight bars of increasingly complex figures, rising to a peak and then spiraling downward, changing the beat as he goes. Every solo of his that follows, whether played on the trumpet or sung, has the same simple-to-complex, balanced pattern, using ideas first stated in that brief introductory solo. On the last chorus, for example, Armstrong rises quickly to a high B-flat and holds the note for almost four bars. When the strain of the note's length and elevation is at its maximum, he releases it, lurching downward again and again with a rhythmically free phrase that he first stated in the middle of the opening solo. This is music that is extraordinarily orderly, balanced, and elegant, and yet, like the very finest jazz, always full of risk and surprise. If some of the other musicians in the group disappoint, they only serve to underline Armstrong's achievement at this point in time.

heard at the back of every hall he played in, even without a microphone. His tone was round and full, his notes seemed unerringly placed for their fullest effect—and even after all these years, virtually every note he recorded seems to be the only possible choice—and yet, none of it ever seems obvious. He was also one of the first popular musicians to use vibrato creatively (classical music notoriously uses vibrato without subtlety or significant variation). Vibrato can be used for many things: as a means of displaying warmth and sincerity, as a cover for faulty intonation and bad pitch, as a way of separating oneself from others. But Armstrong used it to put a single note into forward motion, to swing it. If he held a note long enough, he widened the vibrato near the end and increased its volume, giving it a kind of volatility and intensity not available to a more stable note. There was a cheerful impatience in his playing, an optimistic confidence that led him to risk going over the top. If the musicians around him seemed lackluster (as they usually did), he came out of the ensemble even before the others were finished, launching into his solo hell-for-leather (as musicians used to say at the time). Or he doubled the time in his solo, ripped up to a high note, leaving the notes in between sprinkled at his feet; he attacked notes with such gusto that even the simplest improvisation took on a majesty and even a dignity that the printed page would never suggest. Yet the shape of his solos was always graceful, poised between the dross of pop and the utopia his music suggested.

As if it were not enough that Armstrong would rewire instrumental music for the rest of the century, his singing did the same for vocal music. He sang much as he played (or vice versa), but with a playfulness and a rasp that would forever be part of American culture. Though he was not the first to do scat singing, he was the singer most identified with it, and he took the license to use it on anything he chose. He, more than anyone, made vernacular speech a part of popular song. Before long, you could see his influence on the pop song itself. Harold Arlen, for one, wrote songs whose

Louis Armstrong and Earl Hines, "Weatherbird." *The Smithsonian Collection of Classic Jazz.*

In 1928, only five years after he had recorded this same composition with King Oliver, Armstrong makes it seem eons away as he turns it into a duet with Earl Hines. It's a classic example of the aesthetic of playing "with" and "against," each of them playing together with real independence, neither musician doing quite the same thing nor ever giving ground to the other, Hines renouncing utterly the role of simple accompanist. The form is still three-theme ragtime, but they have managed to so radically transform what one does with ragtime that at moments they seem to have moved forward in time to swing (the lightness of the implied beat), bebop (harmonic substitutions and an angular approach to melody), and even free jazz (moments in which the beat seems to have been withdrawn). This is a record that could be studied profitably for years, and so it has been. Some of both musicians' musical lines on this record were to turn up again and again in jazz over the next twenty-some years (and sometimes quoted at melodies sound like Armstrong solos, "I Got a Right to Sing the Blues," for example, or "Between the Devil and the Deep Blue Sea."

length, as in the conclusion of Gene Krupa's 1941 "After You've Gone," where trumpeter Roy Eldridge and pianist Bob Kitsis assume the Armstrong-Hines duo roles).

Further Listening:

Louis Armstrong: Portrait of the Artist as a Young Man, 1923–1934. Columbia/Legacy C4K 57176. Now out of print, but possibly still around, this is a fine 4-CD boxed set sampling of some of Armstrong's most essential recordings. *This is Jazz: Louis Armstrong*, Columbia/Legacy CK-64613-2, is a good alternative on a single CD.

Armstrong might well have rested his reputation on the first recordings he did under his own name—the Hot Fives and Hot Sevens of 1925 to 1928. Made with a band that existed only in the studio, these records have long been proclaimed as the purest form of New Orleans jazz, though they were hardly that. This is music that was much more carefully planned than much of the music from the Crescent City—innovative at almost every moment, yet brilliantly never straying far from popular taste.

Armstrong continued playing and singing for forty more years, leading big bands into the swing era, starring in films, becoming jazz's first superstar and then its first icon; and though some of the youthful fire and experimentation faded over the years, he seemed forever creative and graceful, in part because it took the public that long to absorb what he was doing and how much he had changed music single-handedly. Though he continued to record pop tunes both good and bad, his playing, and particularly his singing, became more poised and deeply felt with age.

Sidney Bechet

If there was one reed player in Armstrong's league, it was fellow New Orleans clarinetist and soprano saxophonist, Sidney Bechet. In fact, Bechet's style was developed even before Armstrong's. Yet because he played the soprano saxophone (then a rather arcane instrument), and spent much of his life in Europe, his influence was never nearly as great in the United States as Armstrong's. Starting as a clarinetist, Bechet played a highly decorative and detailed line like most other reed players from New Orleans. But he was a far more accomplished musician than other clarinetists, and his solos moved with surprising rhythmic freedom for the time. When early on he switched to the soprano saxophone, his playing became louder and he began to dominate the groups he played with.

Louis Armstrong, "Star Dust." *The Smithsonian Collection of Classic Jazz*. Also *Louis Armstrong & his Orchestra 1931–32*. Classics 536.

Hoagy Carmichael's song "Star Dust" was enormously popular when this recording was made in 1931, and was a part of every dance band's book. Now with his own big band, Armstrong makes almost the whole recording his own, taking great liberties with the tune as he sings and plays over some uninspiring accompaniment. Yet somehow he miraculously keeps the melody's original arc and the lyrics' sentiments in front of him all the while. The audacity and daring of his improvisations are breathtaking, especially the repeated single note with which he opens his vocal or the repetitions he introduces into his trumpet solo. Armstrong recorded an alternate take of this song on the same day, and almost every note he plays and sings on it is different. This is as clear an example you're likely to hear of what improvisation can mean in jazz.

Further Listening: *Louis Armstrong: An American Icon*. Hippo 11032.

But it was his sound that was most striking: his vibrato was intense, fast, and hysterically wide and throbbing, matching his elaborately decorated melody lines and giving an expressive charge to everything he played.

Sidney Bechet, "Summertime." *Jazz Classics, Vol. 1.* Blue Note 789384.

When this Gershwin song was recorded in 1939 Bechet was committed to keeping certain principles of New Orleans jazz in front of the public, but by choosing a song not in the New Orleans repertoire he showed that he was no mere revivalist. The intensity and passion he brings to this song exceed almost any New Orleans performer's abilities (except Armstrong's). There is a careful choice of notes at work here, but also a luxuriousness and beauty that is rare in any music.

Further Listening: *An Introduction to Sidney Bechet: His Best Recordings, 1923–1941.* Best of Jazz 4017.

13 Beyond New Orleans

Outside of New Orleans, across America, jazz was developing quickly in the late 1920s, with witty and sophisticated arrangements of current popular tunes, and harmonies and rhythms that tell us a new kind of musician was beginning to play this music. After Louis Armstrong's mid-twenties recordings, playing in four-beat began to be favored over two, since the rhythms of the melodies played by those who followed him were more appropriate to four relatively even beats. As jazz historian Max Harrison has pointed out, the playing of the soloists who rose up in those early years was beginning to suggest the need for new forms of harmony and a more quickly moving harmonic structure: Louis Armstrong's "Weatherbird" and Bix Beiderbecke's "Davenport Blues" are examples of such pressures for change. In New York City people like Jimmy Dorsey, Red

Nichols, Miff Mole, Eddie Lang, and Joe Venuti were complicating the music with advanced harmonies and new conceptions of rhythm on pieces like Eddie Condon's "That's No Bargain" (1926). But in some respects the music was also becoming simpler. Improvised polyphony began to fade, except when it was conventionalized and turned into a routine by those who hadn't grown up playing it, or it was written out as part of a larger arrangement.

In Chicago, where many New Orleans musicians had gone to ply their trade, a new wave of local musicians—most of them white—were involved in jazz, people like alto saxophonist Charlie Pierce, cornetist Bix Beiderbecke, and the musicians identified with Austin High School, such as tenor saxophonist Bud Freeman, clarinetists Benny Goodman and Frank Teschemacher, and cornetist Jimmy McPartland. Theirs was a different view of the music, and they were often quite accomplished instrumentally, even if they were also rough by intention. Teschemacher, for instance, soloed with eccentric zigzag melody lines and a dry sound that, together, in retrospect, hinted at idiosyncratic soloists yet to come like Ornette Coleman. Jack Teagarden, a Texas-born trombonist whose laconic vocals paralleled those of Jimmy Rogers, the country musician from Mississippi, whose many hit records tied European-derived folk songs to the blues (Rogers himself recorded "Blue Yodel No. 9" with Louis Armstrong in 1930) and became an influence which can still be heard in today's country music.

Musicians began playing instruments new to jazz, or found ways to give new meaning to older instruments: Adrian Rollini, for example, alternated on bass saxophone and vibraphone, both instruments then off the beaten path.

Joe Venuti and Eddie Lang, violinist and guitarist, brought fresh sensibilities to older instruments and played them with great rhythmic drive. The saxophone had been around for nearly eighty years, and dozens of types of horn were available, but it was not until jazz musicians converted the saxophone from its role as a comedy or vaudeville instrument that anyone in music took it seriously. Coleman Hawkins, more than anyone, made the case for the saxophone by changing his own playing and taking on a more serious and wide-ranging approach.

Music whose melodies were played polyphonically was now called Dixieland, suggesting a certain nostalgia for many people's first exposure to jazz some ten years before. This was a different music, however, the polyphony more predictable, with newer melodies, sometimes played in four-beat, sometimes with considerable sophistication. And sophistication was sometimes these new musicians' downfall, as they often overreached the material they were playing, introducing odd voicings (note choice and placement in a chord) for variety's sake, modulating to new keys for no apparent reason, or overburdening simple songs with complex and gratuitous harmonies until they undermined whatever charm they might have had (Jelly Roll Morton's 1929 "Freakish" is a case in point).

Further Listening:

Jazz From the Windy City 1927–1930. Timeless CBC 1021.

Meanwhile, large orchestras developed that played jazz as just one of a number of musics in their repertoires. Jean Goldkette's and Paul Whiteman's were among the best, and though their music was once enormously popular, modern ears do not recognize the irony and charm that folks in the 1920s heard in their fusion of European string orchestras, black hot jazz groups, brass bands, semiclassical exoticism, instrumental novelties, and pop songs. Today they are listened to—if they are listened to at all—for those moments when a Bix Beiderbecke seems to pop out of the pack with a heated solo, or a Joe Venuti is sharply etched against the other string players. But these well-heeled orchestras often had some of the best composers and arrangers in the country working for them, and they created completely new standards of excellence. Paul Whiteman, for example, had in his orchestra's book George

Jean Goldkette's Victor Recording Orchestra, "Clementine (From New Orleans)." Various Artists, *Lost Chords*. Retrieval RTR 79018.

Jean Goldkette ran a series of six dance bands from out of his Detroit booking office, and this particular orchestra was packed with talent, many of whom, such as Frank Trumbauer, Joe Venuti, Eddie Lang, and Bix Beiderbecke, would shortly be bought up by his competitor, Paul Whiteman. On this 1927 recording of a forgotten pop song they manage to get a strong swing feel, several years before the swing era even took hold. The arrangement was collectively reworked from a stock arrangement—a middle-of-the-road version published to enable local bands to play new pop tunes—with each section of the orchestra working out their own parts. Through most of this record, the band floats comfortably over a strong four-beat, the saxophone section phrases in a thoroughly modern fashion, guitarist Eddie Lang and violinist Joe Venuti take their breaks with poise and sophistication, and Chauncey Morehouse punches up the rhythm with little more than a cymbal. And then there's cornetist Bix, filling in the holes, cementing the foundation, and guaranteeing that no one would forget that this band could play jazz.

Further Listening:

Joe Venuti and Eddie Lang, *Stringin' the Blues*. Topaz Jazz TPZ 1015.

Gershwin's "Rhapsody in Blue" (originally written for Whiteman's orchestra to accompany Gershwin's piano), Zez Confrey's flashy piano display piece, "Kitten on the Keys," American classical composer Edward McDowell's "To a Wild Rose," light opera composer Victor Herbert's "Cuban Serenade," Rimsky-Korsakov's "Song of India," the Original Dixieland Jazz Band's "Livery Stable Blues," as well as pop songs of the day such as "Limehouse Blues" and "From Monday On." But ever since a publicist shrewdly labeled Whiteman the "King of Jazz" (an absurd claim, given that he thought of his orchestra as pop in every sense—pop music, pop jazz, pop classics), he has been studiously ignored by most jazz writers. Whiteman used jazz musicians in interesting and quite persuasive ways, however, and helped spread a taste for jazz across the country that culminated in swing becoming the popular music of America within a decade. Orchestras like Whiteman's and Goldkette's were helping to educate a public in what it meant to be culturally American, and, apparently, given the radical mix of their repertoires, what it meant to be postmodern as well.

Bix Beiderbecke

Bix was the kind of person of whom historians say, "If he hadn't been born, he would have had to have been invented." And if Bix Beiderbecke's arrival on the scene was not invented, then it at least seems legendary. Like many of the first white jazz musicians, he was a midwesterner, born in

1903 in Davenport, Indiana, on the Mississippi River in a middle-class German immigrant family. Raised in a European musical tradition, early in life he nonetheless heard some of the best of the first white bands to play jazz, like the Original Dixieland Jazz Band and the New Orleans Rhythm Kings. His first professional work was with the Wolverines, a rough but rhythmically strong college band that became involved with the singer-songwriter Hoagy Carmichael. After a brief, unsuccessful stay at the University of Iowa, Beiderbecke passed through several large bands, later to record with the Frankie Trumbauer group and finally the Paul Whiteman Orchestra.

Beiderbecke was the natural foil to Louis Armstrong. But Beiderbecke's career was limited to eight years (he died in 1931 at age twenty-eight, from alcoholism and pneumonia), which gave his life a romantic sheen. What he brought to the music was something quite different from Armstrong. Bix's horn was the softer, rounder-toned cornet, and he played with a distinctive sound—the fabled "bullet hitting a chime" timbre—and a smaller, sometimes completely absent vibrato. His range was limited, his playing not virtuosic, but rather structured and formal, with a smaller number of notes used. Though he played the blues, he often stressed the bent quality of the note, leaving it hanging in the air, underlining it as if to call attention to it as an artifact. His melodies do not astonish, but they reassure, his notes cascading in an easy, relaxed manner. There were moments of genuine excitement in Beiderbecke's playing—short flurries of notes played loudly—yet they sometimes seem forced, as if he were obligated to show that he at least knew how that kind of jazz was played.

After his 1924 recordings with the Wolverines came the brilliant small band recordings he made with Frankie Trumbauer in 1927 and 1928. "Singing the Blues," for instance, was so influential that Fletcher Henderson hired Bill Challis (Paul Whiteman's and Jean Goldkette's arranger and Beiderbecke's friend) to work this tune up for big band, and on the recording Rex Stewart played Beiderbecke's solo, note for note. Beiderbecke meanwhile moved into the highest of commercial circles as a regular soloist with the Paul Whiteman Orchestra. This all had the makings of some maudlin fiction, and Dorothy Baker's novel *Young Man with a Horn* captured the essence of it using Beiderbecke's life as an inspiration: white musician under the spell of blackness sells out to become a pop star, forgets his debt to black culture, and falls from grace. It's an oversimplification of the blurred lines between race, commerce, and art in the jazz of the 1920s, but it is nonetheless true that Beiderbecke became interested in large orchestras and late nineteenth-century classical music from Europe and the United States. In fact, he composed several pieces that survive because arranger Bill Challis wrote them down and helped arrange them for piano: "Flashes," "Candlelights," "In the Dark," and "In a Mist." For years these short pieces were talked about in hushed seriousness as experimental and advanced works, tantalizing evidence of what might have been had Beiderbecke's life been different; but in retrospect they are very much of their time, and in terms of classical music, behind it. They belong, at best, to the school of "modernistic" piano works sometimes called piano deco—programmatic, impressionistic, local-color works of a gentle though sometimes florid nature, such as Eastwood Lane's "Adirondack

Sketches," or "The Blue-Robed Mandarins," or Rube Bloom's "Southern Charms" or "Silhouette," composers and compositions well known to Beiderbecke. For a dance band musician, such pieces may have seemed ambitious, but they were somewhat out of the jazz tradition, and remain a sidetrack in a shortened career.

It was Beiderbecke the stylist who heightened interest in this cooler form of jazz which offered an alternative to the hot jazz of the 1920s. He demonstrated that this music could be played lyrically, almost gently, with a softer, sweeter sound, while still paying allegiance to the black rhythms and vocal inflections that were driving jazz. His was a path that would be intersected with by many of the players of the late 1920s, including Red Nichols and Lester Young, as well as the cool players of the late 1940s and 1950s.

Frank Trumbauer and his Orchestra, "Crying All Day." Various Artists, *Lost Chords*. Retrieval RTR 79018.

In a blatant attempt to recreate the success Trumbauer had had with his recording of "Singin' the Blues" in 1927, "Crying All Day" from later that year attempted to build this performance on the opening of Trumbauer's solo on the earlier record. This is relaxed, "cool" music that contrasts to the wired, nervous quality of much of 1920s music. Over a loping bass saxophone part played by Adrian Rollini, a saxophone section led by Trumbauer sets up a sweet little melody against which Bix Beiderbecke and the tart-toned clarinetist Pee Wee Russell take solos. It's over quickly, but a mood has been established that's not easily forgotten.

Further Listening:

An Introducton to Bix Beiderbecke: His Best Recordings, 1922–1931, Best of Jazz 4012, offers a full range of Beiderbecke's music, including his work with Whiteman and Goldkette. Mike Polad's *Piano Deco*, Vols. 1 and 2, on Polecat 101 and 102 demonstrate piano works by Lane, Bloom, and Beiderbecke.

Red Nichols

Red Nichols was a post-Louis and post-Bix cornet player from Utah, who gained considerable popularity between the mid-1920s and the 1950s. Red Nichols's Five Pennies was only one of many small jazz groups that blossomed in the late 1920s, some of which continued to add instruments until they had grown to 15- to 19-piece orchestras by the end of the decade. A few of those expanded groups found their real voices in the elaborate arrangements of big band music, thus redefining the next decade. Small bands, on the other hand, were never more than frameworks for their soloists and were not able to expand their format. Nichols's band was a paradox: as a small group their arrangements were rich, fascinating, precisely played, and sounded bigger than they were; but once they expanded in size they lost their focus and their edge. Yet their early records—especially those from 1926 to 1929—defined a new approach to the music. These were white musicians who had grown up and learned to play their instruments just as jazz was beginning to sweep across America. Even though Nichols's bands were regularly staffed by some of the best young

Red Nichols and his Five Pennies, "Carolina in the Morning." Various Artists, *Lost Chords*. Retrieval RTR 79018.

Glenn Miller's arrangement of this old pop tune flirts with boogie-woogie on this 1930 recording, creating an exciting framework for Nichols's trumpet and Benny Goodman's clarinet. This is something of an all-star outfit, with Gene Krupa on drums, Jack Teagarden's trombone, Joe Sullivan's piano, and the ubiquitous Adrian Rollini's bass saxophone flickering in and out. Compared to what other bands were doing with pop songs at the time, this was exceptional in its variety, dynamics, and contrast.

soloists—Jack Teagarden, Jimmy Dorsey, Pee Wee Russell, Fud Livingston, Miff Mole, Joe Venuti, Benny Goodman, Dave Tough, and Gene Krupa—their music was collectively oriented, most of it written out or worked up in advance. Nichols was open to new ideas and combinations of instrumental voices, and he featured the bass saxophone at the bottom of the band, or Vic Berton's tympani drums as melodic instruments—something that would not be tried again in jazz until the 1950s. The musicianship and arrangements of the Nichols little groups were models for big bands to come; and years after they were forgotten by the public, Gil Evans remembered their tight, carefully harmonized effects as influences on his own arrangements for Miles Davis in the 1950s.

14

1925–1940: Swing

As the music of the 1920s illustrates, big bands and orchestras of some kind or other had been around for years in the United States: marching bands, quadrille orchestras, light music or salon orchestras, plantation brass bands, and many other types of groups of ten musicians or more were mainstays of musical life. So to call the 1930s and 1940s the era of the "big bands" is misleading. Swing bands were modeled in part on marching bands and were divided into sections of saxophones (or "reeds"), trumpets, and trombones which were musically arranged so as to play against each other in call-and-response fashion and then to come together for ensembles. The saxophone sections were the real center of the swing bands: they were structured like choirs, with alto, tenor, and baritone saxophones (the most common formation being two altos, one or two tenors, and a baritone). These reed sections were often the most identifiable parts of swing bands, with considerable latitude allowed as to how they were voiced. Instead of an alto, a clarinet might be used as the lead instrument, as it was in the Glenn Miller Orchestra; three tenor saxophones and a baritone might form a section that got a dark, murky sound (as with the famous "Four Brothers" of the Woody Herman band); or a French horn might be mixed in with saxophones and clarinets for a chamber-group feel (the specialty of the Claude Thornhill Orchestra).

The history of the swing era can be divided into two parts: the first, a period of pre-swing from 1924 to 1932, and the second, from 1932 to the mid-1950s. The two can be distinguished by the size of bands and the relationship of their parts, the flowering of swing phrasing and rhythm, and the development of mature and individualized soloists. (The transition to a new kind of swing was probably smoother than it appears, but during the depression of 1930 to 1932, very few records were made, and thus very little documentation exists of this period of change.)

In the 1920s and early 1930s, dance bands were smaller, with few having more than nine to eleven musicians. The ability of bands in this period to hold a steady swing rhythm was limited, and even some of the best of them—Fletcher Henderson's and Duke Ellington's orchestra, for example—were not always consistent. Most bands played in two-beat, and it took the next seven or eight years for them to move to a relatively even four-beat, helped along by the popularity of the string bass that was beginning to replace the heavier-sounding, slower-moving tuba; the move to electronic recording radically improved the sound of records, allowing the bass to be properly heard for the first time. Drummers in the second period of swing became more active participants in arrangements, filling holes, bridging sections of music, all the while rumbling and agitating under the whole ensemble. Explosive as they could be, swing drummers approached the beat itself with a lighter touch, with a small splashing click of the high-hat cymbals and the blurred rush of the big ride cymbal beginning to replace the snare and the bass drum as the heartbeats of the band. Swing rhythm became flexible and variable rather than precise; a forward-driving pulse that seemed to be (and often was) accelerating, the product of the interaction of the members of a rhythm section, each of whom approached the beat differently. Arrangers and soloists as well developed their melodies on rhythmic figures of four beats instead of two, placing accents where they chose over the surface of even beats. The great arrangers could make the band phrase and move as if it were a soloist, so when the actual soloists played they meshed perfectly with the ensemble. No longer would a great player like Armstrong or Beiderbecke stand out against stiff background rhythm or accompaniment, as if they had arrived from a different musical universe.

Riffs had been used by bands for some time, but in the second period of swing they expanded from being accompanying figures behind soloists to becoming melodies in themselves. At times, several contrasting riffs were running simultaneously in different parts of the band, forming complex webs of rhythm. Improvised polyphony began to assume a lesser role in jazz, first becoming simplified and formulaic, then slowly disappearing altogether. For some time America remained nostalgic about Dixieland-styled music, and polyphony lived on in small groups inside the big bands that nightly played a mini-set in a rather routinized fashion (like Tommy Dorsey's Clambake Seven). These little bands placated older listeners and perhaps even the leaders of the bands, many of whom had grown up with that music. (Not surprisingly, the last big band to feature a Dixieland group was Lawrence Welk's.) A few bands—like Bob Crosby's Bob Cats—even tried expanding the Dixieland format into full-scale arrangements. Every once in a while, some group would slip into the hit parade by reviving an old tune, like former Casa Loma trombonist Pee Wee Hunt, whose deliberately corny "12th Street Rag" was number one for eight weeks on the hit charts in 1948.

Swing was made possible by the substantial number of well-educated musicians in the United States who at this point could read or write sophisticated arrangements, and by the development of a number of stylists capable of soloing. The rapidly burgeoning influence of radio, movies, and recordings created a synergy that would spread swing music across the country and around the world with astonishing speed. The development of sound film made motion pictures a hugely attractive medium in the early 1930s, and big bands began to move out of the role of theatrical pit bands and take the stage between films at the biggest theaters; and soon they would be in the films, the leaders sometimes performing as themselves or as actors. Soon, swing seemed to be everywhere. Live music could be heard from all parts of the country every night on radio, and people from different regions could hear musicians and styles previously limited to a local area. "Territory bands" that played in regional styles might with a little luck find themselves catapulted to national fame. Or they might simply disappear without ever recording. In Birmingham, Alabama, for example, blacks in the late 1920s and 1930s regularly heard bands at their dances such as the C.S. Belton Orchestra, Doc Wheeler's Royal Sunset Serenaders, the Carolina Cotton Pickers, Fess Whatley's Sax-O-Society Orchestra, the Black & Tan Serenaders, the Fred Averett Band, and the Magic City Serenaders. But nothing survives of them except their sterling reputations in the memories of a few local musicians who themselves went on to fame.

By the early 1930s swing was firmly established as the pop music of America, and the bands could make almost anything work for them: pop songs and riff tunes, sentimental favorites from the past, marches, waltzes, and arrangements of light classics. There was a form of swing for everyone. A "sweet" form continued from the pre-swing era, and still appealed to an older generation: bands like Guy Lombardo's, Sammy Kaye's, or Freddie Martin's had some elements of the swing style, but often phrased differently, used an older, broader vibrato, played in two, or used an older type of pop song. But these bands were heard by large audiences as well. (It is always surprising to see who the fans of these bands were: Charlie Parker's wife, Chan, said that Parker loved Sammy Kaye's recording of "Slow Boat to China"; Louis Armstrong praised the Guy Lombardo saxophone section; and Sun Ra's arrangements of the light classical works showed his taste for Freddie Martin.)

Further Listening:

Cartoonist R. Crumb has amassed a number of the recordings of the better, but lesser-known, early pop and sweet bands like Rudy Vallee, and the Ray Miller Orchestra on *That's What I Call Sweet Music: American Dance Orchestras of the 1920s.* Songbook 7243 4 96603.

In the Southwest, western swing had developed by the early 1930s, a fusion of country music and swing with big bands playing two-beat, heavy on the blues, fiddles, and electric guitars. Bob Wills and his Light Crust Doughboys, Milton Brown and the Brownies, and Spade Cooley were among the earliest and the best, but for years to come jazz would have a profound influence on country and western music. The links between these musics has not been as well researched as they should have been, but the fact that Ray Charles and guitarist Charlie Christian started in country bands tells us something about the importance of the two musics in their mutual development.

Swing of one form or another unified American taste, reaching every class, age group, and race, despite segregation. Musicians like Duke Ellington ultimately became popular in every group. The big swing orchestras were spectacles of the first order. The music may have sometimes been hot enough to threaten an older generation, but otherwise they were showcases of gentility and splendor. Onstage the musicians were rakishly attired in tuxedos or freshly pressed suits, starched shirts, and patent leather shoes, women singers in evening gowns. Drummers sat amid gleaming foliage of cymbals and gongs, the head of the bass drum painted with

Milton Brown and his Musical Brownies, "Taking Off." Various Artists, *Lost Chords*. Retrieval RTR 70018.

Recorded in 1935, a year before Brown's death, "Taking Off" is not an elaborate arrangement. The band has only eight musicians, but, allowing for a certain degree of cultural lag, the violin, piano, and electric guitar solos illustrate the degree to which country music was forever changed by swing.

tropical scenes and lit softly from behind. Spotlights bounced off gleaming brass and mirrored hanging balls, creating a smoky phantasmagoria. The music could be a solid wall of sound, every voice as one; or a single section of trombones or trumpets or saxophones could suddenly go into sovereign motion, their instruments lifted and swaying, choreographed against other sections, their physical movement miming the call-and-response of the music and encouraging the dancers. Soloists rose from behind the anonymity of music stands to step up to the microphone with personal style. Behind the soloists there were testifying instrumental riffs and verbal cheers of praise and support.

For blacks these bands had special significance, since some groups were as much in demand by whites at the wealthy hotels and country club gatherings as they were among blacks at their own nightclubs. It was a life of elegance, of pride in craft, a life that mocked the social limitations placed upon them. And the leaders were often heroes in the community.

Fletcher Henderson

Fletcher Henderson was such a hero. Born into a family of important educators in Georgia, and educated himself to be a chemist, Henderson instead became an administrator for the Black Swan Recording Company and worked as an accompanying pianist for Bessie Smith and a num-

Fletcher Henderson, "Copenhagen." *Fletcher Henderson 1924, Vol. 3.* Classics 647.

"Copenhagen" was a popular song of the 1920s and was recorded quite frequently. In fact, the Wolverines (with Bix Beiderbecke) had recorded it only

ber of other leading theatrical blues singers of the day. When opportunities arose to lead bands in Broadway shows and at Roseland dance hall in New York City, he became a full-time bandleader, employing some of the finest musicians in the country (among them Coleman Hawkins, Buster Bailey, Louis Armstrong, and Charlie Green), as well as some of the most innovative arrangers (Don Redman at the beginning, and Benny Carter in the 1930s). His bands, more than any other, established what a swing band should sound like, and his versions of "Honeysuckle Rose," "Wrappin' It Up," and "King Porter's Stomp" were state of the art, copied by some, traded for arrangements with other bands such as Jean Goldkette's. After a debilitating automobile accident, Henderson became one of the principal arrangers for Benny

a few months before this 1924 recording. Don Redman is the innovative arranger here, and though this is a very early example of swing, maybe even pre-swing, he established the outline of a pattern with this recording that was to be repeated for years to come by countless bands. The music is distributed between trios of trumpets and clarinets (clarinet trios were very popular at the time, having come from marching bands), the brass section, the entire ensemble, and soloists (most solos written, but with a few passages of collective improvisation). Redman breaks the music of the original song down into four-bar phrases, but two-thirds of the way through the recording, breaks it down even further, into three-, two-, and one-bar phrases. Despite the complexity of his arrangement and the three themes of the original song, there is a logic and a flow to it that gives it coherence and keeps it from being cluttered. Incidentally, there are occasional hints of earlier New Orleans–style music in this arrangement, and the presence of Louis Armstrong in the trumpet section makes them seem even more striking.

Goodman, helping Goodman reach stardom with a band that sounded very much like his own.

Many of the early swing bands are long forgotten and are hard to find on record, if available at all. There was, for example, Luis Russell, up from New Orleans to Chicago, who adapted King Oliver's style for swing and sometimes backed Louis Armstrong on records; the Missourians (later taken over by Cab Calloway), bringing an older, boisterous, energetic St. Louis style into New York City; or Chick Webb's band, with its pure swing driven by the drummer-leader's unfailing time and the band's superb soloists. One other to mention is the Casa Loma Band, a group that began in 1927 as one of Jean Goldkette's bands sent out from Detroit to various resorts, hotels, and dance halls and developed a mixed repertoire of pop vocal hits like "Smoke

The Casa Loma Band, "White Jazz." Various Artists, *Lost Chords.* Retrieval RTR 79018.

In 1931 it might seem like the most obvious thing in the world for a white band from the Midwest with the name of a Toronto hotel to title a composition "White Jazz." It wasn't, though, especially when shortly after they followed this recording with one enigmatically called "Black Jazz." This is a fine piece of swing, with parts being tossed around the sections of the band like a beach ball, soloists fitting their roles as if they'd played this music all their life, the whole band phrasing like one horn on the ensembles, and the rhythm section carrying them forward like a runaway train. This pure riff composition by bassist Gene Gifford is a break with the pop song tradition, and one that leaves the usual melody behind in favor of forward motion and excitement. More than anything, it announces the arrival of a new kind of music, one that would soon have the dancers leaving the floor to listen as they pressed against the bandstand.

Rings" and strictly instrumental features like "No Name Jive." Their impeccable musicianship and fresh solutions to the problem of how to organize the sections of a dance band had immediate influence on the burgeoning swing era. The touch of Casa Loma can be heard in the bands of Jimmie Lunceford and Benny Goodman.

Further Listening:

Various Artists, *Harlem Big Bands.* Timeless CBC 1010.

Swing bands became vehicles for stardom, and some leaders—like Benny Goodman—reached a new teenaged audience, made movies, had weekly radio shows, and gave triumphant concerts at Carnegie Hall. In a sense Goodman's success was the result of having found the midpoint of swing, a place that represented a synthesis of all existing styles. By the early 1950s there had been thousands of swing bands, so many that to generalize about them is as difficult as reducing all of rock and roll to a few pages. But

Jimmie Lunceford, "Organ Grinder's Swing." *The Smithsonian Collection of Classic Jazz.*

"Organ Grinder's Swing" was a much overplayed and rather silly hit song in 1936. But when Sy Oliver turned in his arrangement for the Lunceford band it had become a subtle but sharply drawn miniature, with contrasting sections of tinkling celeste and woodblocks in one key, alternating with a growling, bluesy theme with strong rhythm in another. The two sections were also set apart by strong color contrasts in the sounds of the instruments chosen for each section. This is a perfect example of the arranger's role in jazz: the original tune had been virtually recomposed, but with many small details and flourishes. Incidentally, at dances the tempo of this piece was much slower than on the recording, and the shift between the two sections gave dancers a chance to show their individual styles.

there were two very different bands that seem to best represent the range of what swing achieved: Duke Ellington's and Count Basie's.

Duke Ellington

Because Ellington's career spanned so much of jazz history, his music reflects many styles and musical periods, his compositions number in the thousands, as do his recordings. His sheer output of music alone would qualify him for singular recognition in American cultural history; but when the quality of that music is considered—its incredible inventiveness and originality, its brilliant use of American themes and ideals—he must be reckoned with in the highest of all terms.

Having begun life as a musician in Washington, D.C., where he learned ragtime piano and played for theaters and society affairs, his first arrangements for band not surprisingly display a rag sensibility. When he moved to New York City he continued with a similar music, but he also became fascinated with stride pianists Willie "The Lion" Smith and James P. Johnson. Though he developed a

Duke Ellington, "East St. Louis Toodle-O." *The Smithsonian Collection of Classic Jazz.*

This 1927 recording was jointly worked out by Ellington and his trumpeter Bubber Miley. Miley's talking trumpet carried the first two of three themes, while the saxophones walk in chords behind him. Other soloists join in with these and other themes, the ensemble plays all together, and the record ends quietly as it began. This is not the best composition Ellington ever wrote (he continually changed it over the years), but it sets a mood and holds it, leaving a strong sense of instrumental color behind.

distinctive style of his own—a rich, unique blend which nonetheless was immediately recognizable—at times he could call on all of those styles and put them into play.

From the late 1920s through the late 1930s Ellington and his musicians were installed as the house band at the Cotton Club in Harlem, and it was here that he developed his skills as a composer and arranger. Ellington's music was heavily influenced by his choice of idiosyncratic musicians, and by his practice of building arrangements around their individual styles. Trumpeter Bubber Miley, with his highly expressive, rough, and folkish style especially helped Ellington to move away from some of the sweeter arrangements he began

Duke Ellington, "Cotton Tail." *The Smithsonian Collection of Classic Jazz.*

It was 1940, the very peak of the swing era, and Ellington came up with something that anticipated the coming of bebop. Working from the chords to "I Got Rhythm," a small group from within the band tears into the boppish theme in unison, with no introduction and with the same urgency that boppers would be displaying in their own anthems in the six or seven years to come.

Cootie Williams's trumpet solo is accompanied by saxophones voiced in a very modern style, even for Ellington. Tenor saxophonist Ben Webster follows with a solo packed with tonal and rhythmic variety, one that builds to a powerful climax with the help of the inventiveness of the rhythm section (especially bassist Jimmy Blanton's repeated held tones which briefly suspend the rhythm, and Duke's accompanying chords that suggest two keys at once); the saxophone sections' part seems to extend Webster's solo (there is some evidence that he arranged it); and when the brass come, the rhythm section drives them hard. When Ellington enters next with a stride solo the effect is positively shocking. The saxophone section returns again, the melody is restated, and it's all over in three minutes and eleven seconds. Yet in that time we've heard perhaps the greatest big band performance of the era, with every soloist perfectly placed in an overall scheme that balances the written and the improvised contributions with perfection.

with. Then with musicians such as Sidney Bechet and Sam Nanton in the band, Ellington was able to create music that spanned white and black tastes, and he used anything he wished as raw material for his compositions. There were elements of New Orleans music, for instance, growling, talking trumpets in the manner of King Oliver, and clarinets soaring over the top of the band (and his clarinetists often were from New Orleans). He used as source material everything from sentimental songs to classical themes, and from the blues to rock and roll. Ellington felt free to use any musical form he found useful—the concerto, Indian raga, West Indian folk dances, the most beautiful and the most insipid of pop songs. It was Ellington's alchemy—his ability to transform these materials so completely—that set him apart from his other colleagues in swing.

His own compositions flowered in variety: pop tunes of all sorts, the "jungle" themes, exotic evocations of the desert or the pyramids; praise songs to the city, the high life, and modernity; or his own blues—mood pieces about colored cellophane or misty mornings; dance songs, from the sublime to the profane. The list is endless, for he knew no limits.

Though he led one of the two great swing bands, his swing rhythm was like no one else's. They could, if they wished, get that accelerating, freewheeling, almost-out-of-control drive of the best bands. But just as often, Ellington's band's rhythmic conception was more like a huge animal coiling up to spring into life, or at other times like the old man Ellington pictured coming home from work with his "broken walk" in "East St. Louis Toodle-O." Rhythms bubbled under rhythms with Ellington, like the two hands of a ragtime pianist working with and against each other.

Similarly, though he used the same instruments as other bands, and seated their players in sections on the stage like other bands, beyond that, his methods were often very different. The section, to begin with, might be made up of musicians with radically different sounds and styles—like the trombone section of the smooth, sweet-toned Lawrence Brown, the classically trained valve trombone of Juan Tizol, and the funky, folkish, talking horn of Tricky Sam Nanton—and yet they could all play together, and sound quite different from any other swing band's trombone section. At his most creative, Ellington might assign certain sections of the band other sections' roles, the brass, say, carrying the beat, while the rhythm section coasted.

Though he operated with the conventional distinction between soloists and ensemble, Ellington might assign the soloist the job of varying the melody the ensemble played, only *before* the melody is played; or, again, the soloists might be given melodies to play

Duke Ellington, "In A Mellotone." *The Smithsonian Collection of Classic Jazz.*

The theme to this 1940 tune is simple and not a great composition. It is rather the alto saxophone solo by Johnny Hodges and the trumpet solo by Cootie Williams that make it great, along with the way in which they are balanced by the band—buoyed up, talked to, and cheered on. Ellington was a great composer, but what makes this performance, like many of his others, so compelling is the way in which he has made his orchestra an extension of his composition.

that sounded more like the ensembles' parts, while the ensemble received melodies that seemed more angular, more individual, more improvisational.

His influence is written across the history of jazz, with every era showing their debt to him. It was one thing to see his contemporaries affected by him, to see other bands attempt to copy his hits. But in the 1960s and 1970s, when swing was no longer in favor, he was still a force behind musical innovations. Charles Mingus kept Ellington's compositions and methods in front of musicians through his own work. But avant-gardists like Cecil Taylor, Roswell Rudd, Steve Lacy, Sun Ra, Archie Shepp, and Ran Blake all recorded his works as well. And others—Don Pullen, Anthony Braxton, John Carter, Muhal Richard Abrams, Carla Bley, and Julius Hemphill—adapted his compositional methods for their own purposes. When the inevitable reaction set up against the avant-garde in the 1980s and 1990s, it was Ellington who many of the younger neo-traditional musicians rallied around.

Count Basie

The bands that Basie led over the years presented pop songs or the blues in an unadulterated, danceable manner. His arrangements were seldom innovative, and if anything, grew more conservative. Earlier on, Basie's bands followed the conventions of swing, with various sections of the band answering and cross-talking with the others as a line of soloists took turns at the front. Later, the bands drifted toward arrangements with an ensemble that phrased like a single instrumentalist.

Those are the bare facts, but they miss what Basie was all about. The way the sections of his band talked to each other was unprecedented. True, Mozart had long ago found a way to present complex, simultaneous conversations in *The Magic Flute*. But Basie's instrumental conversations were excited, shouted out, and breathtakingly rhythmic. It might have been an arcane language they talked in, but once it was heard in its rhythmic dress, everyone could understand it. It was rhythm that was Basie's story, his narrative. First off, there was the incredible cohesion and drive of what was called the Basie "All-American Rhythm Section," which stayed together from 1937 to 1947. Jo Jones was at the center, the drummer who surrendered the constant thump of the bass drum on every beat, and relocated the pulse in the cymbals (the high-hats snapping together loosely, the ride cymbal singing and sizzling), one drumstick chattering against the post that holds the high-hats, the other occasionally striking the rim of the snare drum, the bass drum free to highlight and punctuate. Bassist Walter Page now bore the burden of the beat with a powerful walking line; guitarist Freddy Green also shared the timekeeping, but with slow drag-strokes of chords that once were played by pianists. Count Basie sat at the piano, his left hand largely immobile (having given up both rhythm and harmony duties to the bass and guitar), punching in short rhythmic phrases with his right hand, commenting on what the band or a soloist had just played, anticipating a bump from the bass drum with a hammered note of his own, and everything he played spaced by long stretches of silence . . . stretches sometimes so long that the listeners' eager ears might hear a note or a beat when one hadn't yet appeared.

By chance, there is an opportunity to hear what the Basie rhythm section would have sounded like with a different drummer. During a jam session on "Honeysuckle Rose" on Benny Goodman's *The Famous 1938 Carnegie Hall Jazz Concert* (Columbia/Legacy C2K 65143), Gene Krupa was the drummer with Basie, Freddie Green, and Walter Page. Krupa is heavy on the bass drum (playing on every beat), and he does not use the high-hat cymbals at all. The result is a radically different rhythmic feel. Only when Krupa and Basie play very lightly and quietly at one point, and allow the bass and guitar to dominate, does it resemble the Basie rhythm feel.

Bennie Moten, "Toby." *Bennie Moten 1930–1932*. Classics 591.

In December 1932 the Moten band arrived at the RCA record plant in Camden, New Jersey, hungry and without money from an unsuccessful tour, and settled themselves in for a long recording session. But this recording of "Toby" shows no sign of physical strain. They launch into the arrangement at an inhuman pace, spinning off riffs and letting them stack up on each other, building tension and drama while tenor saxophonist Ben Webster, trumpeter Hot Lips Page, and Basie take solos. Basie is at this point still soloing with two hands in classic stride style, but bassist Walter Page is playing with a powerful four-beat, and an energized rhythm section flows torrentially around him.

William Basie was born in Red Bank, New Jersey, and grew up under the spell of East Coast rag, or stride, especially the playing of Fats Waller. Like Ellington, he began playing for movie theaters and nightclub reviews, but he never took composing seriously. Stranded with a vaudeville show in Kansas City in 1925 he stayed on there, and later joined Walter Page's Blue Devils, a fine blues-based local band. When the Bennie Moten band absorbed the Blue Devils, Basie went along with some of their key people—Page himself, singer Jimmy Rushing, and trumpeter Hot Lips Page. Moten was a ragtime pianist who had studied with Scott Joplin. His was the most popular band in Kansas City, but one that remained old-fashioned in some respects—the persistence of two-beat, some leftover ragtime rhythms, arrangements that seemed to be pieced together from different sources, and even an accordion—but their structured riffs and their fierce drive made them something exceptional.

When Moten died in 1935, Basie formed his own band using some of Moten's best musicians and soon went into the recording studio. Those first records he made are among the most important in jazz history.

In later years Basie did not use as many soloists, but often counted on a powerful tenor saxophonist like Illinois Jacquet or Eddie "Lockjaw" Davis to do much of the building of excitement in their

Jones-Smith, Incorporated, "Lady Be Good." *Lester—Amadus!* Phonotastic 7639.

Recording in 1936 under a pseudonym in order to be able to record for two competing recording companies at the same time, Basie used only three-quarters of his All-American Rhythm Section (Freddie Green was not yet part of it), trumpeter Carl Smith, and one of the most revered figures in jazz history, Lester Young, on tenor saxophone. Young's two improvised choruses are what this record was all about.

In a time when tenor saxophonists played with a wide-bodied, often gruff sound, Young's was light and airy, modeled in part on Frank Trumbauer's solo on "Singin' the Blues." Yet, at only twenty-six, Young's style was already fully developed and confident. Young was as idiosyncratic as his playing. His solo on the Gershwins' "Lady Be Good" floats, dances, and sails over the bar lines, rides the rhythm section, and builds a solo from small bits and pieces. Yet he is always careful to connect the dots of these small fragments into long horizontal lines. He plays within a relatively small range of tones, moving mostly in small steps; but with his rhythmic sophistication, his ear for balanced melody, and a harmonic sensibility that allows him to anticipate the next chord through his choice of notes, there is never a sense of limitation in his playing. This was one of the most coherent and satisfying solos played in jazz up to this point in time.

lengthy solos. When the band would come in after them it was often as a massive single voice shouting over what seemed to be the endless clockwork drive of the rhythm section.

Many musicians passed through the Basie band, many arrangers, but the rhythm section gave a distinctive shape to everything put in front of them. Basie played less and less piano as time went by, dropping only the occasional note, or the spare chord in place; yet what he *didn't* play seemed to increasingly define the music. Altogether, the band was an incredible swing machine, the definitive swing band, and it sometimes appeared that every band was trying to sound like Basie's. Singers, too, were caught up in the magic of Basie's swing: although it was the great blues orators like Joe Turner, Jimmy Rushing, or Joe Williams who usually sang with the band, it seemed that every singer—whether Frank Sinatra, Sarah Vaughan, Kay Starr, Sammy Davis, Jr., Ella Fitzgerald, or Tony Bennett—wanted a chance to see what they could do in front of it. Not surprisingly, they often sounded better than they ever had before.

BY THE end of World War II, the big bands of the swing era began to decline in number and in force. The usual explanations are real enough—rising costs that put a damper on large traveling organizations, the development of a pop song industry that valued singers and songs at the cost of instrumentals, shifts in taste following the dislocations of home life in the wake of the war. Radio began to use recorded music in place of live musicians, developing disc jockeys as personalities substituting for band leaders. Fearing the elimination of live music on radio, the American Federation of Musicians began a two-year strike against recording just before America's entry into the war. The resultant absence of musicians on record opened the way for singers to become dominant in pop music, and big bands never again regained their ascendancy in pop culture. (Musi-

Count Basie, "Jumpin' at the Woodside." *The Original American Decca Recordings*. MCA GRP 36112

Count Basie immediately announces the meter of "Jumpin' at the Woodside" as four-beat right at the beginning, bringing his rhythm section in behind him to lead into a riff tune built on a 32-bar pop song form. The two riffs near the beginning (one played by the saxophones, the other by the brass simultaneously) were not new, and had been floating around in swing circles for at least four or five years, but in Basie's hands they were used to generate a larger, more organized composition. Once the soloists begin (Buck Clayton on trumpet, Lester Young on tenor saxophone, Hershel Evans on clarinet, Basie on piano), the initial pair of riffs are put through various transformations as they are turned into accompanying figures and new riffs are added. Clarinet and trombone trade riff figures at one point in call-and-response style, for example, only to have the clarinet move on to solo while the saxophones pick up the riff behind him. There is not a lot of melodic material here to be varied, but the band uses what is there to great effect, maintaining a sense of forward motion and development that climax in a final chorus based on the original riffs. Live, this early Basie band's riff-building process could ecstatically incite dancers, even driving them to create new moves. And more than any other band, they taught other musicians by example what the mysterious element of swing was all about.

cians did continue to record throughout the strike on V-discs, recordings made exclusively for the Armed Services, and between 1943 and 1949 over nine hundred records were made, at least 40 percent of which were jazz and swing. But most of these were never heard by the public at large.)

There were other, less obvious reasons for the decline of big bands and swing. The three- to four-minute time constraints of the single record frustrated the development of an adequate framework for incorporating newer kinds of improvisation and soloing into swing band arrangements. The conventions of big band organization and arranging had begun to grow tired, and in a business driven by novelty, a shift was long overdue. On top of this, the late '30s and early '40s were also a period of revivalism when Dixieland and boogie-woogie got their own shares of the audience, many of whom were often younger people who had missed out on these older musics the first time around.

Count Basie, "Whirly-Bird." *The Complete Atomic Mr. Basie.* Roulette CDP 7932732

This was one of the best of the late Basie bands, and probably the best of the later records. The arrangement is by Neal Hefti, the band is energized, the tempo is top speed, and they aim for the roof. Saxophonist Eddie "Lockjaw" Davis enters ready to chomp his way through his solo, hot, unstoppable, a tenor in full. The high quality of recording picks up the detail of interaction in the rhythm section, and Basie's precise but always surprising accents show just how percussive his role was at the piano. The ensemble roars its way through the arrangement, and at times seems anxious to burst ahead of the rhythm section. But when Basie hangs out those suspended chords and those thunderous exclamation points come forth from the drummer, everything fits together.

PART 3

15 The 1940s: Revivalism

Just at the point when jazz seemed poised for a new era, a strange thing happened: writers, record collectors, and some fans began to look backwards and, through a mixture of research and fantasy, sparked a series of revivals that would help to lay the groundwork for the beginnings of a jazz history. In 1938–1939, for example, a young socialite who had dropped out of Yale named John Hammond organized two spectacular concerts at Carnegie Hall that attempted to locate the origins of jazz in the blues, gospel singing, and black folk song, and to set forth a line of development that followed jazz from New Orleans to boogie-woogie and stride piano (but no ragtime), finally culminating in swing. On another front, a group of fans (some born too late to have experienced the first burst of New Orleans jazz) went to New Orleans in the early 1940s to see what was left of the original musicians and to interview and record them. It was a pilgrimage of sorts, but also an archeological expedition. It was the first of a long series of "rediscoveries" in American music, allowing those who missed it or didn't get it the first time around to have another chance. Coming next down the line would be a boogie-woogie revival, then a folk revival, a bluegrass revival, a blues revival, and a second New Orleans revival in the 1960s.

The amateur researchers and collectors headed for New Orleans to fill in history, to record jazz marching bands, nights at dance halls and social clubs, and the oldest living musicians. But when the first records of newly discovered older New Orleans musicians began to appear, it dawned on close listeners that this music was very different from that of the King Oliver band and Louis Armstrong. Bunk Johnson, a contemporary of Jelly Roll Morton and King Oliver, played trumpet with a pronounced feel for ragtime rhythm, and when he was given freedom to record whatever he wanted in 1947, he chose rags and pop songs of the moment, but no New Orleans–identified instrumentals. The rags were also played as published, with no improvisation ("This music is hot as written," Johnson said). On clarinetist George Lewis's records or those of trumpeter Wooden Joe Nicholas, the lead instrument is not always the trumpet. Sometimes the melody is passed from instrument to instrument, sometimes in the middle of a phrase. The trumpet may switch to the clarinet part, while the clarinet leads the melody. Switch leads are common in gospel quartet singing, but they are seldom if ever found in the classic New Orleans recordings. In fact, compared to the New Orleans music recorded in the 1920s, this music has fewer solos, is lighter and more concerned with texture, and is simpler rhythmically—in other words, a big disappointment to some.

What to make of all this? At the time, some said that these late discoveries were marginal musicians, and thus never recorded or played outside of New Orleans. But this was not true. Bunk Johnson, for example, was widely traveled and well respected among his contemporaries. But there are two other possible solutions to this puzzle. First, these revival musicians might represent an earlier stage of New Orleans jazz before Oliver, Morton, Armstrong et al—a more collective and less soloist-oriented music that had not been heard because most of the musicians who were recorded had left New Orleans some time before and had already adapted to out-of-town tastes and styles. That's possible, but it seems that these changes are too radical to have been carried out within a time span of two or three years. More likely is Max Harrison's suggestion that these late-recorded musicians represent a later stage in the evolution of New Orleans music, but one carried out exclusively at home. Some support for this idea is given by recordings made by Sam Morgan in 1927, one of the few artists to actually record in New Orleans. His "Bogalusa Strut" and "Stepping on the Gas" have the same lighter rhythm, varied textures, and open structure of the revivalists' music. In any case, one important conclusion to be drawn from all of this is that King Oliver's Creole Jazz Band may have represented a more conservative stage of development than what these musicians played.

As the New Orleans revival percolated along in the late 1940s, bands developed that played in all of the New

Orleans styles: the "classic" polyphony and solo style of the King Oliver Creole Jazz Band was represented by such groups as Lu Watter's Yerba Buena Jazz Band, and the bravura Louis Armstrong approach was continued, especially by the Chicagoans and by the likes of Eddie Condon. By the 1960s, a second New Orleans revival occurred, and this time the new-old style of the rediscovered musicians such as George Lewis had a strong influence on people such as Woody Allen. (In Europe, "trad" music revivals have their own particular history.) The New Orleans style(s) thus has had the longest continual run of any jazz style, even if a rather frozen and often uninfluential one.

Further Listening:

Various Artists, *From Spirituals to Swing: The Legendary 1938 & 1939 Carnegie Hall Concerts*. Vanguard 169/71.
George Lewis, *Trios and Bands*. American Music AMCD 4.
Bunk Johnson, *Bunk Johnson 1944*. American Music AMCD 3.
Wooden Joe Nicholas. American Music AMCD 5.
Sam Morgan, *Papa Celestin & Sam Morgan*. Azure Az-CD-12.

16 Five Who Helped Make a Revolution

If you were on the scene before the early 1940s, and were listening hard enough, you might have seen bebop coming in the slowly accumulating innovations of some exceptional swing musicians. Their playing suggested the need to go beyond the recurrent melodies and formulaic harmonic structure of pop tunes, and beyond a straightforward rhythm for dancers. All of them were thoroughly swing-based and much in demand, but their playing contained aspects of bebop several years before it was to be heard and named.

Roy Eldridge

Eldridge is the obvious link between Louis Armstrong and Dizzy Gillespie—though he absorbed the trumpet work of

Rex Stewart, Red Nichols, and Henry Red Allen as well as Armstrong. He was blessed with speed, technical facility, harmonic knowledge, and impeccable rhythm, but he also had a real sense of drama and expression. He could play higher and faster than others, but he also could produce a burr in his sound that gave him an extra edge. And he could move from the bottom of the horn to the top with a shriek that could stop dancers in their paces. Armstrong could do it and make an audience cheer him on like an athlete struggling to break a record, but Roy Eldridge made those top and bottom notes feel like a natural part of what the horn should do.

On Roy Eldridge's *The Big Sound of Little Jazz* (Topaz TPZ 1021) or *Heckler's Hop* (Hep 1030), you can sample his earlier years. The first CD finds him in the company of Mildred Bailey, Billie Holiday, Benny Goodman, Gene Krupa, and dozens of the other fine musicians and singers he worked with. "Heckler's Hop," from 1937, is the standout on the first CD (and also found on the second), but the range of his recording activity is impressive and rewarding for its own sake. "After You've Gone," on the second CD, again from 1937, is a tour de force, full of diving and leaping, careening and careering, with notes dropped, some left hanging on the ledge of the rhythm section. Eldridge often flirted with hotdoggery, but he is simply too spectacular not to forgive. Truly *hot* music.

Charlie Christian

Christian was the first person to bring the electric guitar to its full potential, though his career ended with his death at twenty-six. He seemed to emerge from nowhere in the Midwest, but on his first recordings his style is fully in place. His playing was distinct and clean, with long hornlike lines, and full of riff figures that generated a powerful rhythmic charge on records like Benny Goodman's "Gone with What Draft" (*The Genius of the Electric Guitar*, Columbia 460612). On the legendary recordings made at Minton's in 1941, such as "Swing to Bop" (*Charlie Christian*, Laserlight 17032, or *Swing to Bop*, Natasha 4020), his single-note playing moved away from the swing feel he displayed with Goodman's band, taking on a modern rhythmic quality, drawing his long lines across the underlying chord structure and giving his music a head-down, stubborn quality. Christian riffs furiously throughout, allowing one to edge into another until he reaches the bridge, where he attends to the harmony more closely and stacks notes up until they tumble back into riffs again. Behind him, drummer Kenny Clarke is accenting more irregularly than a swing drummer, as is pianist Thelonious Monk.

Art Tatum

Jazz has its fair share of singular performers, musicians so individual that they often turn up surrounded by musicians of different styles, confounding historians who seek to describe their contribution. Art Tatum was a pianist who absorbed everything that came before him, and he could play it all—boogie-woogie, pop tunes, stride, and swing—but at top speed and with pianistic technique unheard of before in jazz. He seemed to rearrange everything he played so casually that even the simplest tunes looked new. But it was his harmonic inventiveness that caught the ears of musicians. He regularly used the upper notes of chords or threw in substitute chords so smoothly and at such speed that many listeners never noticed. But horn players and pianists did, and he was a principal influence on a whole generation, especially Bud Powell, Al Haig, and the first bebop pianists.

Despite his incredible technique and inventiveness, there are those who think of Tatum not so much as an improviser but as a decorator of melodies, a glorified cocktail pianist. But the word of pianists has usually won out. And consider this: every recording that Tatum made seems to be played at the highest level. On "Willow Weep for Me" (in the *Smithsonian Collection of Classic Jazz*), the original melody is highly repetitious, but rather than vary it for interest, Tatum stays close to the repetitions, introducing even more repetitions in the form of a recurring vamp. What he does vary is first the harmony, making it more complex as he goes along, and second the rhythm, by double-timing the melody. These changes are subtle, but they give the piece a feeling of development absent in the original melody.

Jimmy Blanton

Bassists are seldom innovators and hardly ever influences. But Jimmy Blanton, despite a short career (like Charlie Christian, he died young, at twenty-three), changed the future of jazz by combining a strong rhythmic foundation with melodic and countermelodic playing that could lift a band on any night. Most of his playing life was with the Duke Ellington band, and fortunately Ellington featured him and had him recorded well. (Charles Mingus recalled hearing him clearly over the Ellington band from the back of the concert hall.) Anything on which he plays on Duke Ellington's *The Blanton-Webster Band* (Bluebird 7432113181) shows off the difference he made, but "Jack the Bear" was a feature for him, and a first for the bass. After Blanton, bass players knew what was possible on the instrument and how much it could add to what the melody instruments were playing.

Lester Young

Lester Young is the musician who reversed the direction set for the tenor saxophone by Coleman Hawkins. In the Count Basie band, he was used as a counterweight to big-toned tenor player Hershel Evans, and behind Billie Holiday's singing he was her alter ego: Young played higher and lighter, with great harmonic and rhythmic sophistication, and without vibrato. His solos used small elements of melodic material strung together creatively so that there was a linear, unfolding, narrative quality to his playing. As Young himself might have put it, he "told a story." Young's influence was such that he helped shape bebop *and* cool jazz.

Young is well represented in a number of musical settings on *Lester Leaps In*, ASV Living Era AJA 5176.

17 Bebop

It was an odd name to give to music. It seems even stranger in retrospect, since bebop today seems not so much comic, or inept, or chaotic (all of which it was once accused of being), but secretly formal and almost like chamber music in its seriousness. It was a music of World War II, and though some of its key players were never in military service, musicians on the home front experienced their own displacements and upheavals in the form of strikes, the injustices of segregation, discrimination, and economic inequality. (Langston Hughes once said bebop reminded him of the sound of police nightsticks on black people's heads.)

Many of the black musicians who first played bebop were migrants from the South and the Southwest, their musical abilities developed within a framework of local intellectual activity and political thinking, and they often presented themselves in a kind of double face of artiste/bohemian and a simultaneous parody of those roles. Dizzy Gillespie would at times appear dressed in a large, flowing bow tie *à la Bohème*, with beret, goatee, and horn-rimmed glasses (with plain glass in them), speaking in the vocabulary of the hip. Though Gillespie did offend some (Ralph Ellison, and even Charlie Parker, from time to time), he continued in the kind of performer/entertainer tradition that Louis Armstrong had mastered, and like Armstrong was much beloved, even by people who weren't sure of what it was he was playing.

To non-jazz fans or swing devotees, bop was a musical affront, a deliberate provocation, a scandal. Outside of a small number of people in a few key cities, most people who had heard of it thought bop was a mysterious side trip for a group of strange young musicians. "Revolutionary" is what its fans called it during its beginnings, or "innovative," or "modern." Bop does, in retrospect, seem the most unique and clearly differentiated style of jazz. But its development took place during one of the longest of a number of recording bans created by a strike of the American Federation of Musicians; and the absence of new music on recordings made the transition from swing to bebop seem less smooth than it may have been. Bop bands were small units—combos, as they were called—but unlike the rhythm and blues bands they closely resembled and often shared personnel with, bebop bands were not stripped-down big bands with a trumpet and a saxophone representing whole brass and reed sections. The parts of the bebop combo were organized differently, often playing in unison. The aim was not to play for dancers or floor shows at nightclubs only, and certainly not to play for a pop market.

A case could be made for swing and bebop having more in common than any other two styles of jazz. In fact it was possible in this period to hear some of the giants of each style playing together in comfortable aggregations. On Red Norvo's "Get Happy" in 1945, swing masters Norvo, Slam Stewart, and Teddy Wilson combined easily with boppers Dizzy Gillespie and Charlie Parker. On Slim Gaillard's "Slim's Jam" (1945), rhythm and blues players Gaillard and Jack McVea came together with New Orleans drummer Zutty Singleton and Parker, Gillespie, and bop pianist Dodo Marmarosa. But by the late 1930s and early 1940s swing had become a stable, even predictable music. The formal experimentation of Jelly Roll Morton, the breathless invention of Louis Armstrong's solo work, the wild, accelerating tempos of youthful big bands, all of it was in the process of becoming standardized and formulaic as the innovations of the first twenty or thirty years of jazz were consolidated. Swing was no longer an ethnic music or even the music of a cult: in becoming the pop music of America it risked becoming a music in which repeating success and pleasing audiences was the primary goal. The fact that the country was still segregated insured that the largest part of the population was not hearing what many black bands and singers were doing until after they had moved on to something else, a culture lag that kept swing in place far longer than it otherwise might have been.

When younger players appeared in the years of World War II, they began to tinker with pop tunes, sometimes keeping the older harmonic structures and putting new melodies over them, or radically paraphrasing the older songs, and at other times varying the older harmonic structures as well. Old staples like "Sweet Georgia Brown" (which later became the theme song of the Harlem Globetrotters) could be turned into a cascading, start-and-stop display piece like "Hollywood Stampede" in 1943 by Coleman Hawkins; years later, stripped down to its skeleton, it would emerge as Thelonious Monk's "Bright Mississippi" (1964). But instead of simply following the phrasing set by pop singers or by swing riff melodies (those evenly and symmetrically placed one- or two-bar fragments like Glenn Miller's "In the Mood" or Benny Goodman's "Stomping at the Savoy"), bop melodic phrases were longer and less repetitious, but at the same time unevenly structured and irregularly placed. The melody of Dizzy Gillespie's 1946 recording of "Anthropology," for example (based on the harmonic structure of George Gershwin's "I Got Rhythm"), is made up of five phrases, each one differing in length and beginning on a different beat of the measure, even while remaining within the conventional AABA song form. But if pop songs were being reexamined and transformed, the blues was making a strong return in bop, where it was played with great respect for its originators.

Further Listening:

Various Artists, *Birth of Bebop: Wichita–New York 1940–1945*. Frémeaux FA 046.
Various Artists, *The Birth of Bebop*. Charly CPCD 8194.

The new bop melodies were more angular than conventional pop tunes and even other jazz tunes, as the intervals between notes in bebop grew wider, often moving up or down a sixth, seventh, or an octave (as in the melody of Dizzy Gillespie's "That's Earl, Brother" [1946]). Passing notes (the notes not strictly part of the chords being played) were widely used in bop as they were in other musics, but here these notes were typically left unresolved—that is, left hanging, without moving on to the notes of the next chord. In the playing of Charlie Parker, the phrases were typically irregular and often quite distinct and separate from each other. He might, for example, be playing in the lower register, then leap upwards without warning. Yet once the syntax of his music was grasped, his solos seemed coherent, even organic. In general, then, the melodies of bebop were less symmetrical, more chromatic (that is, drew on all twelve notes of the octave), and less well made than those of swing.

Bebop was a period

Charlie Parker, "Ko-Ko." *The Smithsonian Collection of Classic Jazz.*

In the late 1930s, British band leader Ray Noble recorded a series of impressions of Native American life, and though the rest of them are long forgotten, "Cherokee" became a part of the standard jazz repertoire. It was a simple, stereotypically exotic melody—something like walking up the black keys on the piano—but the rapidly moving chord changes of the bridge were a killer for improvisers, especially when tried at high speed. Charlie Parker had been playing it in clubs for years, but when he went into the studio to record it in 1945, his young trumpeter Miles Davis didn't yet know Parker's 32-bar introduction to the piece, so Dizzy Gillespie played it on the first take. But they were barely into the melody when Parker called a halt to the recording, apparently figuring that if they played the longish introduction and the 64-bar AABA melody, there would be no time left for his solo on a three-minute recording. So on the second take he cut out the melody and moved directly from the introduction to his solo—and what an astonishing solo it was, faster than of great experimentation with harmony, its players often knowing the work of current classical composers, such as Stravinsky and Bartok (the very composers admired by the intellectuals who often dismissed bebop). Chords were often extended or altered, with new ones substituted for the conventional chords of songs. Though this harmonic experimentation was not as radical as it might have appeared to pop fans at the beginning of the 1940s, it can still be surprising, as when—in brief moments in the melody of Dizzy Gillespie's 1946 "Street Theme"—the musicians lunge into small moments of polytonality (playing simultaneously in different keys).

But it is in the rhythm of bebop where we really feel the giddiness of experimentation. Just as the melodies were broken up and somewhat discontinuous, so was the rhythm, such that on first hearing this music, both rhythm and melody may seem erratic or disorganized. Charlie Parker's use of rests (in those brief moments when he is not playing) is part of the melody *and* the rhythm. These pauses spring up in surprising places, not at those moments of silence usually left at the ends of phrases in pop songs or the blues. Parker's "Thriving on a Riff"—also based on "I Got Rhythm"—is a good example. When this kind of staggered, unusual use of silences occurs along with offbeat accents

people can talk, seemingly faster than people can think. Yet in spite of the pace, he creates a seamless improvisation that hurtles recklessly forward. Notes fly in from everywhere, but always with a logic behind them. At one point he quotes a famous clarinet part from the old New Orleans march "High Society," folding it into the total improvisation with accuracy and grace.

and sudden shifts in speed, and is played over the steady beat of the bass and drummer Max Roach's jagged accents, moments of fleeting polymeter are heard.

Charlie Parker, "Embraceable You." *The Smithsonian Collection of Classic Jazz.*

Instead of using George Gershwin's original melody, Parker's first recording of this song essentially ignores it, though at a number of points he comes close, especially near the end of each eight bars. In place of the original phrases of the song, he instead borrows from the opening bars of a now-forgotten pop song from 1939, "A Table in the Corner" (recorded by Artie Shaw with a vocal by Helen Forrest). Though it fits like a glove rhythmically and harmonically, the quoted notes are all from the top of the original chords of the Gershwin song, giving his solo a floating, spacious feel. Parker begins by hovering close to the four-bar phrases of the latter melody, but when he breaks loose for his improvisation he seems to play as long as his breath holds out.

Parker was always surprising in his improvisations, even when he played the same song night after night. Only a few minutes later on the same day in 1947 Parker recorded "Embraceable You" again, this time sticking closer to the original melody and never refer-

What made bebop seem even wilder and more of a break with the past was the sheer virtuosity of its players. There were Charlie Parker's lightning lines, the relentless flow and power of Bud Powell's piano, Dizzy Gillespie's soaring solos charging into the bridges of tunes as if they were hills to be taken, or J.J. Johnson's nimble elevation of the trombone to the solo status of the trumpet or the saxophone. The bebop players found within themselves resources that carried the moods and emotions of swing music forward, adding to them, and breaking through to what was previously thought to be impossible in music.

Big dance bands were

in decline in the early forties, but a handful of younger bandleaders sympathetic to bop attempted to revive them with the new music. Billy Eckstine, for instance, put together an all-star grouping, and Dizzy Gillespie used some of the most creative arrangers in the new music to find a way to make the swing band form work with small band ideas. The result often re-excited listeners tired of swing formulas or those too young to have been interested in them in the first place. Gillespie also tapped into the new Latin music scene in New York City, bringing from it new ideas about rhythm, culture, and religion, many of which ultimately could be traced to Africa. In Cuban drummer Chano Pozo, he found a musician who could create

ring to "A Table in the Corner." Though he played the Gershwin tune on many occasions after this (it can be heard in at least eight other transformations on bootleg and legitimate live recordings), only once again did he ever refer to the Artie Shaw record. At a Birdland date in June 1950, Parker played a good portion of the original melody, but then went on to play further out than on any other version, sounding for all the world like Ornette Coleman almost twenty years before Coleman could be heard on record.

Dizzy Gillespie, "Cubano Be/Cubano Bop." *The Complete RCA Victor Recordings*. Bluebird 66528.

In 1947 George Russell wrote a Latin-flavored composition for Gillespie which would take advantage of the presence in the band of the great Cuban *congero*, Chano Pozo. There was nothing obvious about this piece. Russell constructed it on a single scale, in the manner that would be called modal jazz ten years later, bringing in the horns with staggered entry. There was a seriousness about it which was unusual for big bands at the time, but also a funky boisterousness. Just after the band's first performance of the composition, Russell heard Chano Pozo jamming on the bus on the way to Boston, and he suggested that Dizzy let Chano chant and sing alone somewhere in the middle of the piece. So by the time it was recorded a few months later it had become a six-minute performance. The middle of the arrangement was now opened up to allow for a call-and-response exchange between Gillespie's trumpet and Pozo's conga drum, leading in turn to a startling interlude in which Afro-Cuban religious chants in a Nigerian-derived dialect were answered by members of the band, who did not understand the language.

What Gillespie, Russell, and Pozo had pulled off in this first Latin jazz recording was nothing less than a highly experimental and prescient composition which at the same time exposed the African, Latin, Deep South, and New York roots of bebop.

ever greater subdivisions to the beat, even as his Cuban religious chanting would add an exotic charge to the music. With arrangers like George Russell and Gil Fuller, Gillespie was able to construct Latin jazz suites and extended works (like "Cubano Be/Cubano Bop") that were thrillingly alien, even while somehow familiar, a music that would be perceived by many much the way the first jazz had been: as both primitive and modern at the same moment.

Bebop may have begun as a scandal, but it soon began to make swing seem tired, prewar, symmetrical, a thinly veiled pop music suddenly laid bare. Some older swing bands tried to make a connection with the new music. Benny Goodman briefly fronted a small bebop band, awkwardly trying to remake his older hits like "Stealin' Apples" in new clothes, and with younger soloists like Wardell Gray and Doug Metome. Goodman's old drummer, Gene Krupa, would himself use arrangers like Gerry Mulligan and Eddie Finckel to get a new sound, though his drumming kept the band firmly within swing territory. A '30s dance band with waning popularity like Woody Herman's was able to reinvent itself, making the transition into new popularity by using excited young musicians and arrangers, and experimenting with new tonalities and instrument combinations. Younger singers like Babs Gonzales, Joe Carroll, and Sarah Vaughan would continue the scat tradition in bebop style by inventing new sounds ("oop—bop-sh'bam," "ool-ya-koo") to fit the rhythms and attitude. Saxophonist Charlie Ventura, a veteran of Gene Krupa's band, had some success with his "Bop for the People" concept, a pop-bebop band with singers Jackie Cain and Roy Kral scatting out well-known melodies like "I'm Forever Blowing Bubbles." The George Shearing Quintet also found success in a mixture of bop and lounge music.

Many musicians who returned after the war took advantage of the G.I. Bill to study in conservatories, where they encounted modern composers such as Hindemith, Stravinsky, and Stefan Wolpe, who themselves had already been influenced by jazz. Bands like Stan Kenton's would take some of the bop experiments and move even further away from swing, sometimes crossing completely into Latin territory, or into the domain of the concert band. Even Claude Thornhill, a pianist whose dance band was cast in the mold of a smaller classical unit with its use of French horns, tuba, flutes, and tinkling piano, would bring in Gil Evans, an arranger who not only wanted to play bebop compositions but also wanted to make the band phrase and move like a small bebop band.

Bud Powell

Much as Earl Hines was Louis Armstrong's interpreter on the piano, Bud Powell adapted Charlie Parker's ideas to the piano. Again as with Hines, the ideas first expressed on a horn took on a different feel. In the Powell-Parker case, there was a touch of neoclassical in the translation. But not too fine a point should be put on that, however: Powell brought Art Tatum's frightening technique to the piano, yet stripped it of the florid decorations that often crept into Tatum's playing. Powell's keyboard attack (that's what it was) was unrelenting, as aggressively fiery and unpredictable as Parker's on saxophone. Solo, Powell could imply the beat without playing stride or using a walking bass line, and the listener never missed the rhythm section. He stabbed out chords of a few notes only, avoiding the on-the-beat left-hand routines of his swing predecessors, while his right hand sailed through his

170

Bud Powell, "Un Poco Loco" (takes 1,2 and 4). *The Amazing Bud Powell.* Blue Note 81503.

In 1951 even the most astute musicians knew very little about African music, and aside from Machito's band, the most important Cuban group in New York City in the 1940s, very little about how Latin music could be applied to jazz of the moment. All the more astonishing, then, is the level of creativity, and even authenticity, with which Powell's trio brings off this purest of Latin jazz etudes. Over a hypnotically obsessive left-hand figure, Powell seemingly explores everything that could be done in bebop piano. But then we turn to the other takes of this piece and learn that his inventiveness is ceaseless and constantly surprising. At the time, there was no obvious form of rhythm accompaniment for this kind of playing, but Max Roach's innovative cowbell rhythms provide the perfect match to Powell's rhythm figures.

improvisations, accenting the unexpected even at lightning tempos. He was the quintessential bop pianist, never equaled and exceptionally difficult to imitate.

Thelonious Monk

Monk was, to say the least, not your usual pianist. On first listen, many think him amateurish and reckless in his disregard for conventional technique. Yet repeated hearings reveal that he had considered the mechanics of the piano closely and managed to get a variety of timbres and sonorities by means of several types of articulation. He also found a way to use tonal clusters, giving the notes a crushed sound. He coaxed blue notes and sonorities out of the piano, and he approached the damping pedal uniquely, evaporating certain notes within the chord as it sounded, leaving only a wisp behind. These were simply not things that you were supposed to be able to do with an acoustic piano.

Though Monk was known initially as an accompanist in bebop circles, he has often been considered to be more a composer than a pianist (his improvisations are frequently difficult to distinguish from his compositions). But his unique approach to the piano has also had enormous impact, especially in recent years. Both his compositions and his improvisations are simple inasmuch as they remain true to the 12-bar blues and 32-bar pop song forms that served as the frameworks for improvisation in the bebop era (though he did occasionally depart from these quite radically and creatively). But he differed from other beboppers in avoiding the harmonic density of bop and the seemingly endless flow of its melody lines. Instead, he favored spare, calculated melodies and carefully chosen notes, graced with silences which were treated as a part of the melody. Monk's chords seem blunt, desiccated, and strangely voiced. His apparent simplicity is deceptive: his work is filled with a rhythmic complexity and harmonic sophistication rare in jazz composition and improvisation. He manages to isolate and dissect the harmonic, melodic, and rhythmic clichés of both swing and bop, so much so that he sometimes seems to be parodying them. Better, he made both swing and bop sound strange, and in doing so rose to the highest standard of each.

While beboppers were using altered chords to emphasize the harmonic structure of pop tunes in their improvisations, Monk was improvising on melodies, taking parts of the tune and using them to recompose it. He sometimes played older pop tunes relatively straight, in stride fashion, but with bop harmonies and chord voicings; even there his approach was so crafted that every note was set in relief against its harmonic and rhythmic background. His own compositions did not resemble pop tunes, nor were they programmatic or atmospheric. They were instead "rigorous investigations of musical ideas," as French critic André Hodier put it. Sometimes only one idea was explored per song (intervals, rhythmic figures, clusters of notes, a certain type of chord) and then improvised on melodically. In "Well, You Needn't" (1947), he turns a swing cliché into a disorienting figure by means of new rhythmic emphasis. "I Should Care" (1948) frustrates the listener's expectations about steady tempo, a uniform piano sound, and normal harmonic resolution of a song's progression. In "Straight No Chaser" (1951), a single melodic motive is repeated at different points in each bar so as to confuse the meter and create rhythmic and harmonic surprise. On "Introspection" (1947) he can play several bars with offbeat accents, then contract the rhythm by playing on the beat, so alternatively displacing the beat, then conforming to it.

Only a few musicians—such as John Coltrane, Johnny Griffin, Milt Jackson, and Sonny Rollins—were comfortable playing Monk's compositions with him as accompanist, since he demanded that no shortcuts be taken and that their original intention be adhered to, even if the intention was nothing more than a recurring element. He accompanied other players by hammering out certain required figures like a drummer or, at the opposite extreme, by getting up and walking away from the piano and leaving only the bass to carry the harmonic burden for long stretches of time.

Thelonious Monk is difficult to place within a conventional notion of style: he was a bebopper, but he went beyond the conventions of bop with his conceptions of rhythm and harmony. He also had a deep feel for tradition, for stride piano and gospel music, and he worked them both into his performances. Yet his use of space, intervals, and sonority, as well as his expansion and contraction of rhythm, make a good case for calling him a precursor of free jazz.

Thelonious Monk, "Misterioso" (1948). *The Best of Thelonious Monk: The Blue Note Years.* Blue Note 795636.

This is a blues, though you might not think so, what with a melody that clomps up and down the scale in stair-step intervals of sixths that sounds like a beginner's exercise. Very little swing in sight here, though it does manage to suggest two tempos running at once. Milt Jackson's one-chorus solo on the vibraphone is a perfectly respectable improvisitory exercise on the blues, but the ear is drawn away from him to the small gesture that Monk makes behind him on the piano: a repeated interval of a seventh, which breaks up the flow of Jackson's solo, or restructures it, depending on how you hear it. Monk's solo, on the other hand, is shocking in its resistance to the logic of conventional blues. Phrases seem to end on the wrong note, the intervals he chooses sound wrong, he seems to fall behind at one point, and he repeatedly strikes clashing seconds. Then a return to the melody, this time with only Jackson playing it, while Monk drops unpredictable single notes all over the keyboard, scattering the melody, turning a realistic painting into a pointillistic shocker. Monk then rejoins Jackson, and they wind to a stop with the original melody. By the end, the single interval that began the piece has been repeated, re-sequenced, and expanded, creating an extended phrase that rhythmically contradicts the prevailing meter, and finally fragments it altogether.

18 The 1950s: Cool Jazz

By comparison to what is called cool jazz, even the wide variety of musics known as bebop seem to make up a coherent style. "Cool" from the beginning seemed to embrace too much, and perhaps even to mark as new a playing style that had effectively been around for over twenty-five years in the music of Frankie Trumbauer and Bix Beiderbecke. In the same way, many of the principles of swing playing that persisted in bebop also continued into cool playing.

More complicated yet, cool soon became associated with whiteness, which, as it turned out, was both a burden and a benefit. This was doubly ironic, since "cool" as a term for an attitude of understatement began as an African-American concept. You could hear it used in the late 1940s, especially in reference to Stan Getz, a tenor saxophonist whose style

Stan Getz and Kenny Barron, *People Time*. Verve 314 510 823.

Music from the end of Stan Getz's career, a piano and saxophone duo, recorded three months before his death. Getz had begun his recording career in the late 1940s as the coolest of the cool, with an icy, weightless sound that chilled his ballads below the temperature of sentiment. But here, almost forty-five years later, his tone warmed, the melody lines worn smooth, his vibrato widened with age, "cool" may no longer adequately describe Getz. Kenny Barron provides a frame for Getz to ruminate on tunes he has played for years, and the saxophonist responds with a finely woven interaction. Though it lacks the fire that youth and a rhythm section might provide, this is jazz of great maturity and rare beauty.

derived in part from Lester Young's sonority and Charlie Parker's musical vocabulary but was played by him with a light, dry tone. Getz's way with melodic ideas was the envy of many saxophonists. But it was Getz's "sound" that was the subject of a buzz, which he responded to with self-conscious irony on a recording titled, "Long Island Sound." He was part of the "four brothers" saxophone section of Woody Herman's First Herd, all of whom were to some degree beboppers but who played with a soft edge and slight vibrato. Coming after the anxious and emotional overflow of bebop, cool players had the look of musicians in retreat, reacting to the wave which had just hit.

Miles Davis

At the very end of the 1940s, Gil Evans joined with Miles Davis to find a way to move the big band not just away from swing but away from bebop as well. Earlier in the 1940s

Evans wrote for the Claude Thornhill Orchestra, a swing chamber ensemble of French horns, tuba, flutes, muted brass, and mixed reeds, which played a surprising lamination of Charlie Parker's phrasing, French impressionist orchestration, and chinoiserie in a time when other dance bands were unambiguously sweet or hot. It was Evans's treatments of bebop tunes for Thornhill (such as "Donna Lee" and "Yardbird Suite") that suggested to Davis a model for the "Birth of the Cool" nonet that ushered in a new style of music in the 1950s.

When Miles Davis assembled this group, his intention was to use some of the best young arrangers in New York to create a band book of jazz compositions, one not dependent on pop tunes, as were most big bands of the day. Miles's group anticipated the future of jazz and helped spur it into existence. There were beboppers like Max Roach and Miles in the band, as well as musicians from Lennie Tristano's circle such as altoist Lee Konitz. The relationship between Evans and Davis later resulted in some of

Miles Davis, "Move." *Birth of the Cool.* Capitol CDP 792862 (1949).

"Move" (1949) has the tightly coiled, jaggedly wired melody line of a bebop tune and wears its rhythm up front (it was written by drummer Denzil Best). But this arrangement by John Lewis softens the edges by its voicing and light phrasing, and by the introduction of a tranquil countermelody. It was a 78-rpm single with only three minutes to play with, but everyone makes the most of it. Davis's solo is concise and to the point (he had written out the introductory and concluding phrases to assure continuity in the short solo space). There is a residue of big band conventions in the passage surrounding Max Roach's drum breaks, but the independent tuba line, the interplay of the horns, and the restraint of the rhythm section all signaled that an alternative to the big band was in the air.

the great albums of the 1950s: *Sketches of Spain*, *Porgy and Bess*, and *Miles Ahead*, all of which carried the marks of the Birth of the Cool band. In fact, many of the key trends in jazz were initiated in this band. Gerry Mulligan's arrangements and his presence in the group resulted in the formation of the Gerry Mulligan Quartet with Chet Baker; and similarly, John Lewis's writing for them led to the formation of the Modern Jazz Quartet. Some of the compositions for Davis's band (such as Johnny Carisi's "Israel") also presaged the modal compositions that would appear in the late 1950s.

Though the Birth of the Cool band existed for only a few studio recording dates and a couple of weeks of live playing and had little direct public impact, it influenced many musicians, especially those on the West Coast—Dave Brubeck, Shorty Rogers, and Dave Pell—who followed its instrumentation and flowing style on their own recordings. More important, the Davis band showed all of its contemporaries that it was possible to write for larger ensembles in a manner that went beyond the music of the previous twenty years, while still respecting the traditions of jazz by framing improvised solos with band arrangements that made the outcome sound coherent and logical.

Lennie Tristano

Tristano is a name not known by most jazz fans, and one often misused by writers of jazz histories. Beginning on the fringes of music as a blind vaudevillian performer, he developed piano skills that suggested he had absorbed not only Art Tatum's musical vocabulary but, later on, Bud Powell's as well. He was fully committed to jazz as a tradition, carefully studying the improvisations of the best musicians, especially Armstrong, Lester Young, and Billie Holiday. By the same token, he viewed jazz as having built a tradition of melodic improvisation based on harmonic structure, feeling that it was possible to play forever on conventional chord progressions without exhausting all of their possibilities. For much of his life, he appeared less interested in the rhythmic contributions of jazz, often playing and recording with a very quiet, uncomplicated rhythm section, or with only a metronome. If his own rhythmic figures were less varied than most jazz players', his melodic lines were long, coherent, and especially well thought out. Later, some musicians and many critics would accuse him of being too cerebral, too stiff for jazz, but giants like Charlie Parker and Miles Davis had great respect for his work.

Despite a promising beginning as a performer (he was also heavily pro-

Lennie Tristano, "I Can't Get Started." *The Complete Lennie Tristano.* Mercury 830921.

By the time Tristano recorded "I Can't Get Started," it had been around for some years, having already been a hit for big band leader Bunny Berigan. Though this is only a piano trio recording, and a short one at that, with only one and a half choruses of the original, it is still startling a half-century later. Guitarist Billy Bauer begins as if he is going to play the original melody line simply and without embellishment, but within two measures he and the group have doubled the time, and doubled it again just as quickly. Tristano's piano meanwhile surrounds Bauer's line with two-handed chromatic chords, making the piece seem atonal. In the last 16 bars, the group finds its way out of 4/4 into 3/4 and, briefly, into 2/4, ending with 3/8 over 4/4. Despite these devices, it's a short, unpretentious piece of work; but since it was recorded in 1946, before cool jazz, and just after bebop had begun, it seems impossible to categorize. Free jazz? Maybe.

moted by Barry Ulanov, the editor of *Metronome* magazine), Tristano ultimately chose not to perform and settled for being an influential if cultish teacher. His earliest students—Lee Konitz and Warne Marsh, especially—became heavily identified with Tristano's style, but over the years he also had students as diverse as show pianist Roger Williams and guitar wizard Joe Satriani. In his own bands and those of his students, he encouraged the use of collective improvisation, even though his model often seemed to be so not much that of New Orleans' collectivity as it was European counterpoint and polyphony (his students often played Bach as warm-up exercises, or even as performance pieces). Though it might at first appear that Tristano was a musician of limited palette, he made music so innovative and diverse as to render him stylistically unclassifiable. In 1949 he recorded (under Lee Konitz's name) "Digression" and "Intuition," two brief pieces that were free of fixed chord structure and key, thus anticipating free jazz by some ten or so years. Though he appeared rhythmically conservative, in 1954 he recorded "Turkish Mambo," a complex exercise for three multitracked left-hand parts, each in different meters, each of which shifted as he improvised against them; and "Requiem," on which the tape of the piano solo was speeded up and slowed down as it proceeded. Such experiments earned him even more condemnation from critics, who saw him as creating a fake and mechanical music. But Tristano was one of the first to understand the potential of the recording studio in music making, and the role it could play in composition. Far from crude, his first experiments were completely musical and remarkably polished.

The Modern Jazz Quartet

Pianist John Lewis was a solid member of the school of bebop, having worked in most of the key bands of the 1940s, including Miles Davis's Birth of the Cool. When he became part of the Modern Jazz Quartet—the group initially built around vibraphonist Milt Jackson—he found the perfect medium for his music for years to come. Like some others who were called cool, Lewis looked to the past for some of his orchestral ideas, drawing on forms and musical devices (such as counterpoint) from the baroque era and unifying them with the blues, bebop, and contemporary classical music.

It was a daring concept, seemingly contradictory but brilliantly realized. Onstage, there were the four musicians in sleek tuxedos or three-piece suits. Jackson's volatile, yet always soulful and elegant vibraphone solos were at its center, flanked by a propulsive but delicate rhythm section of bass and drums, with Lewis's fastidious but quietly funky piano orga-

Modern Jazz Quartet, "Django." *The Smithsonian Collection of Classic Jazz.*

John Lewis's 1954 composition for the death of Belgian guitarist Django Reinhardt is a simple but triumphant reassertion of form in jazz composition. The principal theme is a halting, stately melody that suggests a European funeral cortege. This is followed by a light, spirited section for improvised solos that seems closer to a New Orleans jazz funeral. This impression is reinforced by a recurrent bass figure drawn from King Oliver's 1926 recording of "Snag It." Lewis here creates a perfect vehicle for the four instrumentalists: the work underscores the contrast between Lewis's understated, subtle piano figures and the assertive, blues-based vibraphone of Milt Jackson, while still allowing the improvisations and the melody to flow together as one.

nizing it all. They often took ballads like "Willow Weep for Me" or "Softly as in a Morning Sunrise" at a tempo that seemed too slow to get off the ground. But with the vibrators on Jackson's instrument turned low, there was a passionate throb to his melodic statements; when they inevitably doubled the tempos, it was as if they had gone back to Kansas City swing to reinvigorate bebop. It was a financially as well as musically successful concept, and one which provoked them to try a seemingly endless series of new ideas and experiments. There were suites and fugues, and works that paired them with chamber orchestras, classical guitarists, and string quartets.

It was a formula for success made in jazz heaven. There were those who thought the Modern Jazz Quartet effete, even pretentious; but being African-American, "East Coast," and bearing impeccable jazz credentials, they made most observers uncomfortable with the idea of tossing them in with other cool musicians, dismissing them as a wrong turn in the evolution of jazz. For jazz fans they came to occupy a unique place somewhere outside of the usual streams of jazz, while those who seldom listened to jazz also thought of them as an exception to what they conceived of as jazz.

Lee Konitz

Konitz was the star student of the Lennie Tristano school, and one of the few alto saxophonists to appear in the wake of Charlie Parker who was able to resist the lure of his sound. Instead, Konitz favors a light, airy tone in the upper register, generally free of vibrato that makes him immediately recognizable. Anything Konitz plays—even a straight, unembellished melody—comes out as sounding improvised.

Lee Konitz, *Jazz at Storyville*. Black Lion BCD 760901.

"These Foolish Things" and "Foolin' Myself" from 1954 are brilliantly unique readings of these songs, though the latter also captures in its own icy way some of the same spirit that Billie Holiday brought to it on her own recording. The band behind Konitz is quiet, the dynamics and interaction are minimal, but they are perfect for his purposes. His long, endlessly inventive ideas flow over an undecorated plain of rhythm with a scrupulousness that verges on the stark.

For a different-yet-same Konitz, *Motion* (Verve 5557107) from 1961 has Elvin Jones on drums, who illuminates the saxophone lines with the same rhythmic textures he brought to John Coltrane's music at that time.

19 West Coast Jazz

More successful as a marketing label than it ever was as a unified style of music, West Coast jazz has lost much of its luster since the principals have faded and the force of the coastal reference has worn off. But looking back, it's easy to see why it was victorious in packaging and selling a loosely associated body of music. In the 1950s California was poised to become the golden alternative to the East Coast (the latter symbolized by a New York City that had begun to lose some of its influence and its population). The New West was in need of a soundtrack that reflected the freshly minted feel of the place, and West Coast jazz arrived right on schedule, straight from Central Casting, as Lenny Bruce used to say, all sunlight, surf, and celluloid. And all white as well, if you read the press reports. Dave Brubeck, Gerry Mulligan, Jimmy Giuffre, Art Pepper, Cal Tjader,

Shorty Rogers, Chet Baker—all these young men were back from the war and enrolled in music schools, turning California into the Paris of the 1920s, finding their Bohemia in Redondo Beach, Santa Monica, or North Beach. If the West Coast at the time lacked the music magazines, the recording centers, and the club activity of New York City, it at least had the movies, with opportunities for work in studio orchestras; a few key record companies—Pacific Jazz, Contemporary, Dial, Fantasy, and Capitol; and its own history of jazz, almost as old as the beginnings of jazz itself. It was that history that was ignored by those who promoted West Coast jazz.

In Los Angeles, especially, there was a vital black community in the first decades of the twentieth century, and the area known as Central Avenue was the focus of what has only lately been wisely recognized as an important black jazz community. Even before 1910, Jelly Roll Morton was playing in Los Angeles, and before 1920 many other groups, now almost forgotten, had developed there: the Wood-Wilson Syncopators, for example, were perhaps the first group to use the word *jazz* in their ads ("the famous jass band"). By the 1920s Paul Howard's Quality Serenaders included musicians such as Lionel Hampton, Lawrence Brown, and others soon to become nationally known. Reb Spikes and his brother had formed their own record company and recorded Kid Ory's Creole Jazz Orchestra in 1922. Throughout the 1930s and especially the years of World War II, the black population of Los Angeles grew, and with it musical groups and clubs and dance halls. Bebop took root in Los Angeles almost immediately, spearheaded by Howard McGhee with the Coleman Hawkins band in 1945, and then by Dizzy

Gillespie and Charlie Parker, both of whom recorded on the Coast. An array of fine boppers quickly developed in the Los Angeles area, such as Teddy Edwards, Dexter Gordon, Sonny Criss, Harold Land, Roy Porter, Charles Mingus, and Wardell Gray. There were more to come in this only-recently-documented history of jazz on the West Coast: Buddy Collette, Hampton Hawes, Eric Dolphy, Frank Morgan, and Lucky Thompson, to name a few.

But "West Coast" was too good a label not to use in the early 1950s, so new music percolating up from California's shores was grouped together and, more to the point, put in opposition to what was seen as East Coast—the largely black and bebop-based music heard on Prestige, Savoy, and Blue Note records. You could see the strategy at work on the record album covers. If Blue Note records were all dark tones, interiors, stark club shots, and African-American males, Contemporary and Pacific Jazz were sunbeams and waves, models in swim suits, motorbikes, pastel abstract art, and white musicians. When Sonny Rollins recorded *Way Out West* for Contemporary, instead of the noirish shadows and shot-from-the-floor colossus images, he was suited up as a cowboy and placed out on the desert. Similarly, Stan Getz (a quintessential East Coaster who cringed at being called West Coast) was often cast in a California role, posed to look as if he had just strolled in from the beach. (No surprise, really, that the next music that would come to be identified with California would be surf music.)

If the music was easy to label, when looked at in retrospect it is another case of a variety of styles being treated as if they were one. In part, this situation was caused by a continuing problem in the development of jazz: the relation of the improviser to the composer. The dilemma began early in the history of the jazz. with the question of what the soloist should improvise *on*, and if it was to be a song or a composition, how much of the original should be presented? What should the relationship of the soloist to the original be? How should the whole performance be held together? Is it possible to maintain spontaneity inside of a written framework? These were problems wrestled with most successfully by Jelly Roll Morton and Duke Ellington early on, and continued by Thelonious Monk, Gil Evans, and the other writers for Miles Davis's Birth of the Cool band, and by John Lewis with the Modern Jazz Quartet. Many West Coast musicians were consumed by these questions, and their solutions were substantial. Though largely forgotten today, their adroit use of European compositional elements broadened jazz's palette and gave it new directions to explore. Shorty Rogers and Teddy Charles on *Collaboration West* (1954), for example, were using modes as a basis for improvisation well before Miles Davis's *Kind of Blue*. There were many heavily composed pieces as well, notably those by Gerry Mulligan for his tentet and Jimmy Giuffre's many experiments in small groups; and there were those who pushed jazz in directions that no one else wanted to take: Lyle Murphy's *12-Tone Compositions and Arrangements* (1955), Duane Tatro's *Jazz for Moderns* (1954–1955), or Bob

Further Listening:

For an overview of West Coast jazz try *The West Coast Jazz Box: An Anthology of California Jazz*, Contemporary 4CCD-4425-2, a 4-CD boxed set. For a broader view, strong on black California jazz and rhythm and blues, there is *Central Avenue Sounds: Jazz in Los Angeles (1921–1956)*, Rhino R2 75872, a 4-CD boxed set.

Graettinger's arrangements for Stan Kenton in the 1940s and 1950s. There was good musicianship on the coast, extensive use of formal counterpoint and uncluttered surfaces, a certain reserve in expression and in its use of vibrato and volume; but in other ways much of the music seemed very "East Coast" in its use of show tunes, Latin rhythms, and bebop vocabulary.

Gerry Mulligan

Like so many West Coast musicians, baritone saxophonist, arranger, and composer Gerry Mulligan was from the East. He began as a bebopper, though with a strong commitment to the principles of swing. As arranger, Mulligan worked his way through some of the more interesting of the late swing-era bands, such as the bebop-infected orchestras of Elliot Lawrence and Gene Krupa. Like Gil Evans, he could make bebop themes work with standard swing dance rhythms, writing arrangements that made otherwise conventional musicians seem reborn as boppers. He, too, was one of the important elements of Miles Davis's Birth of the Cool band.

Working in California in 1952, Mulligan put together a quartet he reduced to the essentials: baritone saxophone, trumpet, bass, and drums. With none of the chordal instruments to direct and frame them, Mulligan's quartet was free to explore rhythms and textures, and produced a light, airy jazz, though heavy on interplay and dialogue. Mulligan's baritone saxophone had a rich, energetic quality and a bubbling optimism ran through his solos. His shadow self was the estimable Chet Baker, a trumpeter with a model's mien and that rare ability to make you think he sounded the way he looked. These were young white men who could be taken for undergraduates at USC, creating an aura of hip that matched the American moment with sweet and sorrowful ballads and uptempo originals that were cheerful and full of sunlight. They had rubbed the rougher edges off bebop and brought it back with a clarity of expression that even the squares could get.

After a few years as a cool musician, in the early 1960s Mulligan began to be considered the essence of all that was "mainstream," a term that was meant to indicate players who had a sense of the entire jazz tradition and could play with almost anyone who had come before them. This was the position he held for the rest of his life, and though he conducted and wrote for big bands from time to time, his main preoccupation was the small group with his wonderful baritone sound at its center.

Gerry Mulligan, "Bernie's Tune." *The Best of the Gerry Mulligan Quartet with Chet Baker.* Pacific Jazz 95481.

The first of Mulligan's pianoless quartets had that lean, naked feel of Miles Davis's Birth of the Cool. In retrospect, however, it may seem a bit *too* spare, too close to flirting with the morose, its inevitable sections of counterpoint somehow baroque and calculated. But in 1952 Mulligan was reversing decades of small band tradition, going for the bare essentials, letting the rhythm show through the bop-derived lines, slowing the tempos, lowering the volume . . . cooling it. "Bernie's Tune" was a favorite tune for jamming—a theme in a minor key fitted to a pop song format—and there was no reason to think that something special would come out of it. But there is something new here, something sophisticated about horn lines clear enough to be listened to, something refreshing about the return of riffs, countermelodies, and polyphony. Still, it's hard to imagine them pulling it off without the confidence that Mulligan's tumbling and rolling baritone saxophone lines provided.

While his records varied in quality and interest, he was one of the few musicians who never made a bad one.

Jimmy Giuffre

Giuffre is not widely known, even in hard-core jazz circles, but he is one of the most widely recorded musicians of his time, and an influential figure. Like Stan Getz, he first became known for his work with the "Four Brothers" saxophone section of Woody Herman's 1940s band—in fact, it was his composition of the same name that featured the saxophone section that gave them their name. He could be found on many of the records coming from the West Coast in the '50s, either as arranger or soloist, and his own records in the late '50s and early '60s broke with precedent. His quartet on *Tangents in Jazz* in 1955, like many groups of the period, used no piano, but it was the new roles he assigned to the drums and bass that surprised: instead of strictly maintaining rhythm, they were given melodic roles and frequently exchanged tasks with the horns. *The Jimmy Giuffre 3* (1956) took as its model Debussy's "Sonata for Flute, Viola, and Harp" but used folkish, almost country and western compositions for its book, with an added soft edge of the blues. It was an original sound, and one that many would have stuck with. But in 1961 Giuffre radically reformed his thinking about trios by adding Paul Bley on piano and Steve Swallow on bass, while he himself began to play the clarinet exclusively, hardening his tone and reducing its vibrato (on records like *Free Fall* (1962). Although now sometimes playing free of fixed keys and tempos, theirs was still a quiet form of chamber jazz and seemed a strange anomaly in an era in which many musicians overreached their abilities or, worse, aimed low.

Today Giuffre's records may seem less radical than they were, if for no other reason than that the group played at low volume, often in the lower ranges of their instruments, as if what they were offering was too dangerous to let out all at once. Yet four years before the changes in jazz that were marked in 1959 by the innovations of Ornette Coleman, Miles Davis, and John Coltrane, Giuffre was pointing the way toward them with new means of collective improvisation, fragmented melody lines, reexamination of the conventional roles of instruments, and the presence of an implied rather than a stated beat. The use of sound itself became a basis for improvising and for organizing a performance. Not many musicians have been able to weather the stylistic changes in jazz or to accommodate those shifts in their own playing and still sound vital in the process. Coleman Hawkins is one, Miles Davis another, and if Jimmy Giuffre has not always been seen as such a survivor, it is because he has been self-effacing and chose to work outside of the jazz mainstream.

20 Hard Bop, Soul Music, and Funk

If bebop was seen on one hand as musically revolutionary and on the other as merely strange, and if cool and West Coast jazz were received as a series of experiments well within the jazz tradition, some of the music that followed in their footsteps—hard bop, soul, and funk—was given a more self-consciously racial interpretation. Between the mid-'50s and the mid-'60s, new forms of jazz emerged—Eastern, black, urban, industrial musics that picked up themes and stylistic features from the whole spectrum of black music, from folk to church to pop. The genesis of these new forms is complex, a mixture of shifts in demographics and social expectations combined with technological developments and changes in taste.

Musical tastes were more organic and communal in America in the 1950s, especially in black communities, and small boutique-like neighborhood record stores could shape and reinforce local tastes, as did radio DJs who catered to communities of listeners. Jukeboxes in restaurants and bars played jazz singles. Local bars were still centers for live entertainment, where trios made up of the newly-invented portable electric organs, drums, and guitar or saxophone ruled: new organ stars such as Shirley Scott, Jimmy Smith, and Big John Patton appeared, along with full-bodied tenor saxophonists like Jimmy Forrest and Gene Ammons. At dances, big bands like those of James Brown and Ray Charles could perform the whole panoply of African-American musics, from blues to pop to jazz. A string of East Coast record companies—most notably Blue Note, Savoy, and Prestige—catered to these black communities and acted as talent scouts in cities that had no labels of their own, such as Detroit, Newark, and Philadelphia. Before the 1960s were over, the shared culture of black communities was weakened by the civil rights movement and the diffusion of black economic power, the rise of rock and roll, the staging of festivals and large concerts, and multiracial programming on radio and TV. But this late burst of black artistic activity left an indelible mark on the history of jazz nonetheless.

By the late 1950s a number of musical and technological changes had altered expectations about music. Long-playing records had extended the amount of time that musicians were expected to play, and longer solos were a cheap way of extending play without requiring longer and more complex arrangements—fortuitous, as it turned out, since musicians' approach to improvisation had been evolving for some time and they were ready to play longer solos. Rhythm and blues, still popular in black neighborhoods, had lost some of its force among white listeners, though a few performers like Ray Charles and Mahalia Jackson had crossover hits and could draw interracial crowds to their performances. A folk revival was also under way, with older black blues performers being brought out of retirement and lionized by young white audiences. "Soul," a black term of cultural approval and the password of new black consciousness, made its way into music, becoming the rallying cry of musicians who sought to reform jazz to regain the audiences they had lost over the last decade to pop music and, more recently, to rock and roll. But it was also a point of safe retreat from free jazz, which was also on the rise.

The period between the mid-'50s and mid-'60s was a era in which the resources of jazz were consolidated and refined, and the range of sources broadened. Some of the jazz of this period reached across class and age and unified African-American audiences. Young people could see this music as "bad" in the same sense that James Brown used

Horace Silver, "Blowin' the Blues Away." *Blowing the Blues Away.* Blue Note B21Y-46526.

Silver's little band had an *au courant* sound in 1959: crisp, terse horns, assertive rhythm section, altogether as funky, soulful, and tight as Ray Charles's band might sound if it was shrunk to five pieces. And that was the clue: Silver thought of his quintet as a miniature big band, thoroughly organized and arranged, but up to date. Trumpeter Blue Mitchell and tenor saxophonist Junior Cook take solos that radiate an awareness of what is happening in Silver's piano accompaniment, responding to its urgency as if it were a sax or brass section riffing behind them. Their solos are also perfectly realized, balanced, strong statements in spite of the fast tempo. It was music of the moment, to be sure, but of such strength and richness that it still impresses long after the shibboleths of funk have been forgotten.

the word, and older people could also see its links to past black traditions.

"Hard bop" as a name for music of this period has always been a bit simplistic. Some musicians disliked it from the beginning, finding it glib and misleading ("What was bebop, soft?"), a press agent's term. As critic Gary Giddins once suggested, hard bop has come to be defined by what it is not—not bop, cool, fusion, or free jazz. Once again the music produced in this period was far too varied and diverse to be contained by a single name. There was, first off, the most popular form, a music often called soul, for its folk- or pseudo-folk-based melodies and its rhythm and blues and 3/4 or 6/8 church rhythms: things like Horace Silver's 1959 "Sister Sadie" or Cannonball Adderley's recording of Bobby Timmon's "This Here" in the same year; or organ trios, such as those of Jimmy Smith, Jimmy McGriff, and Shirley Scott. Some soul music was called funk—"funk" being a word derived not from the English word for "fearful," or "dejected," but most likely from the Ki-Kongo word *lu-fuki*, a word used to praise the sweat and body odor of those who "work out" in their performances—a music with repeating bass figures, the drums playing with a strong emphasis on the second and fourth beats of the measure (the high-hat cymbals loudly snapping shut on those beats, emulating clapping), straightforward melodies, and simplified harmony. In effect, however, it sounded closer to gospel music than to rhythm and blues. But soul was more than a style. Like the blues, it vividly evoked black history. In 1958 and 1959 soul became such a polarizing subject that *Down Beat* ran interviews and acrimonious panel discussions where musicians debated whether the ability to play this music was culturally- or genetically-determined.

Latin rhythm increased in popularity during this period, to the point that it constituted something of a sub-style. Two of the key bands of the period, Horace Silver's and Art Blakey's, used so many Latin-influenced compositions that they became an expected part of their records and performances. Conga drummer Ray Barretto virtually became a house band musician for Blue Note Records, complicating and stirring up even the most straightforward of sessions. And every once in awhile, Blue Note issued records like Kenny Dorham's *Afro-Cuban* or Sabu Martinez's *Palo Congo* which were almost entirely Latin in concept.

Other hard boppers played in a style difficult to separate from bebop, except that they explored one or another area in greater depth. Some were lyricists, like Art Farmer, Hank Jones, or Miles Davis (who was now on his third style of jazz), or they were highly individualized bebop players, like Jackie McLean or Elmo Hope. There was also an experimental wing of musicians who intensified the elements of bebop: people like Sonny Rollins, Andrew Hill, John Coltrane, Thelonious Monk, or Charles Mingus. But even this group seems too diverse to lump together. Many of these players changed from one approach to another as time went on, or worked in several styles simultaneously. Even more complicating, as quickly as these disparate styles were established, a new, equally diverse generation entered the scene in the 1960s: musicians like Joe Chambers, Bobby Hutcherson, Joe Henderson, Woody Shaw.

If this music was coded black by listeners, some critics found it excessively so. The English poet and conservative jazz critic Philip Larkin complained that the civil rights movement was destroying jazz. Other white writers complained of the anger and hostility apparent in this music, while some found it regressive or monotonous, rightly or wrongly hearing it as too close to rock and roll.

Further Listening:

Charlie Parker, "A Night in Tunisia." *The Legendary Dial Masters.* Jazz Classics 5003.
Art Blakey, "A Night in Tunisia." *A Night at Birdland, Vol. 1.* Blue Note 46519.
Art Blakey, "A Night in Tunisia." *A Night in Tunisia.* Blue Note 784949.
Further Listening: Various Artists, *Blue 45s: The Ultimate Jukebox.* Blue Note 4 94030.

There were some real departures from classic bebop in this music: drummers played more aggressively, moving beyond merely supporting and encouraging soloists to actually enclosing them, framing them in rhythm (though admittedly this effect was exaggerated by the new recording technology that made it easier to record drums). Where bebop tunes were often based on well-known pop songs, hard bop more typically used new melodies, although as in bebop, these still provided something to play with and against, creating a horizon for soloists. Yet players like Sonny Rollins or Miles Davis could take older pop tunes ignored by beboppers like "Bye, Bye Blackbird" or "Toot, Toot, Tootsie" and turn them into new standards. The differences (and similarities) between bebop and hard bop may best be heard by comparing the recordings of "A Night in Tunisia" by Charlie Parker in 1946 with those of Art Blakey in 1954, and again in 1959: the interaction of players becomes increasingly conversational against a roiling rhythmic background that sometimes threatens to drown the soloists.

21 The Organ Trio

The Hammond B-3 organ was the people's instrument of choice in certain neighborhoods for several decades (then forgotten, and now back with a vengeance). As big as a coffin, and tough enough (they say) to stop a bullet from a .45, an instrument that when cranked up has the percussive crunch of a locomotive; but played softly it resonates with Sunday morning majesty. The organ reached prominence at the same time that funk and soul pianists like Horace Silver and Ray Charles gained fame, and both keyboard instruments had been influenced by church organ music. Some think of the organ as more of a liability than an asset, but the great players (Jimmy Smith, Shirley Scott, or Big John Patton) have always made virtues out of its weaknesses. If the bass pedals could not be worked as fast as a string bassist played, they could nonetheless be moved with the elegance of a dancer's feet. If its sound seemed alien to the sonorities of late bebop, the B-3 at least had a distinctive voice, and the best players could make it talk in their own dialects. Even today, though there are electric keyboards and synthesizers that come close to the B-3's sound, none gets it right, for the whirling, motor-driven Leslie speakers that give it voice stubbornly resist sampling.

Further Listening:

Various Artists, *Kickin' the 3: The Best of Organ Trio Jazz.* Shanachie 5034.

Organ trios consisted of drums, bass, and organ, and played a repertoire of pop tunes, sentimental ballads, down home soul favorites, dance tunes, and all-out stompers. Sometimes a saxophone might be added to these trios, and some of the great tenor saxophone players of the 1960s came up this way, "walking the bar," literally walking up and down the counter as they played those little mom and pop neighborhood bars. It was a setting that helped shape the aesthetic that can always be heard somewhere in the playing of John Coltrane or Sonny Rollins.

22

Post-Bebop

Improvisation, c. 1956

For some years, musicians had been quoting from other songs in their improvisations or interpolating fragments of older songs into new ones (Nat "King" Cole, for instance, regularly built his entire improvisation of "Body and Soul" from fragments of other songs). This practice became even more self-conscious and common in the 1950s. Dexter Gordon could work seemingly endless references to other songs into his solos. Such quotations could be no more than phrases that fit harmonically and rhythmically, or they could be humorous commentaries

Sonny Rollins, "Blue 7." *Saxophone Colossus*. Original Jazz Classics OJC 291.

In an analysis of this recording of a 12-bar blues, Gunther Schuller suggested that Rollins's solution to some of the problems that were beginning to plague improvisers in the 1950s was to find a way to unify the source material and on the current song or merely citations to connect to an existing musical literature.

Quotation and citation point to a problem with jazz improvisation that was becoming more apparent in the 1950s. Musicians were either improvising by playing on the chord structure, with the chorus as their formal unit, or they were decorating or embellishing the given melody. The problem was that there was a lack of cohesion and unity in the performance as a whole: soloists often linked unrelated ideas together as they occurred to them, and one musician's solo was usually unrelated to the next. One solution to the problem was to arrange and compose music that structured the improvisations. This was a method common

the improvisation by varying small portions (motives) of the original composition and then linking them together with other portions, though not necessarily in their original order. He might therefore play a variation of a few significant notes (X), then vary another few notes (Y), another few (Z), then possibly vary Y, then X again, etc.

In the case of "Blue 7," Rollins played only with drums and bass, and the freedom from the usual chordal instruments (piano and guitar) seemed to liberate his thinking. At times his variations were Parkeresque bursts of notes that doubled the tempo, but at others they were merely a stripping down to essentials—say, only two notes, a single interval, but shrewdly chosen ones. (The same two notes can be heard in other recordings like "Vierd Blues" or "Pent-Up House"; so, small as they are, they constituted something of a signature figure.) It was the sort of device that Thelonious Monk had explored in recordings such as "Misterioso," and something that Rollins may have learned from Monk during his stay with his band. "Blue 7" rewards close listening by showing just how much can be done by a masterly improviser with a theme of such few notes and how a coherent composition can be constructed out of them. (Rollins's "Blues for Philly Joe" from 1957 is another example.)

among musicians who were involved with Miles Davis's Birth of the Cool (Gerry Mulligan or John Lewis), and others such as Jimmy Giuffre.

Another solution was to improvise on the melody (rather than the harmony), and yet another was to build up solos from motives or shorter melody units. It was perhaps Sonny Rollins, more than any other player of this time, who best exemplified these methods.

Miles Davis, *Cookin'*. Original Jazz Classics OJC 128.

The first great Miles Davis quintet in 1956, with John Coltrane, Red Garland, Philly Joe Jones, and Paul Chambers, a group whose every record is worthy of attention, since each draws from this exceptional group's nightly club repertoire (*Cookin'* opens with "My Funny Valentine," just as Davis often opened with it on gigs during this period, demanding quiet and respect). This record gets a slight edge over others of this series through its balance of ballads, blues, and hard bop warhorses. Coltrane at this point lacked the consistency and otherworldly inspiration of his later work, but here he plays with a force and sometimes even a recklessness that contrasts nicely with Davis's quiet ruminations. Davis is inspired and witty, and Coltrane matches him all the way. Meanwhile, one of the great rhythm sections follows them at every step, helping to create a unity among equals almost unprecedented in jazz before this group.

Charles Mingus

By the 1950s, the important figures of jazz were either pianists (most of whom were also arrangers and composers) or horn players with extraordinary improvisational abilities. Drummers and bassists were merely the journeymen, toiling away in the rhythm section. Drummers might function as leaders, riding on their flash and charisma, but bassists were semi-anonymous at best. It was all the more surprising, then, that one of the key figures of the 1950s was Charles Mingus, a bassist—but a great bassist, with a volatile and virtuosic approach to a notoriously inflexible instrument. While drummers were laying claim to becoming equal partners with horns, Mingus showed that it was possible for a bassist to do the same, through sheer volume and musical imagination. Musicians in Mingus's group would find themselves supported, challenged, bullied, and cajoled by contrapuntal figures, a room-shaking pulse, and a bass line that talked—literally conversed—like the best of the vocalized horn players. In addition to the powerful walking 4/4 beat typical of bassists, Mingus doubled time at the drop of a hat, or suspended time altogether to play free of the beat.

Miles Davis, *L'Ascenseur pour l'échafaud.* Fontana 836305.

This was music for a 1957 movie by Louis Malle that would come to make us think that every film noir had always sounded that way—slow-walking bass beats and muted, slithering horn lines miming the characters on the screen and underscoring their emotions. The melodies are brief fragments, sometimes surfacing only for a few moments and then disappearing. This is Miles with European musicians he hadn't worked with before, playing in the moment, improvising musical impressions as he watched the screen. What he played managed to capture the era of postwar everywhere, while offering him the freedom to test his compositional skills within a minimalist context. How many other beboppers who worked in the shadow of Charlie Parker could have recorded these little gems of quiet passion?

Born in New Mexico and raised in Los Angeles, Mingus had at one time or another played with Louis Armstrong, Duke Ellington, Lionel Hampton, Art Tatum, Red Norvo, and Charlie Parker. He had worked in classical settings, Latin bands, rhythm and blues groups—in short, with most of the masters of

Miles Davis, *Sketches of Spain*. Columbia CK 65142.

In the late 1950s Gil Evans and Miles Davis collaborated on a number of projects that continued directions first started with Claude Thornhill's orchestra and Davis's Birth of the Cool band: the early-morning feel of the front-line harmonizations, the opalescence of the shifting registers and voicings behind the soloists, the shadow plays of riffs. Evans seems to test each chord for density, creating tension by using instruments in startling ways—say, an upper-register tuba lead, with flutes and trumpets near the bottom of the chord; or Stravinsky-like bassoon over French horn and flute—placing motion and energy in the harmonics rather than the rhythm. *Sketches of Spain* and other projects (*Miles Ahead* and *Porgy and Bess*) are suites held together not so much thematically as by shared voices and implied moods. Gershwin's music seems literally recomposed in the *Porgy and Bess* album, as is Roderigo's "Concerto de Aranjuez" in 1959–1960's *Sketches of Spain*. *Sketches* is music very much of its time, evocative, romantic, and deeply felt, but also, at its weakest moments, a bit obvious, and occasionally over the top. But Davis's playing throughout (and especially on "Solea") is remarkable, bringing new colors and emotions into jazz. Once heard, it remains unforgettable.

jazz and in every conceivable setting. He applied all of these experiences to his own music, using the blues, Latin music of the Southwest, fundamentalist church music, bebop, classical forms, and the totalizing embrace of Ellington's arrangements. Some of his finest moments occurred when he crammed a number of these musical influences into a single work, such as *New Tijuana Moods* of 1957, or the 1963 "Better Get Hit in Yo' Soul."

In one way or another, Mingus announced the seriousness of his ambitions like no one else in his time: he wrote an outrageous semifictional autobiography, founded his own record company, and never missed an opportunity to lecture or harangue an audience into listening. He organized a group he called his Jazz

Workshop, staffing it with some of the most advanced musicians of the time. His compositional process, like Ellington's, involved using the individuality of his musicians, teaching them by ear, encouraging them to contribute. His compositions often began merely as rough outlines, but by the time they had been played for a few nights they became complex and flowing. He reflected on Jelly Roll Morton and Duke Ellington and their use of collective improvisation, multiple themes, and wide use of source material. At the same time, he anticipated jazz to come: he broke up the repetitive patterns of 32-bar pop songs (his "Minor Intru-

Charles Mingus, "Folk Forms, No. 1." *Charles Mingus Presents Charles Mingus.* Candid CCD 79005.

It takes only a few seconds of this 12-bar blues to know that this is going to be jazz played at the highest level. Four musicians battle, support, and struggle with one another as equals—no mean feat, given that two of them are a drummer and a bassist. But Charles Mingus was a model to his musicians, making the bass talk, sing, and walk—like a natural man, as the blues singers used to say. This meant that the rhythm section would have to surrender part of its strictly powerhouse function, without forgetting it entirely, for Mingus wanted to be able to turn a band on a dime, stopping and starting at will, engaging rhythm and tempo gears without regard for the strain it put on the players. The same went for the horns. In this 1960 piece there are no soloists and accompanists in the strict sense of the words. For that matter, there are no composers and improvisers, either. The players move from the written to the improvised with such ease and authority that it is not always easy to know what's what, especially as they are constantly shifting configuration, so that duets are passed around among all four of the instruments.

sion" of 1954, for example, rocks back and forth between alternating modes); his use of pedal points or single chords anticipated modal playing; and his constant shifts in tempo, accelerations, and occasional wholesale abandonment of a fixed rhythm presage free jazz and some of the experiments in rhythm that continue today.

PART 4

23 1959: Multiple Revolutions

Though we should always be wary of using single dates as markers for points of change, 1959 begs to be seen as the moment at which jazz ceased to follow an evolutionary handbook. It was if not the beginning, then at least the moment at which we can first see jazz moving into a state of permanent diversity. Confidence in jazz was still high, with recordings of an extraordinary range appearing almost daily. The mainstream was still flowing nicely: Louis Armstrong recorded with Duke Ellington, affirming the wholeness of the tradition. Dave Brubeck had just recorded *Time Out*, an album of compositions with unusual and provocative meters: this was experimental music, but gently so, and his quartet sounded friendly to those who followed him. (Even today, "Take Five," a piece from that album, remains so popular that it turns up behind automobile ads on TV.) Cannonball

Adderley recorded *The Cannonball Adderley Quintet in San Francisco,* one of the most popular of the soul jazz albums. Charles Mingus produced *Mingus Ah Um,* which showed just how such folk and soul elements could be used not just for popular consumption but in compositions of great seriousness and emotional power. Many other musicians at this time were recording "jazz" versions of Broadway and private eye TV show scores: *Gypsy, Flower Drum Song, Porgy and Bess, Peter Gunn,* and *77 Sunset Strip.* It was evidence that America as a whole thought of jazz as a single style of music, unaware that hard-core jazz followers were at that very moment finding it increasingly difficult to say exactly what kind (or kinds) of the new jazz they favored.

But 1959 was also a year in which three very innovative albums appeared, each producing its own form of shock. First, John Coltrane recorded *Giant Steps,* with music that might have seemed to those not listening closely to be merely bebop of the highest order. But something seemed to be shaking loose inside the album. The title piece, "Giant Steps," was fast, thick with constant chord changes (moving at the rate of a new chord on every other beat) and with a melody whose endlessly unfolding odd intervals—giant steps—appeared to be designed to make life difficult for its tenor saxophone soloist. It was difficult music, and Coltrane's virtuoso performance drew attention to the tedium that formulaic bebop could produce. It was a constant stream of notes, relentlessly navigating the guides and barriers the chords erected; a tour de force, to be sure, but also a statement about the exhaustion of a bold idea. To underline the point, on the same album John Coltrane provided another composition that could not have been more different: "Naima" was a slow, meditative piece built on a single note, almost a drone, which was repeated over and over by the bassist for eight bars, then a second note repeated for a second eight bars, a pair of fulcrums on which the entire composition was lifted.

John Coltrane was at the time working with Miles Davis, and perhaps it should not have been surprising that "Naima" paralleled the second of the three signal albums of 1959, one on which Coltrane played, Miles Davis's *Kind of Blue*. The idea was simple, the music of the most basic order, the session unrehearsed, and every piece on the record was a first take save one. Davis had been talking to George Russell, one of the music's most thoughtful and provocative composers, about his wish to play on something simpler than chord progressions. During their conversations Russell explained to him that it was not necessary to change with the chords—that an improviser might play only on one or two scales or chords.

Kind of Blue became over the years the one jazz record owned by people who don't listen to jazz, and with good reason. The band itself is extraordinary (proof of Miles Davis's masterful casting skills, if not of God's existence), listing John Coltrane and Julian "Cannonball" Adderley on saxophones, Bill Evans (or, on "Freddie Freeloader," Wynton Kelly) on piano, and the crack rhythm unit of Paul Chambers on bass and Jimmy Cobb on drums. Coltrane's astringency on tenor is counterpoised to Adderley's funky self on alto, with Davis moderating between them as Bill Evans conjures up a still lake of sound on which they walk. Meanwhile, the rhythm partnership of Cobb and Chambers is prepared to click off time until eternity. It was the key recording of what became modal jazz, a music free of the fixed harmonies and cadences of pop songs. In the Davis musicians' hands it was a weightless music, but one that refused to fade into the background. In retrospect, every note seems perfect.

What Davis did with "So What" is typical of what made this album unique. The introduction begins deceptively, out of tempo and slow, the main theme a short figure played on bass; a two-note, "so what" phrase answers, stated first by piano and drums and then by trumpet and saxophones. (The title was suggested by Beverly Bentley, a friend of his at the time, who said it sounded like his favorite dismissive remark.) The form is the conventional pop song AABA, with the musicians beginning on a single chord, then moving up a half step to another once they reach the B section, then back. The two chords seem to disturb each other when first heard, as neither is especially strongly allied to the other. When Davis solos, he makes sure that he states at the beginning the tonic (E) of the single chord he is playing on, repeating it again and again throughout. It's a procedure he follows once more when he shifts to the second chord. But the flow of his ideas and the poise of his phrases keep the listener grounded without calling attention to the process or becoming repetitious.

It is hard to recapture the shock that accompanied the arrival of Ornette Coleman's *The Shape of Jazz to Come*, the third stunning record of 1959. Though it was a pianoless quartet from the West Coast, what they played had little in common with cool musicians like Gerry Mulligan and Chet Baker. Coleman's quartet played no jazz standards or ballads, only his compositions: themes like "Lonely Woman," in which Coleman's alto cries and wanders freely over a fast beat; or "Congeniality," where a short theme in a slow 3/4 alternates with another in fast 4/4. When Coleman enters to solo he seems to be ignoring most of the spare harmonic base underneath him.

There were two contrary tendencies at work in jazz at this point: to simplify the existing vocabulary of music and to complicate it. On the one hand, "Giant Steps" attempted to increase the complexity of melody and chords over which a musician played; on the other, "Naima," *Kind of Blue,* and *Change of the Century* were freeing up the melody by reducing the number of chords. It was the kind of contrary moment unique to times when the arts are in foment. You could hear it earlier in bebop when Charlie Parker was thickening the mix, heaping on the notes and expanding the vocabulary, even as Thelonious Monk was simplifying that very approach. (The same thing had happened in the novel when, in the 1930s, James Joyce was overloading its vocabulary while Samuel Beckett or Franz Kafka was trimming it back, distilling it.)

Kind of Blue was constructed from what has come to be called by some modes. A mode is technically a scale, and in theory there are thousands of scales available to music. But by and large, scales other than the major and the minor did not make much impact on jazz, with the exception of George Russell's writing in the late 1940s for bands such as Dizzy Gillespie's and the influence of Latin music on Gillespie's pieces such as "Mantecca." Later, as rock, soul, and funk entered jazz, there was a tendency with each for the music to simplify and reduce harmonic rhythm—the speed at which chords change. With chordal movement reduced, new room was made for melody—the vertical dimension of music—to move, which made bar divisions and solos of a fixed length less meaningful, even unnecessary.

Ethnic musics were beginning to have more influence on jazz in the 1950s as the musicians traveled more widely—Art Blakey and Max Roach were exploring Latin and African rhythms, and Duke Ellington was working Latin, African, and Asian musics into his suites. New modes were becoming a conscious part of many players' repertoires (Ron Carter said that he had begun to adjust his bass patterns to every country in which he traveled). Soul music had also brought modes of church music into use.

But typically it was not exotic scales that were used by musicians, but only one or two chords that could be used to slow harmonic change while still containing enough notes to fit into a scale. Or a drone or a pedal point might be used—single tones, most often on the bass or in the left hand of the piano, which were sounded again and again. The "modal tunes" that jazz musicians wrote to fit these new harmonic patterns were not so much used to determine an improvisation but were rather a reservoir to be dipped into. Instead of chord changes, musicians could now play on these few chords or drones or go beyond them. At first, modal improvisers fit these minimal harmonic materials into a fixed order in pop song formats such as Miles Davis's "So What." But they soon found that they could manipulate these modal elements into different sequences or stay on a single mode as long as they liked (Bill Evans's "Peace Piece," for example, is a simple melody built on only two chords in a single mode, and it is in turn used as an introduction to "Flamenco Sketches" on *Kind of Blue*). But simple modal patterns did not mean that the melodies had to be simple: Eddie Harris's "Freedom Jazz Dance" uses only one chord, but its twisting and hopping melody never seems simple or repetitious, especially as played by Miles Davis.

Modal playing freed musicians from the syntax and timing of conventional harmony and songs, and even of fixed lengths of solos. It also provided new kinds of melodies and arrangements with a freer sense of rhythm, as modal pieces often have a floating, impressionistic quality (like Herbie Hancock's "Cantaloupe Island"). In the hands of a musician such as John Coltrane, modality had an enormously liberating effect, allowing him to play irregular phrases, using notes from beyond the modes. Whether he was playing a pop tune like "My Favorite Things" or an original like "India," he brought modal feeling to bear.

Miles Davis, *Highlights from the Complete Live at the Plugged Nickel.* Columbia 481434.

Davis's second great quintet had been together only a little over a year when they recorded all of their stay at the Plugged Nickel in December of 1965 in Chicago (this CD presents some strong moments drawn from the larger 8-CD set). Everyone in this band was destined to be a star, and close listening to any one of them is rewarding. Bassist Ron Carter erects the scaffolding, while Herbie Hancock's piano adds filigree and lace, and drummer Tony Williams thunders and sparks (for once, mixed metaphors reflect exactly what was going on). Miles is sublime, but it is Wayne Shorter who is busy making his place in jazz history here, secure with the freshness and volatility of his ideas and the beauty of his sound. The band holds together miraculously, always balancing their risks with nuance and the subtlest of dynamics. An irresistible record, essential for hearing one of the great musical organizations at work.

MILES DAVIS

Davis was as emblematic of his era as Armstrong

was of his, and by innovating in every aspect of jazz, he left a mark on this music that only Ellington could match. Like Ellington, Davis mocked musical categories. Was he a bebopper, a cool jazz player, hard bopper, modal jazz musician, free jazz revolutionary, a fusioneer, a pop instrumentalist? He was all of the above, and the fact that we are still coming to terms with his music years after his death reminds us of just how remarkable were his range, sweep, and daring.

Yet Davis was not a virtuoso trumpet player. Indeed, at points in his career he had the reputation of being too timid and technically inept, a second-rate musician at best. But he could turn his alleged weaknesses into an aesthetic vulnerability that would fascinate generation after generation of listeners. Add this to an unerring sense of the lyrical and the dramatic, and a largeness that could reconcile Broadway show tunes and the blues, and you had the makings of a superstar, perhaps the last, some say, that jazz would produce.

John Coltrane

It was a period in which fundamentals were being rethought, John Coltrane was one of the most serious musical thinkers of the era. One possible implication of playing with a reduced number of chords is to play only one chord, he thought; another is to recognize that all 12 tones in an octave are equal, and therefore that all intervals are possible, that all melodies and all chords can be contained in one chord at the same time. Would there be "mistakes" in such a conception? Coltrane did not go all the way with these ideas, but his search is fascinating to follow. At one point he stacked chords on top of chords, as the beboppers did, but while attempting to play all of the notes at once. "Sheets of sound" is what that effort was labeled by sympathizers, while skeptics said he was trying to play chords on a saxophone, or that he sounded like he was trying to ingest too many peanut butter sandwiches. But that would not be all. Coltrane became interested in foreign musics, especially those of India, and he brought foreign modes and performance techniques into his own work, along with their spiritual concerns. As he pursued new spiritual disciplines his solos became longer and more complex, leading his detractors to blame him for what they perceived to be the decline of jazz. Philip Larkin wrote on the occasion of

John Coltrane, *John Coltrane: The Classic Quartet—Complete Impulse! Studio Recordings.* Impulse D8-280.

There have been many Coltrane compilations and boxed sets over the years since the saxophonist's death in 1967, but this 8-CD complete collection of his quartet's studio recordings between 1961 and 1965 is the centerpiece. Jazz may be blessed with dazzling soloists, yet few groups in its history seem to perfectly match the intentions of their leaders: Louis Armstrong's Hot Five and Hot Seven, Bill Evans's trio of 1960–1961, or Miles Davis's mid-'60s quintet are among the few who come to mind. Coltrane's quartet of pianist McCoy Tyner, drummer Elvin Jones, and bassist Jimmy Garrison was another, a group so finely attuned to his playing that it is difficult to imagine him without them. Tyner, for example, could immerse the group in restless chords and showers of single notes; Jones played with stentorian power, tempering it with well-etched detail and a strong sense of melody; and Garrison anchored them all with drones and deeply rooted vamps. Over this roiling mass, Coltrane strode fearlessly ahead. So powerful was his group conception that even when ringers like Art Davis and Roy Haynes turn up on a couple of tracks, they, too, carry out his aims, their individual differences worked into the scheme. On the sixty-six tracks included in this set, it's possible to follow the evolution of this extraordinary band from Coltrane's ascetic approach on relatively straightforward albums such as *Ballads* and *The John Coltrane Quartet Plays,* through devotional efforts like *A Love Supreme* and *First Meditations*, and on to *Living Space* and *Sun Ship*, those last moments before his leap of faith into the unknown in his last few years.

This quartet's music is marked by a seriousness of purpose that bursts the boundaries of jazz, and with a display of authority rare for any music. Yet despite its exploratory passion, this music was grounded in the blues and even the distant memory of swing. Coltrane, always the seeker, had found his kindred spirits and poured himself and all he knew into these performances. Even those who never shared an enthusiasm for his music recognized this much.

The final disk of the set contains music that was previously spread across eighteen albums and here has been collated and reassembled chronologically. There are also seven unreleased tracks, including significantly different versions of "Bessie's Blues" and "Resolution" from *A Love Supreme,* and others discovered by Ravi Coltrane on his father's original reference records. (For those interested in the culture of the

Coltrane's death at forty that the only compliment one could pay him was one of stature: "If he was boring, he was enormously boring. If he was ugly, he was massively ugly."

It is astonishing that Coltrane's entire recorded output—the music that we have to reckon with—occurred within the twelve-year period of 1955–1967. Where most musicians can take thirteen years just to get up to speed, Coltrane was creating whole styles, new musical conceptions, new senses of self every two years or so. Perhaps even more astonishing, in this brief stretch of time he passed from journeyman Blue Note respectability to semi-pop-star status, and then from jazz icon to extreme avant-gardist. It was almost too much, even for his copiers (who were legion), and for most people there is much Coltrane left to be discovered.

studio, it is fascinating to learn that despite the apparent simplicity and inevitability of its melody, a gem like "Dear Lord" began its life with a glaring series of false starts.)

This is an essential set for understanding jazz at its highest level of achievement, but if money is an object, three essential CDs would be *John Coltrane Live at the Village Vanguard: The Master Takes* (Impulse IMP 125120), *A Love Supreme* (Impulse 11552), and *Interstellar Space* (GRP 11102).

Ornette Coleman

By the late 1950s, most jazz musicians had accepted Charlie Parker's musical view of the world as their own, using the same musical vocabulary, the same syntax. For all the talk about bebop's radicalism, it became an orthodoxy surprisingly fast and without noticeable disruption. Parker's musical language could soon be heard in even the sweetest of dance bands, behind comedians on *The Ed Sullivan Show,* even in TV commercials. Virtually every alto saxophonist emulated Parker's tone and phrasing, struggling to negotiate the chords at the speed necessary to display bebop competence. It was perhaps because alto saxophonist Ornette Coleman embraced aspects of the Parker orthodoxy that the rest of what he played seemed so strange to listeners when he first appeared on the scene. Coleman had reinterpreted Parker's musical language, the standard language, and made it appear just another dialect of jazz, to be used or not.

In hindsight, the hubbub that attended Coleman's first appearance at the Five Spot in New York City in 1959 seems odd. His way had already been eased by the imprimatur of admiring mainstream musical figures like John Lewis,

Gunther Schuller, and critic Martin Williams; Leonard Bernstein attended his appearances, and columnist Dorothy Kilgallen touted him as a showbiz phenomenon. You could hear references to Charlie Parker in most of what he and his trumpeter Don Cherry played. His rhythm section of Billy Higgins and Charlie Haden worked with unrelenting drive, and his tunes, though a bit quirky, were attractive. Yet musicians like Charles Mingus, Miles Davis, Roy Eldridge, and Coleman Hawkins were indignant, seeing them as a group of put-ons and incompetents.

Ornette Coleman, "Rambling." *Change of the Century*. Atlantic 781341.

Ornette Coleman, "Lonely Woman." *The Shape of Jazz to Come*. Atlantic 78139.

Coleman is from Fort Worth, Texas, and two of the other members of this quartet are from Iowa and Oklahoma. Though too much can be made of this, it's undeniable that the influence of the blues runs through much of Coleman's music (he himself has expressed admiration for blues guitarist Robert Johnson's sense of rhythm). "Rambling" gets at least somewhere in the vicinity of a southwestern blues. The rhythm has a peculiar double quality, sounding like both a raga and a shuffle, but when Coleman enters for his solo there's no doubt among any of the members of the quartet that it's the blues, and they're off (Charlie Haden gives a whoop!). But things are never that simple with Coleman, and the improvisations are in 16- and 12-bar units. Even the rhythm, physically compelling as it is, allows for the bass player to move well beyond the timekeeping role of a funky bassist.

His tone was the hurdle that many couldn't get over. Was he off-pitch? out-of-tune? playing the wrong note? Tonality had always been discussed in terms of a received European conception of the rightness or wrongness of tones. Never mind that the European idea of pitch and intonation was itself a compromise reached in the eighteenth century to deal with some everyday musical problems, not something handed down from God. Yet after Coleman, unconventional ideas of tonality reigned everywhere: without Ornette, voices such as John Lydon's (say, on PIL's recording of "Swan Lake" on *Second Edition*) would not be so readily accepted today, even on the hard-core fringes.

"Lonely Woman," a 41-bar ballad, begins with drums and bass expressing different rhythms, and the horns enter in yet a third rhythm, on a freely phrased dirge-like theme. Throughout much of the piece bassist Haden stays on a pedal point, a repeated, droning figure that leaves the horns considerable harmonic leeway. Combined with trilevel rhythm, they feel free to try out ideas, turn them around, abandon them, or go somewhere else. The playing is open, but also emotional and expressive. As free as it may be, it is also an appealing melody, much covered by everyone from punk bands to pop singers.

The '60s were a time when many musicians were pushing the limits of the music, but Coleman went a step further. His instruments seemed strange: he played a white plastic saxophone that looked like a toy, as did the pocket trumpet—a tiny horn used by the mounted infantry in India—played by Don Cherry. The music seemed stranger yet. Coleman aimed to liberate musicians from having to improvise on chordal patterns—the structures that set up the cycles of repeats, returns, and closing figures, and determined what would be played next. Instead, he let the limits of his breath determine structures (much like some then-contemporary poets); he was more interested in melody than harmony, and his tunes became more irregular and asymmetrical (made even more so by his wide-ranging and free sense of pitch) than beboppers had ever imagined. Though he minimized harmony, his work remained strongly rhythmic in a conventional way, appealing to a physical sense of pulse or heartbeat, and his phrases were often predictable and even blues-like. As revolutionary as he was, he seemed to know how far out *not* to go.

It didn't hurt that Coleman was perfect for the role he assumed. Quiet, focused, strikingly dressed, in interviews he was a master of the one-liner, of the Zen zinger. Asked about the key he was playing in, he might answer that the only keys you need to worry about were in your pocket. Or if someone worried about what note he was building a chord on, he might reply, where is the tonic? Should we even recognize the tonic? He might tell you that he was playing feelings, not notes. Told he was playing sharp, he could say that you can play sharp in tune and flat in tune.

His revenge, as well as his curse, would be that within ten years, this music would no longer be shocking.

24 Free Jazz

Before the 1960s, jazz had reached a certain level of comfort. It was clearly marked off from classical and popular music and had an audience that had grown with it over the previous thirty years and knew what to expect. There were informal rules as to what was acceptable and effective in improvisation, and there were objective standards of success, even if they were difficult to articulate. The evolution of jazz had minimized the decisions musicians had to make before the playing began. True, bebop had something of the cachet of radicalism because it had attacked the conventional symmetry of the pop songs that underlay older jazz, but it had also retained and even expanded the role of harmony by extending and altering the chords of the very pop melodies bop musicians were eliminating. Bebop had also subdivided and complicated the conventional rhythms of pop music, but it still had a beat, along with the cycle of climaxes and repeats that organized harmony and melody and helped listeners locate themselves physically within a performance. Jazz had of course stretched and bent time, and those variations were called swing, but an overall beat was kept nonetheless, and listeners still felt comfortable. A new music began to percolate in the late 1950s, flowering fully in the 1960s, one which seemed less interested in harmonic advances and, at its extremes, would make rhythm unreliable for listeners, leaving them with no sense of regularity. Soon, some new jazz players would use volume, texture, grain, tone color, and other sonic variables to create variation and interest, demanding of the listener a focus and appreciation of sound for its own sake. At times, the results of free jazz and classical experimental music would sound similar: the improvised collectivity of Ornette Coleman's *Free Jazz* and John Coltrane's *Ascension* seemed to converge with Karlheinz Stockhausen's *Zeitmasse*.

The new jazz of the 1960s began on the margins. Trumpeter Bill Dixon first announced its arrival at the October Revolution of 1964, a self-produced festival at an uptown coffeehouse way off the beaten jazz trail in New York City. The musicians who played the festival—Cecil Taylor, Sun Ra, Paul and Carla Bley, Jimmy Giuffre, and others—later continued to work in a motley assortment of bars and coffeehouses. Before long, these musicians would attempt to take over every aspect of the business, turning their occupied lofts into clubs, doing their own booking, disrupting the taping of TV shows to protest the absence of black musicians in the studios, even starting their own recording companies and record distribution services. The players of free jazz had come from everywhere in America—Ornette Coleman and Dewey Redman from Fort Worth, Albert Ayler from Cleveland, Cecil Taylor from Long Island, Bill Dixon from Nantucket, drummer Rashied Ali from Philadelphia—but it was on the Lower East Side of Manhattan that the music first found itself, among the new community of musicians who settled there in the early 1960s.

New York City was also the stronghold of classical experimental music, where people like John Cage, Earle Brown, and Morton Feldman worked, and you might have thought that people would have noticed the connections and parallels in the two musics. But free jazz lacked the European art and studio hallmarks that would make it recognizable, if not necessarily appreciated. What people outside the scene were likely to have noticed was what one musician called "squeaking, howling music, people looking and dressing strange—unkempt, raggedy, with bad hair and wacked-out talk; musicians were accused of having just bought their instruments in pawnshops and going right onstage and pretending they could play them." But in fact there was a great variety of music in free jazz: it could be loud and insistent, ready to contend with newly amplified rock music, but also exceptionally soft, unamplified, and chamberlike. It was physical, but intensely emotional as well. Some of the musicians were amateurs, and amateurism was honored, because it brought fresh ears to the music, yet many free players were among the most virtuosic of their time. Free jazz's openness to all alien musical codes frustrated easy characterization.

At first called "the new thing," the term "free jazz" came into use to capture the spirit of the moment, the politics of liberation and even utopianism that crossed the land. (Later it would be called avant-garde by some, though frequently in disdain.) From the beginning, many musicians disliked the label free jazz, sometimes because it made the music sound too easy, too "natural" to reflect the thought and preparation that went into it. Many had worked for "free" enough and were not amused by the irony (stories persist today of audiences showing up at free jazz concerts and expecting to be admitted without paying). Once again, the name given to a period of music is inadequate to express what was accomplished, compressing, as it does, a wide variety of musics. There was a range of political music that included several types of black nationalism, as well as other forms of agitprop musics that mixed poetry, song, and political manifestos in its performances (Archie Shepp, Charlie Haden's Liberation Orchestra). There were some who took jazz so far back to its beginnings that what resulted might be called folk jazz (Jimmy Giuffre's early trios, and at least some of Ornette Coleman's, Stanley Cowell's, Frank Wright's, and Albert Ayler's music). Others were neo-traditionalist for at least part of their career: Sun Ra's re-creations of Ellington's and Fletcher Henderson's early music, or the bebop revisionism of Don Cherry, Ornette Coleman, and John Coltrane were typical. There was a deeply spiritual or religious subgroup of players (such as John Coltrane, Frank Wright, Albert Ayler, and Sun Ra), as well as an experimental, almost academic wing (in the work of the Art Ensemble of Chicago, Jimmy Giuffre, Bill Dixon, Leo Smith, and Cecil Taylor). And for some—such as Don Cherry and Jan Garberek—there was a convergence of jazz with the folk musics of the world that gave them a claim on being the first to play what is now called "world music." This list shows that some of these musicians played in several of these styles, sometimes simultaneously, which makes discussion of this period all the more difficult.

Much of what some thought was primitive or parody in free jazz was in fact an honoring of the past—homage, with serious attention to the details and achievements of jazz history. (If New Yorker critic Whitney Balliett could say that Ornette Coleman "like all true revolutionaries, appeared as a highbrow disguised as a primitive," then it could equally be said that many free jazz players were neo-traditionalists camouflaged as storm troopers.) Many played their instruments with the vocalized, speech-inflected qualities of the blues, early New Orleans, and Ellington's music; they returned to the simultaneous improvisation of early jazz; multi-instrumentalism became highly valued (especially where the instruments played were old—such as the bass saxophone or the C-Melody saxophone); exotic (instruments identified with third world peoples); or—in the case of the Art Ensemble of Chicago—toys, or what they called "small instruments." Some rediscovered fundamental principles of jazz such as call-and-response, with players like John Coltrane or Eric Dolphy splitting their solo instrumental lines into two or more related parts. A new kind of physicality was introduced to the music, the players bending, twisting, jumping, even dancing, as they did at the rhythm and blues bar bands of the 1940s and 1950s. As these older styles of performance began to reappear in modern dress, critics and audiences alike were often baffled or offended, fearing they were being conned. Audiences used to an avant-garde who made the simple look complex were thrown by an

Albert Ayler or an Ornette Coleman, who made the complex look simple.

Musicians of free jazz also absorbed current practices from other music: intense emotionalism was brought into the music, paralleling what was happening among soul singers such as Aretha Franklin, Otis Redding, or James Brown. Some followed contemporary developments in the theater, using costumes and even makeup, along with poetry readings, dance and multimedia presentations. Even the way these musicians positioned themselves at performances changed. Some formed a circle facing in that left the audience out, others scattered across the stage or throughout the building.

But everything these musicians did was not retrofitted and borrowed from pop and ethnic musics. Solo performances by instruments other than the piano became common for the first time in jazz history (saxophonist Anthony Braxton, for example, felt he could perform solo after he heard classical composer Arnold Schoenberg's "little" compositions for solo piano). New conceptions of pitch, tonality, and vibrato arose, along with extremes of register, new tone colors, and new textures ("textural improvisation" became a common term); the concepts of swing and timekeeping—the most basic of all jazz features—were redefined; instrumental virtuosity became critically important for some musicians, especially drummers and bassists, who were being called upon to perform melody as well as rhythm.

It was a highly compressed, intense period of creativity, much of it occurring outside of recording studios and the public's hearing. But within a few short years these musicians had interrogated and redefined many of the conventions of jazz. They completed the erasure of the line between composer and improviser that earlier jazz had hinted at, and reinvented or rediscovered older techniques. They moved pitch away from the question of playing "in or out of tune" and made tonality a conscious choice, in the same way that timekeeping or swing were turned into resources to be drawn on, rather than obligatory procedures. New techniques were applied to traditional instruments—drummers might play with knitting needles or tree branches with the leaves still on them, or play the cymbals with a violin bow; pianists discovered the inside of the piano, bassists played above the bridge, horn players found ways to produce chords or sustain notes seemingly forever by circular breathing. New instruments appeared—plastic saxophones, Middle Eastern double-reed horns, African and Asian drums, bells, and whistles. Old ones, like the soprano saxophone, the cello, and the tuba, were revived. Free jazz was competitive, daring, and risky, but it also spawned communalism and cooperative institutions like the AACM (Association for the Advancement of Creative Musicians in Chicago), BAG (Black Artists Group in St. Louis), the Jazz Composers Guild of New York City, and the Union of God's Musicians and Artists Ascension of Oakland. To clarify these developments and the departures they made from orthodox jazz, new metaphors were introduced, the most important of which were derived from the domains of energy, spirituality, metaphysicality, and freedom.

The idea of freedom as expressed in these new definitions of improvisation was echoed and adapted well beyond the bounds of music during the late 1960s and early 1970s—in drama (The Living Theater, Judson Poets Theater, Squat

Theater, Open Theater), in dance (Judith Dunn, Fred Herko, Molissa Fenley, Trisha Brown), film (Shirley Clarke, John Cassavetes), in classical and academic experimental music (John Adams, Terry Riley, La Monte Young, Steve Reich, Philip Glass), and even in rock (Captain Beefheart, Iggy Pop, Frank Zappa, the MC5, and the UK's Rip, Rig and Panic). Free jazz also quickly expanded the musical languages of musicians all over the world, but especially those in Russia and Eastern Europe, where "freedom" had urgent connotations and where they saw within this music a means for their own liberation. As the 1970s began, the new music had become a kind of internationalism.

Then a strange thing happened. As quickly as if someone had flipped a switch, free jazz was persona non grata in the jazz world. Someone put the word out that it was dead, purportedly of its own excesses, charlatanism, and Black Nationalist politicization. "Free" and "jazz" were quickly quote-unquoted, to put even their prior existence into question. Key records were cut out by the manufacturers, and textbooks went mum about post-Ornette, post-Coltrane, post-Ayler music. With what some writers had called "anti-jazz" out of the way, it was now possible for them to put jazz back on the evolutionary track by returning their attention to the hard bop of the 1950s. Jazz festivals soon wiped the free musicians off the programs, and the clubs—never that friendly to free jazz in the first place—would return to a policy of booking only mainstream players. Soon most free musicians would be forgotten. This could all seem like an Eastern European totalitarian nightmare, except that in Eastern Europe free jazz was thriving.

How could this have happened? How could all that passion, fire, and spirituality liberated by the new jazz be moribund? A music so frankly heated that Albert Ayler's playing at the Salle Pleyel in Paris in 1966 had people screaming? How could this have happened to all those spiritual soldiers who, along with soul singers, led black music back to its roots, and then expanded it outward to the unknown?

Some of the blame lay in the weakening of the civil rights movement, with its spreading disillusionment and racial backlash; many had missed the reassertion of black tradition in the new music, hearing, instead, only rebellion. Nor did it help that some in the music industry were feeling vengeful for the guerrilla warfare that had sometimes been fought on its turf over the past decade as newer musicians struggled to be recorded. In the mid-1970s, the fevered reassertion of the hegemony of tradition made it difficult to stabilize and maintain *any* new musical style in America. Cultural fatigue was also taking hold, a weariness from too much emotion, engagement, and improvisation, and 45-minute solos now seemed both atavistic and scary. On the horizon, instead, was the promise of the eclecticism of minimalism, the cool surfaces of electronics, the open-ended structure of repetition in disco, and the somebody-else's emotion of reggae, Afro-pop, and salsa.

FREE JAZZ had posed a problem for jazz: it raised questions about the limits of invention and creativity, about collectivity, and about the nature of jazz itself. It attacked the artificiality of boundaries and cultural constraints, insisting on access to all cultural resources. Yet instead of embracing these questions seriously, jazz history has treated it as a

Further Listening:

Various Artists, *Jazz Loft Sessions.* Douglas Music ASC3.

pariah, and attempted to restore a safer evolutionary model by portraying free jazz as a failed attempt and giving it Neanderthal status on the flow charts.

Albert Ayler

A.A., as poet Ted Joans called him, first arrived in New York City in 1963, at age twenty-seven, to run the jazz gauntlet. He had a huge sound on the tenor saxophone, a devastating sonority, a warbling vibrato; he could play at hyperspeed, or as slowly as evolution itself, making octave leaps and dives that took him to low B flat and far above C into the so-called false upper register, which the honking, screaming neighborhood barroom players knew was in the true range of the tenor saxophone. In a time of fire music and revolution, Ayler was talking peace and revelation, writing compositions with titles like "Witches and Devils," "Holy, Holy," "Alpha," "Omega," "Saints," "Mothers," "Children," "Bells," "Jesus," and "Ghosts." (Don Cherry once called "Ghosts" "mankind's national anthem.")

Ayler was to become the last scandal in a music that was born in scandal. Even musicians as perceptive as Steve Lacy were turned around by Ayler. Was he serious or joking? an amateur of the worst sort? or an avant-gardist so far ahead that no one got it? Only after he had heard Ayler several times could Lacy say that he was like an airplane ticket for musicians—he took you further and faster.

Critics heard all sorts of things in Ayler: Sidney Bechet, Johnny Dodds, Bubber Miley, or Illinois Jacquet; waltzes, circus music, polkas, folk dances, bebop, children's songs, calypsos, dirges, blues, hymns, military marches, hymns played as military marches, Native American chants, subway singers, Charlie Barnet, and Freddy Martin. This multiplicity of allusions in his playing made it difficult to verbalize his music's essence, but Amiri Baraka got it best when he called it "the changing same."

In a lifetime as short as Eric Dolphy's and Wardell Gray's (Ayler died at thirty-four), he played with everyone—blues harpist Little Walter, new music composer Harold Budd, Cecil Taylor, Don Cherry—though he is best known, among the few who are familiar with him at all, for his remarkable trio with Sunny Murray and Gary Peacock. At one time or another he also played with a rhythm and blues rhythm section, backup singers, a harpsichord, bagpipes, a rock guitarist, even a string quartet—and when he added his brother Donald on trumpet, you could hear New Orleans polyphony poised against Lisztian cadenzas.

The payoff was that his music was called ridiculous, grotesque, comical; he was accused of mockery, of being a naif, and—that faintest of all praises—an outsider artist. But he could draw the best out of writers and musicians. Stanley Crouch, for example, in 1972 wrote that Ayler's big-hearted power and warmth came from country gospel, a

Albert Ayler, "Summertime." *My Name Is Albert Ayler.* Black Lion BLCD 760211.

In this, one of his earliest recordings, Ayler seems not so much a radical as a casual traditionalist. His method of improvisation is melodic paraphrase, though a somewhat gnarled paraphrase. The melody is there but hard fought for, chiseled into place, his restless intonation making it all the more unsettling.

music that challenged Western mysticism by bringing to it a sensuality that links the body to the spirit of God and the music of the spheres. Anthony Braxton said of Ayler that he pushed the vocabulary of John Coltrane and Pharoah Sanders as far as it could be pushed, and that everything after him would be post-Ayler. And "post-Ayler," Braxton said, meant having to stop and consider what had been done, having to put a new order in place of the chaos that resulted when lesser musicians attempted to step through the door that a visionary like Ayler had opened. ("All we were guilty of," said Don Ayler, "was breathing.")

Heady claims, to be sure, but not unjustified. Ayler's was a music that rattled the cage, splitting all those who heard it into permanently armed camps. When he was found dead in the East River in New York City in 1970, stories spun out from the few facts known about him and turned him into a minor legend.

As with Thelonious Monk, there is no Albert Ayler school of musicians. People now spend more time trying to explain him away as an aberration of the times than answering his challenge. Yet who can deny that he heard the music of the universe differently? Ayler was an end-of-the-century musician if there ever was one.

Albert Ayler, "Ghosts." *Spiritual Unity*. ESP 1002.

This is the Ayler that scared New York. With a rhythm section of the volatile drummer Sonny Murray and the pinpoint-accurate bassist Gary Peacock, Ayler states a melody so simple that it could be a country song, or, with a different rhythm, a calypso or reggae tune. Just as quickly as it is stated, he pushes the intervals of the melody to the point of—what? absurdity? parody? a place where Western music refuses to go? All the while he hews to the structure of the tune.

Sun Ra

How do you make sense of a musician who thrived on paradox and mystery, and made contradiction a part of his art? How do you come to terms with a man who obscured many of the facts of his earlier life (named Herman Poole Blount at birth in Birmingham, Alabama), all of which, if known, would only have shown him to be a prodigy, an outstanding scholar, and a musician who had more than paid his dues into the jazz tradition? From his own bands in Birmingham he went on to play with Wynonie Harris and Fletcher Henderson, and to work with artists ranging from Katherine Dunham, Lil Green, and Olatunji to LeRoi Jones, John Coltrane, and John Cage. The contradictions never ceased: he was the first to bring electronics into jazz, but at the same time kept alive the preswing repertory of Fletcher Henderson and Duke Ellington; he was so devoted to the written page that he often re-

Sun Ra, *Jazz in Silhouette*. Evidence ECD 22012.

Silhouette, from 1958, was the Arkestra's first major statement, helped by the addition of Hobart Dotson, an exceptional trumpet player who later worked with Lionel Hampton and Charles Mingus. Dotson's composition "Enlightenment," the first of the Arkestra's "space marches," became a nightly staple for the next thirty-six years, a vehicle on which the whole group stood or marched or sang in unison. It loped along like some cartoon score, quickly transforming itself by turns into a hard bop anthem and a rhapsodic theme cut by cha-cha, march, and 4/4 swing rhythms, all of this accomplished without the melody repeating itself. "Ancient Aiethopia" calls up the spirit of Ellington's programmatic "African" themes like "Pyramid" or "Menelik." What the Arkestra achieved in this piece was unprecedented in jazz (though Ravel's

Bolero might be claimed as a distant relative): by means of the simplest of structures (a single chord and a crisp but subtly shifting "Latin tinge" rhythm) the Arkestra was set free from the conventions of the pop song and its grip on the swing era, but also liberated from the harmonic residue of the same songs left over from the beboppers' appropriation.

Once the ensemble states the melody, two flutes improvise at the same time; a poised Dotson solo takes full advantage of the harmonic freedom that we would now call modal; Sun Ra plays with the bass tones of the piano ringing out rhythmically against the drums; musicians blow through their mouthpieces without their horns; and two singers intone words so softly that their parts cancel each other out. Improvised and open as "Aiethopia" is, there is always a sense of direction about the piece. And as with all of Sun Ra's work, compositions as prophetic as this coexist on the same record with slightly outré two-beat compositions like "Hours After." The album cover proclaims that "This is the sound of silhouettes, images and forecasts of tomorrow disguised as jazz," and who could deny it?

Further Listening: *The Magic City*. Evidence ECD 22069; *The Heliocentric Worlds of Sun Ra, Vol. I.* ESP 1014.

wrote an arrangement again and again, but he also introduced collective improvisation into big band free jazz in the 1960s. His work went well beyond music, to include poetry, painting, light shows, film, and fashion design, and his influence was ubiquitous during the '60s and '70s. He never let his listeners forget that he had a larger calling than music. He tirelessly communicated through interviews and lectures from the bandstand that it was time to rethink the assumptions on which our daily existence rests, and that, unlike most philosophies and religions, his message affirmed life and not death.

It was easy to be puzzled by Sun Ra's Afro-Platonism, or to laugh at his excesses. But his six-hour multimedia barrages could be genuinely frightening experiences. The music moved from stasis to chaos and back again, with shrieks and howls pouring out of what he called his Arkestra, whose members were dressed like the archers of Arboria (from Buck Rogers). Dancers swirled through the audience; fire-eaters, gilded musclemen, and midgets paraded in front of masks, shadow puppets, and films of the pyramids. The performance rules of jazz were broken one-per-minute. Nothing like it had been seen since Wagner's spectacles at Bayreuth. Somehow Sun Ra's shows seemed to capture all the promise and the threat of the '60s—especially since no one in the audience had a clue as to what was going on. Sun Ra was jazz's great Romantic, who, like the great Romantics who preceded him in European music, understood that music could symbolize the unity in diversity that makes up the cosmos. But for him, the big band was his space vehicle, and African-American aesthetics his culture-synthesizing principle.

By the time his self-produced El Saturn records began to appear in the '50s, commercial record companies had perfected a style that assured the recording process would be invisible, the machinery of phonography being used to provide a "picture window" through which an illusion was created of "being there" with the musicians. But Sun Ra emphasized the opposite by recording live at strange sites, using feedback, distortion, high delay or reverb, unusual microphone placement, abrupt fades or edits, and any number of other effects, noises, or accidents that called attention to the recording process. (On some records you can hear a phone ringing, or someone walking near the microphone.) It was a rough style of production, an anti-style, which anticipated both free jazz and punk production to come, but also reflected a shrewd sense of how one could shape album-sized works out of hours of rehearsal recordings and at the same time make the studio a part of the performance. Sun Ra's recorded output was so great that not only has no one analyzed it all, no one can even claim to have heard it all.

Cecil Taylor

Now some forty years after his first record, there's still talk about Cecil Taylor's music in terms of the degree to which he swings or doesn't swing, or whether he is or isn't a product of the jazz tradition. Some, for example, insisted on seeing him as "European" or "classical." But this won't do. What does "classical" mean? It might be possible to say that, for example, "free" though his playing seems, and improvised though it is, there is nonetheless a baroque quality to his lines, a density so great that they are heard as textures, rather than as distinct "classical" lines. Yet at the same time his ideas are often put in opposition to each other and worked more for their sound value than for their identifiable ideas or motives. He also layers his lines so densely that they can sometimes obscure one another. Who or what in the European tradition does this resemble?

In the face of what Taylor actually does at the piano, and of the undeniable uniqueness of his invention, it seems a stretch to say he plays

Cecil Taylor, *One Too Many Salty Swift and Not Goodbye*. hat ART 2-6090.

There's no way to approach Cecil Taylor lightly, or to expect an easy way in to his musical world. Why not plunge in all the way? If you're looking to be classical music, and no one has come forward to add anything else to the description. Taylor, then, might be listened to without concern for swinging or not swinging, for European versus African-American sources. But unless Taylor is to be considered as a tradition of one, jazz is as good a framework as any, especially if we consider his personal musical history of playing in jazz contexts. Besides, it could be argued that his approach to the piano echoes much in the jazz tradition: the thunderous but free-of-tempo 1963 Duke Ellington recording of "Summertime"; the lagging but explosive phrasing of Erroll Garner; or the on-the-beat feel of Dave Brubeck. Consider a typical Taylor musical procedure: he states a small figure on the piano, to have it instantly taken up by a horn or two, sometimes one after the other. From a European classical

overwhelmed, you could do no better than to start with this superb concert from Germany. This might be heard as a suite with sections for unaccompanied piano, duos, trio, quartet, and full sextet, riding over a variety of rhythms suggesting marches, jump tunes, mazurkas, ballads. In fact, Jelly Roll Morton's Red Hot Peppers come to mind as one of the few orchestras that could accomplish so much in a single piece. (Granted, Morton did it in three and a half minutes, and Taylor takes two and a half hours, but the extra time is not wasted.) A few highlights of this piece: Taylor's exhausting perpetual-motion solo in the first fifty minutes of the recording; the violin-bass-piano trip in the second half hour; alto saxophonist Jimmy Lyon's pensive alto tone an hour or so in; and the duo of Taylor and violinist Ramsey Ameen, which concludes the piece with a tough yet nostalgic meditation. It's drummer Ronald Shannon Jackson who pushes Taylor's group on this record. Jackson is fulminous, swelling and bursting, combining retards with decrescendos, heavy on the drums and light on the cymbals. This record is a wonder of collective improvisation, and of cohesiveness and order.

point of hearing, this could be understood as canon, imitation, a form of conventional polyphonic byplay. But it could be heard just as easily as the homophony or "loose unison" of the classic New Orleans bands, and thus be placed in a line of descent from Buddy Bolden, rather than Messiaen, the French classical composer with whom he is sometimes compared.

Taylor is doomed to remain a puzzle for some and a problem for jazz historians. But he remains one of the great performer/composer/improvisers of our time, and seeing him play can be a life-changing experience.

The Art Ensemble of Chicago

The story of the Association for the Advancement of Creative Musicians (AACM) of Chicago is one of the great triumphs of music in the 1960s. In a time of political and racial turmoil, a genuine institution was built in black Chicago without the help of press, recording companies, and government grants, an institution that would continue to influence the arts through the rest of the century. Chicago was a very different town from New York for musicians: the community of players was more stable, and most of them knew each other. From the testimony of its inhabitants, it was also less competitive and information was more freely shared and communicated than in New York.

The first recorded results of the AACM'S activities were Roscoe Mitchell's *Sound* (Delmark DE 408) from 1967, Lester Bowie's *Numbers 1 & 2* from 1967 (included with *Art Ensemble 1967–1968*, Nessa NCD-2500), Joseph Jarman's 1967 *Song For* (Delmark DD 410), Muhal Richard Abrams's

Levels and Degrees of Light (Delmark DD 413) from 1968, and Anthony Braxton's *Three Compositions of New Jazz* (Delmark DS 423), also from 1968. These records give us only a partial view of a more complex movement, since the AACM also had interests in dance, theater, and literature. But they are sufficient to tell us that there was no orthodoxy here, no party line, except that they demonstrated their openness to everything they could use, European and American avant-garde experiments, scaled-down free jazz exercises, minimalism, and the whole history of African-American music. No surprise, then, when several of their key members formed the Art Ensemble of Chicago, their stage appearances in Europe were accompanied by a banner that read "Great Black Music—Ancient to the Future."

The Art Ensemble's performances were a mixture of modern theater, church pageants, swing-era band flash, and hippie freak-outs, with a music that shifted style, meter, and attitude as it flowed across the stage and into the audience. Tradition was freely mixed with experimentation, satire with ponderousness. The records never captured their impact, and some of their best—made for small European labels—are no longer available. But what they announced at the time was that jazz would never again be bound by a single historical moment, by a certain kind of rhythm, or by a single sensibility.

Other Musicians of the 1960s

Eric Dolphy, *Out to Lunch*. Blue Note CDP 746522.

"Out" in the 1960s carried powerful meanings among certain musicians—an orientation away from an existing music, a certain relationship with society, a kind of musician, a way of playing around chords. If anyone embodied all of those meanings, it was Eric Dolphy. A saxophonist who surfaced in the 1950s, he quickly established impeccable credentials by being able to play post-swing big band music, cool jazz, modal improvising, and "the new thing." But once he joined Charles Mingus's group, it became clear that his real role was as an explosive player whose speech-inflected solos seemed to come zooming in from another planet. His method of improvisation was determined in part by the existing chord structures of compositions, which he followed only to skim over them or mock them.

Dolphy remains an ambiguous figure in the history of jazz and a puzzle for writers, perhaps because he could play in so many contexts. *Out to Lunch* (1964) was his last studio recording before his death at thirty-six, so it has taken on extraordinary weight in his evaluation. Fortunately, it is his masterpiece, and one of the most fully realized recordings in jazz. For the only time in his recording career, his own compositions are dominant, and the quintet is finely tuned to his intentions. This is chamber jazz, to be sure, creating a small world of its own, drawing the listener in and closing the doors on the rest of jazz. What is especially arresting is the free sense of rhythm created by drummer Tony Williams and bassist Richard Davis even as they generally hold to a fixed tempo. Dolphy's solos—on flute on "Gazzeloni" particularly—are the best he ever recorded.

Archie Shepp, *Four for Trane*. Impulse IMP 12182.

If Coltrane had put American music on notice that something was up, these homages from 1964 warned that there were yet more surprises in store. The Coltrane compositions here are attempted with Ellingtonian flourishes ("Naima") and blues inflections ("Syeeda's Song Flute"), the music deeply and unforgettably etched, each instrumentalist drawing on shades of the past and driven by the urgency of the moment. There is not a minute of music here that is not marked with passion and the thrill of the new.

Gary Burton, *A Genuine Tong Funeral.* RCA 07863 66748.

Carla Bley wrote this "dark opera without words" in 1967 for Gary Burton's quartet and an all-star orchestra of Steve Lacy, Mike Mantler, Gato Barbieri, Jimmy Knepper, Howard Johnson, and herself on piano and organ. At over forty minutes, it is one of the most fully realized long jazz compositions yet written, yet one that makes room for the individual voices in this orchestra. Throughout, there are hints of Brecht and Weill, rock, Mingus, circus music, and Ellington, but it is Bley's strong melodic sense and uncluttered spaces that give it its strength. Ten years later Henry Threadgill would produce works on the same scale, but in the mid-1960s Bley had the field to herself among younger jazz musicians.

25 Third Stream

Gunther Schuller first coined the term "third stream," meaning music in which jazz and classical elements interfaced, fused, and directly affected each other. And who better than he, since Schuller had distinguished careers as a musician and scholar in both musics. He knew that the groundwork had already been laid for this connection, and that it is older and richer than most people realize. Although some classical composers did not use jazz elements per se, they borrowed from pre-jazz African-American music and therefore share some of the same premises with jazz: Delius, for example, whose *Appalachia* is subtitled "Variations on an Old Slave Song"; or Anton Dvorák's *String Quartet* ("The American"), and Claude Debussy's "Golliwogg's Cake-Walk." Later composers entered jazz at various points in time and used whatever hit them hardest: Maurice Ravel's *G*

Major Sonata for Left Hand, Igor Stravinsky's "Ragtime," Eric Satie's *Parade*, Kurt Weill's *The Rise and Fall of the City of Mahagonny*, Paul Hindemith's *Suite for Piano*, Alban Berg's *Lulu*, Darius Milhaud's *La Creation du Monde*, and compositions by Poulenc, Auric, Honegger, Copland, William Walton, Louis Gruenberg, Constant Lambert, John Powell, Charles Ives, and Henry F. Gilbert, and more recently Michael Tippett, Henry Brant, and Stefan Wolpe.

Yet when Gunther Schuller first proposed a music built on the two forms in the late 1950s, he was greeted with suspicion, if not hostility from the jazz side. "Europe" and "classical" were terms of insult to some in the jazz camp. Looking backward, this seems odd, since some key figures in jazz at that time were already attempting such works (John Lewis, Teo Macero, Duke Ellington, Charles Mingus, George Russell, David Amram, and Stan Kenton), and some were just about to begin (Ornette Coleman, Eric Dolphy, and Friedrich Gulda).

Schuller has said that the problem was that there were not many musicians who could meet the demands of both types of music. But things have changed. Among composers, for example, there is now a much greater range of musical background: John Adams played Duke Ellington's music and rock and roll early in life; Meredith Monk lists Ella Fitzgerald, Mildred Bailey, and Albert Ayler among her influences; Steve Reich grew up under the sway of Kenny Clarke's brushwork; and Terry Riley and La Monte Young were deeply involved with 1960s jazz. Now it's also more common for jazz musicians to play between the two forms. George Lewis, Richard Teitelbaum, Anthony Braxton, Wynton Marsalis, Muhal Richard Abrams, Leroy Jenkins, Roscoe

Mitchell, Butch Morris, Ran Blake, and John Zorn may not all share the same aesthetic, but they have all worked comfortably within what could be called classical music. In Europe, there are composers who work in both areas such as George Grawe, Giorgio Gaslini, Franz Koglmann, and Terje Rypdal. The problem now, as in the 1950s, is that there is no institutional structure to sustain such music. The clas-

Stan Kenton, *City of Glass*. Capitol 832084-2.

Stan Kenton might easily be placed under swing, bebop, and, with a little effort, West Coast jazz—or just left out altogether, if some had their way. A leader of a big band from 1940 through the 1970s, he recorded prolifically, and at one time or other embraced everything coming down the pike—Latin music, country and western, Wagner, pop music, exotica, or cool jazz. Though he called his music "progressive," much of what he did was pretentious and tasteless. Still, his restlessness paid off big every now and then, and the compositions and arrangements done for him by Bob Graettinger from 1947 to 1953 included in *City of Glass* are a case in point. The big pieces here are "City of Glass" and "A Modern Opus," luminous, shimmering concert works whose brilliant use of instruments can still shock fifty years later. Also included are a few pop tunes of the day, and they too are revelations. Though there are few solos here, and the music at times is a little too reminiscent of Vienna, c. 1910, Graettinger's methods were essentially Ellingtonian, and these are works whose texture, phrasing, and rhythm could only have been conceived by a jazz musician. Third stream? Why not.

Further Listening: A recreation of "City of Glass" and other works by some of Kenton's more "progressive" composers appears on the Ebony Band's *City of Glass*, Channel Crossings CCS 6394. Stan Kenton's *The Innovation Orchestra* on Capitol 59965-2 offers a 2-CD set of some of the most interesting compositions performed by the 1950–1951 band.

sical establishment is timid about introducing any new works at all, jazz lacks both performance spaces and recording companies to support new ventures, and there are very few in the press knowledgeable or interested in these efforts. The music, as always, continues to expand without help, somehow getting played, and each generation of musicians seems more comfortable with the idea.

PART 5

26 The 1970s

The '60s, as everyone knows, extended into the mid-'70s, and what might have seemed like fads or dead ends a few years before began to look as if they were here to stay. The splintering of the jazz tradition into new styles and substyles was becoming more apparent, and judging by the jazz magazines of the time, it was clear that no one had a fix on what was happening. Many of the old gods were fading away: Ellington and Armstrong had passed on, Monk was no longer performing; Miles Davis was in the midst of changing directions yet again; and the death of John Coltrane in 1967 had taken away the most visible and most admired figure in the new jazz. Rock and roll had strengthened its grip on the musical consciousness of the country, and jazz seemed less chic, even tired. On the other hand, rock itself was fracturing into styles, some of which were absorbing the excitement that jazz had always claimed for itself. Some progressive bands—like Gong or Soft Machine—were closing in on the same territory as free jazz, and groups like the Grateful Dead said they were improvising. There was more music out there than even the most rabid fan could hope to hear, and recording industry money and publicity were being thrown at youth. In the flush of commerce, many jazz clubs either folded or converted to rock, and later to disco. Jazz magazines began to cover rock, and—who could believe it?—Duke Ellington proclaimed that rock and roll was another form of jazz.

One reaction to the new shifts in musical taste was to go back in time in search of past glories. Three or four jazz repertory bands were created, and though all of them were underfunded and ultimately disappeared, it was the first step toward establishing the jazz tradition as a living performance art. But new jazz also continued to develop, even though it was often ignored in the press: a second wave of free players arrived with new agendas, although like their predecessors, they continued to honor the jazz tradition in their own way. Much as in jazz of the mid-1950s, these new musicians were following a generation of great improvisers, and they continued to search for an appropriate compositional framework in which to place these new forms of improvisation. Saxophonist Henry Threadgill, for example, came from a background of traveling with gospel musicians and blues bands and an apprenticeship with the AACM collective in Chicago, and became a founding member of Air, a trio that explored everything from ragtime to African music with a confidence that suggested they were comfortable with every aspect of jazz. As Threadgill's compositional efforts continued, he formed his own orchestra, for which he wrote programmatic suites such as *Just the Facts and Pass the Bucket* (About Time AT-1005, in 1983), which is filled with achingly evocative, cinematic melodies balanced by moments of primal funk. Even if some could grouse that it sounded composed, it was still apparent that only an improvising jazz musician could have composed it.

Saxophonist Arthur Blythe seemed to surface from nowhere, though he had long been learning his trade in the musical workshops of the legendary Los Angeles composer Horace Tapscott. Blythe had a ripe, fat, old-time alto sound, a strong rhythmic and melodic sense, and, as one musician put it, the ability to play the entire history of the music in one phrase. *In Concert* (Indian Navigation IN 1029) finds him in 1977 with a tuba-based quintet that explodes with fresh ideas. But it was *Lennox Avenue Breakdown* (Koch 7871) from 1979 that most fascinated listeners. The band was small, but their spirited, carnivalesque mix of funk, Latin, and free playing was exhilarating, especially with the dense textures added by James Newton's flute and James "Blood" Ulmer's guitar.

Since the 1950s it had become increasingly difficult for new jazz to break through to public awareness, and by the 1970s the new Philistinisms of market research and niche programming joined with a downturn in the economy to drive new musics ever further to the margins. Older jazz styles were no longer hip, and the new ones didn't fit the acceptable image. This meant that all sorts of fine music

Anthony Braxton, *Town Hall (Trio & Quintet), 1972*. hat ART 6119 CD.

Only in his fourth year of recording, Braxton in his Town Hall concert brought together two pieces for trio—his own Compositions 6N and 6 (O), and Jerome Kern's "All the Things You Are"—with bassist Dave Holland and drummer Philip Wilson, and Compositions 6PI and 6PII for a quintet that included vocalist Jeanne Lee. The Braxton compositions are balanced between the written material and the individuals' choices built into the piece, and in this Braxton caught the spirit of Duke Ellington perfectly. But it is the Kern song that is the real revelation here, a marvel of energy and fire, the three players seemingly unstoppable in their drive to rework the original tune. Braxton goes all out, playing everything in his arsenal on the alto saxophone, changing his tone and his attacks, moving from swing to bebop to free to "legitimate," spitting, howling, barking, and roaring his way through, finding parallel melodies to the original (the theme from *The Andy Griffith Show,* for one). Braxton and Holland are so intertwined that they often depart together from the structure and harmony of the original melody in order to heighten the intensity. Yet there is never any doubt as to what they're playing.

slipped past without notice, either unrecorded or unheralded.

Still, once in a while there was a breakthrough, and the sudden rise to fame of Anthony Braxton was a signal event in the 1970s. Braxton had been a member of the AACM in Chicago and had toured Europe with the Creative Construction Company. When he returned to the United States, he released his solo double LP album, *For Alto*, in 1971 and created a stir: for some it was the height of arrogance for a young alto saxophonist to make a solo record; for others it was an act of liberation. In any case, within a few years, other jazz musicians were recording solo, even some of those who had initially criticized Braxton. Meanwhile, he had been touring with Chick Corea's Circle, a quartet that played a stringent but highly energized collectively improvised music. Suddenly, Braxton was everywhere: concerts at Town Hall and Carnegie Hall, in Europe with experimental groups like Musica Elettronica Viva, and at festivals across the globe. The buzz was that he was a new kind of jazz musician, a polite, thoughtful conversationalist, a man notably unconcerned with hipness (his compositions were titled with formulas or schematics, which increasingly took on mystical and, later on, artful dimensions). He was an intellectual who was interested in chess, literature, classical experimental music, theater, and painting. And for those who felt jazz was in the doldrums and had no interest in jazz-rock, Braxton was the man.

Right on cue, he was signed to Arista, a major label, and began pouring out works for conventional jazz combos, marching bands, and symphony orchestras—even for four orchestras at once. Braxton had developed a system for composing and improvising that provided a means of generating improvisation while framing it orchestrally at the same time. But unlike most composers, he was

Anthony Braxton, *Creative Orchestra (Köln) 1978*. hat ART 2–6171 CD.

Having recently produced a well-received record (*Creative Orchestra Music 1976*, Arista 4080), Braxton took these same compositions to Europe for a fast barnstorming tour with an all-star assemblage of younger players. This is Braxton's big band extravaganza—though here "big band" should be read to mean everything from marching band to Duke Ellington to Charles Ives—in which he applies his compositional methods to a more familiar orchestral form. Even doubters understood his achievement. Compositionally, this is one of the more interesting records of the second half of the twentieth century, and it is played with an energy and optimism that have largely disappeared in modern music.

not interested in controlling all of a performance, but rather in having some part of the composed material put to work. Though he often wrote for specific musicians, he also intended that any part he wrote could be played by any instrument (in his small group performances, especially, parts were traded about, the drummer playing the piano part, the piano playing the bass's, etc.). Furthermore, he intended that any composition he wrote could be put together with any of his other compositions and played at the same time, making for literally millions of possible combinations. He prepared explanatory notes for every composition he wrote and published them, along with his musical and philosophical notes, as the *Tri-axium Writings*.

Braxton refused to be pigeonholed and limited by the jazz musician's role. When critics complained that he didn't play jazz standards, he answered by recording some ballads and traditional jazz compositions in two albums called *In the Tradition*. When they argued that he was not part of the jazz tradition, he pointed to inspirations such as Lennie Tristano and Warne Marsh, white musicians who were not on the A-list of most jazz fans. Braxton was too knowledgeable about jazz and too strong as an instrumentalist to be dismissed as a fraud, and a few writers and fans complained that in reality he was a European experimental composer—speaking as if such summary judgments by those who had little or no knowledge of that music put an end to the matter. But what European (or American) experimentalist composers—or jazz composers, for that matter—had ever given individual players as much freedom in their compositions as Braxton? Even in his most strictly composed materials he had opened up the forms to new possibilities or (in his operas) changed the fundamental meaning of the forms.

THOUGH THEY were very different kinds of musicians, Cecil Taylor and Anthony Braxton shared some similarities that signaled that a new kind of musician was beginning to appear. Both were scholars and theorists of music, not just performers, and they insisted that no one set limits on what their music might be. Their models were players or entire bodies of musics largely ignored by the mainstream jazz musicians and fans. But both Braxton and Taylor quickly established their own high standards and doggedly stuck to them through times of little work and adversity. Their success did not go unnoticed, even by those who had no interest in their music. Thanks to them, the rest of the century would see musicians develop who no longer heeded the imposed limits of the jazz genre—David Murray, Julius Hemphill, Evan Parker, the World Saxophone Quartet, John Zorn, Myra Melford, Keith Jarrett, Don Byron, Marilyn Crispell, Derek Bailey, Bill Frisell, Anthony Davis, James Newton, Carla Bley, John Carter, Pat Metheny, Joe McPhee, James Carter, or John Surman.

Some Other Sides of Free Jazz of the 1970s

Marion Brown, *Afternoon of a Georgia Faun*. ECM 1004

One of the tenets of free jazz was the importance of honoring the insights and inspiration of the amateur. In this very open work from

1970, Marion Brown himself (regarded by some as an amateur on the alto saxophone) pulled off an amazingly organized piece using Chick Corea's piano, Jeanne Lee's vocals, Bennie Maupin and Anthony Braxton on reeds, and seven percussionists, three of whom were nonmusicians. The results are not for everyone, but the spirit of the times is in this music, a spirit that was sometimes gentle and meditative. Some would complain that it was too "classical," others that it was too random. But this is collective music of the first order, and, as a portrait of forest life, a tour de force of mimetic art.

Dave Holland, *Conference of the Birds*. ECM 1027.

When this was recorded in 1972, free jazz was in high gear but about to be hit by another wave of pop music that would drive it even further to the fringes. Bassist Dave Holland, saxophonist Anthony Braxton, and drummer Barry Altschul had been touring with Circle, and for this record Holland added saxophonist Sam Rivers. These musicians were hard-core free jazz, but this recording will strike most as well worked out, even lyrical. There are some mood pieces, some programmatic music, and some neo-bebop (anticipating by thirteen years Steve Coleman's M-Base). Braxton's bebop is especially convincing here, and Sam Rivers gears his tenor explorations to the forms laid out by Holland. The flute duos are delicate and evocative, belying much of today's talk about free jazz. In fact, this is a fine introductory record for those who think they don't like free jazz—or, for that matter, who think they don't like jazz.

Jan Garbarek, *Triptykon*. ECM 1029.

Norwegian saxophonist Garbarek worked with George Russell during Russell's lengthy stay in Scandinavia in the late '60s, and his earliest records document a player committed to free playing shaped by John Coltrane and Albert Ayler. Within a few years he would move toward a quieter, almost folkish aesthetic that drew on Nowegian folk song and church music. But here, in 1973, Garbarek straddles the two sides of his music with a set of compositions that are sometimes meditative or elegiac, sometimes speech-inflected to the point of being conversational, in free rhythm. This is a solidly Nordic set (backed by Norwegian bassist Arild Andersen and the Finnish drummer Edward Vesela), and one that reminds us of how rapidly free jazz was internationalized.

27 Jazz-Rock

Not surprisingly, the first efforts at jazz-rock were made by younger players, most of whom had not yet established themselves in jazz. Free Spirit, for example, a band built around guitarist Larry Coryell and saxophonist Jim Pepper, recorded the first jazz-rock album in 1967, and by 1968 they were followed by Jeremy Steig, Gary Burton, Charles Lloyd, Steve Marcus, The Electric Flag, and (in England) Soft Machine. The instruments on these recordings were amplified, but amplification had been used in jazz long before this. Guitars

Miles Davis, *Bitches Brew*. Columbia/Legacy 65774.

The revolution was recorded in 1969. When it appeared, *Bitches Brew* sent a musical shiver through a country already quaking from social upheaval, the breakup of the Beatles, the violence at Altamont, and the death of Jimi Hendrix. *BB* was a recording were first amplified in jazz, Sun Ra and Paul Bley had used synthesizers and electric keyboards almost from the day they were invented, and the electric organ had long been a jazz mainstay. Eddie Harris was using electronics on his saxophone by 1963, and Pharoah Sanders's *Tauhid* with Sonny Sharrock in 1966 hinted at what might be possible with electricity. Even the electric bass may have been used first in jazz, as well as in Latin settings.

Miles Davis had flirted with rock first on the 1968 recording *Filles de Kilimanjaro* (Columbia 467088). Gil Evans had recently become interested in Jimi Hendrix's new recordings and had arranged the material for the *Kilimanjaro* session, shaping the title tune from the chords of Hendrix's "The Wind Cries Mary." Herbie Hancock's electric piano, Ron Carter's modal bass vamps, and Tony Williams's relentless beat may

whose sound, production methods, album cover art, and two-LP length, all signaled that jazz would never be the same. Over three days in the studio, confusion, anger, and exhilaration reigned, and the sonic themes, scraps, grooves, and sheer will and emotion that resulted were distilled and edited into an astonishingly organic work. This was not a simple hyphenated hybrid like jazz-rock, but a new way of thinking about improvisation and the studio. Too abstract for a rock record, its tonality too ambiguous for conventional jazz, *Bitches Brew* sold well, and drew a new audience into Davis's camp.

The original record has now been remixed: the murk of the original recording is gone, the instruments are newly defined and brightened, and the dark energy of the original sounds fresh. Keyboardist Joe Zawinul's and bass clarinetist Bennie Maupin's roles have been especially clarified. A bonus track of "Feio" has been added—a Wayne Shorter composition recorded five months later—serving both as a warm-down for *Bitches Brew* and as a promise of Weather Report to come.

not yet have been rock in the strict sense of the word, but it was not quite jazz, either. Then, with Davis's *In a Silent Way* in 1969 (Columbia 450982), three of the seven instruments had become electric, and producer Teo Macero (who himself had a background in electronic music) cut, stitched, and stretched the music into a full-length album. The stage was set for *Bitches Brew.*

It's worth repeating that these were not rock bands. Collective improvisation, the range of volume (from great howls to whispers), the importance of space, the rapid shifts in meter, tempo, and mood, the absence of vocals—these were not the characteristics of a rock band. Davis's groups stood at a midpoint between free jazz and rock. The fact that their records were made with a new kind of production, heavily edited, with the studio used as a

Miles Davis, *Jack Johnson.* Columbia 471003.

Miles Davis was a fan of film soundtracks (after seeing *A Streetcar Named Desire,* he told his brother, "Forget jazz. Alex North is the man!"). He did several over the years, and this one is arguably his best. A boxer himself, Davis had a feel for movement in the ring, and this recording overflows with his admiration for the grace and confidence of fighters like Sugar Ray Robinson. *Jack Johnson* (1970) was for a long time Miles's favorite of his own recordings, and you can hear why from the first note: guitarist John McLaughlin steps out and strides across a shuffling groove that is closer to barroom rhythm and blues than to rock; Davis weighs in with that clipped but plaintive sound that promises you that no matter what kind of music he takes on next, he will always be Miles; a Motown bass player fails to notice a key change and continues in the old key, creating delicious tension; and then, midway through the first of two long jams, when Herbie Hancock muscles his way into the mix—on organ, of all things—it seems to dawn on everyone that music like this could go on forever.

kind of instrument, made them important to both jazz and rock. The "live" performances from *Live-Evil* to *Agharta* (which were also heavily edited, sometimes with studio material added) grew increasingly dense and freer in conception over the next five years. The music seemed closer to free jazz with a strong beat than it was to jazz-rock. The complaint heard most often at the time was that Davis had "sold out"—but to whom? And for what? For a long time much of this music was not especially popular with rock fans, and jazz fans by and large hated it. Some of it was not even issued in the United States until years later.

Just as Davis's '70s music was not rock, and not always jazz-rock, it is not clear that those who followed in his footsteps fit easily under those rubrics. Herbie Hancock, for instance, slowly felt his way into electronics, starting first with big band funk in *Fat Albert Rotunda* (1970), then with electro-atmospherics in *Mwandishi* (1971) and *Crossings* (1972), all three of which are available on CD as *Mwandishi: The Complete Warner Brothers Recordings* (Warner 245732). With *Sextant*, in 1973, Hancock seemed to be headed for what might be best called psychedelic jazz, but he turned hard toward funk with *Head Hunters* (Columbia 471239) in 1973, a tribute to Sly and the Family Stone which became the best-selling jazz record up until that time.

Guitarist John McLaughlin had made several first-rate jazz records in England before he joined Miles Davis, and when he left him he formed the Indian-music–inspired Mahavishnu Orchestra, the first step toward the world jazz he would play for many years to come. Chick Corea's Return to Forever was the most jazz-rock oriented of the post-Miles groups, but even this band leaned toward world jazz by combining Latin rhythms with rock. Weather Report—with Joe Zawinul and Wayne Shorter—may be the most musically successful of these spin-off bands, even though it had no guitar and often aimed for the sound of a big band.

Later in the '70s, musicians such as Grover Washington, Earl Klugh, George Benson, and Chuck Mangione began to produce a music called fusion (though smooth jazz has since taken that name), a form of simpler, more direct instrumental pop music played by musicians who had earlier been identified with straight-ahead jazz. Others who followed in their footsteps—the Yellowjackets, Spyro Gyra, and the Rippingtons—play heavily arranged, sometimes synthesizer-driven melodies over a ground bass (or repeated bass), sometimes with a surfeit of virtuoso technique and few improvisations.

Smooth jazz (or "lite jazz" or "contemporary jazz") developed out of fusion as a radio station formula, an updating of the easy-listening stations of the past, using music that is rhythmically bright and melodically recognizable. It is unambiguous, non-ethnic music, generally without surprises, in which it is often difficult to distinguish one player from another. But it is professionally played and often recorded with audiophile sensibilities in mind (especially by groups on the GRP recording label). The first generation of this music's players are musicians who manage to move back and forth between "traditional" jazz (as the smooth-jazz DJs call it) and the smooth, but not without cost. Saxophonist David Sanborn is one such adaptable musician. He has recorded with a wide array of musicians (such as John Zorn and Gil Evans), and while he was host of the TV show *Night Music*, he played with everyone from Sun Ra to Sonny

Rollins, Bootsie Collins, Carla Bley, and rappers and rhythm and blues stars. Yet his very identifiable sound has been copied relentlessly in pop instrumental circles, and in his own recordings he struggles to find new ways to avoid becoming a caricature of himself. Guitarist Pat Metheny, too, has worked with Ornette Coleman, Derek Bailey, Charlie Haden, and from the beginning skirted involvement with fusion. But he is a favorite of smooth-jazz radio, where his records are often faded when the improvisation begins. The second generation of smooth-jazz players owe much less to "traditional" jazz, and do not have such problems.

Ornette Coleman II: Harmolodics

In 1977, six years after making his last recording with a jazz group, Coleman's *Dancing in Your Head* (A&M 396999) appeared. Now with two electric guitars and electric bass in the group, the word was that it was jazz-rock. But the drummer was not playing a backbeat, the bassist was not running repeated rhythm patterns, and the two guitars were thickly intertwined. It was "harmolodics," said Coleman. Though he has never spelled out his concept of harmolodics in great detail, it would seem to be a way of thinking about relationships; and though his principal concern is music, he has also spoken about doing other things harmolodically—writing poetry, cooking, etc. In musical terms, harmolodics is a way of conceiving how instruments fit together, whether it be in unison, in harmony, or in counterpoint.

Coleman has apparently always seen unison as a more interpretive, individualized way of playing than the "everyone plays the same notes the same way" conception that

Western music has developed. He has questioned even the standard tuning of instruments, and explored what happens in music when instruments in different keys do not transpose into an equivalent key. The results of this kind of thinking for harmony in a jazz group can be heard on 1968's *New York Is Now* (Blue Note 84287), and for symphonic orchestra, on 1972's *The Skies of America* (Columbia CK 63568). His way of interlocking melodies seems to return to the earliest days of Western composition in order to throw the resulting rules and conventions into question. The elements of melody, harmony, and rhythm also come under scrutiny, and as Coleman himself has said, a melody can be used in the conventional sense, or as a bass line, or as a second part against a melody, or as a rhythm. The point of harmolodics, Coleman insists, is to liberate the individual by breaking down the constraints and barriers created by conventional music theory and practice. In his music everyone is a soloist all the time, with form, melody, harmony, and rhythm emerging from spontaneous collective improvisation. When he doubled the instruments in his late-'70s Prime Time band—two basses, two guitars, etc.—his music became denser by making each instrument's conventional role problematic. With so much going on at one time, some listeners find such density frustrating. But Coleman might respond by saying that too many people expect him to be the soloist, so they wrongly hear everything going on behind him as if it were accompaniment.

Musicians who have played with Coleman have often answered questions about harmolodics by saying that whatever else it is, it is playing with Ornette Coleman. Given the overriding similarities in the music played by the disparate groups he has had over the years, there is a certain logic to that.

During the late '70s some of the punk rock bands in New York City were influenced by the free jazz that was developing right on their doorsteps. Ornette Coleman's early bands had already inspired groups as diverse and far afield as Captain Beefheart's Magic Band and the Plastic Ono Band. But once Coleman's Prime Time amplified and doubled the instruments in the band, the funky swirl of popping basses and the scratch of crosshatched guitars were something of an epiphany for bands like Defunct, Material, and James Chance and the Whites, who saw that it was possible to combine '60s emotionalism with heavy funk. Within a few years you could hear traces of Coleman's harmolodic electric bands in the music of Curlew, Alfonia Timms & His Flying Tigers, the Contortions, Jody Harris, Leroy Jenkin's Sting, Saccharine Trust, or Universal Congress Of. Outside America, Coleman's new music showed musicians that material other than the usual jazz themes could be used—children's ditties and simple folk songs, for example—and if used

Ornette Coleman, *Virgin Beauty.* Columbia RK 44301.

Considered by many the most accessible of Coleman's Prime Time band recordings—in part because of the presence of Jerry Garcia—this collection of short and varied themes (ballads, riff tunes, programmatic themes, and a country song) may also be the least interesting of this band's records. The rhythm is straightforward and uncomplicated (and uncomplex as well); Garcia's role is minimal, the mix is soft, and the production is sometimes frustratingly cut and edited. But since Coleman's electric bands have probably never been recorded adequately, this record offers at least a better chance of hearing the interaction of the instruments.

correctly, they too could be considered *out*, or music beyond the norm. In the U.K., Pinski Zoo heard the message; so did Poland's Pick Up, Japan's Dr. Umezu, and Canada's Not King Fudge and N.O.M.A. Coleman's harmolodics seemed to suggest to some of the out-rock groups that it was not necessary to actually play jazz, but merely to *imply* it, or even just to *be* it.

28 The 1980s and 1990s

Understanding the directions taken by jazz since the '80s is not easy. The continued diffusion of various jazz styles, the disappearance of regular reviews in most newspapers and magazines, an economic slump in the record business, the shift of some of the most vital recording activity to small recording labels and to overseas, the confusion that followed the change in record formats from vinyl to CD, all contributed to the difficulty. But none of this meant that interesting music was not being played as the '80s began or that no new musicians were emerging. In fact, what was most interesting about the music of this period was the breadth and ambition of the players and composers.

Alto saxophonist Julius Hemphill is a case in point. Like Dewey Redman and Ornette Coleman, he came from Fort Worth, and played, as they did, with a grip on all of the music of the Southwest. By the time he got to New York City in the mid-'70s, he had already founded his own record company and produced two brilliant records: *Dogon A.D.* (Arista AL 1028, out of print) and *'Coon Bid'ness* (now available as *Reflections* on Freedom 741012). These were pieces for quartet and quintet, respectively, but they were huge in conception, claiming everything as their subject and often sounding as funky as history itself. From here he collaborated on several theatrical productions (including *Long Tongues: A Saxophone Opera* in 1990), co-founded the World Saxophone Quartet, formed the Julius Hemphill Big Band, and, before his untimely death, the Julius Hemphill Sextet.

Anthony Davis was another improviser-composer who came of age in this period, a fine improvising pianist whose compositions drew on classical and Eastern musics (*The Ghost Factory*, Gramavision R2-79429), and whose operas (*X: The Life and Times of Malcolm X*, Gramavision R2–79470) were distinctively voiced and rich with vernacular detail. Davis often worked with James Newton, a flutist with interests in contemporary classical composition and Eastern flute techniques, whose records honor the tradition (Ellington and Strayhorn on *The African Flower*, Blue Note 46292, from 1985, out of print) and yet blaze ahead to new forms and ideas (*Suite for Frida Kahlo*, Audioquest AQ 1023, from 1994).

The late John Carter is a third example, a clarinetist and composer (also from Fort Worth) who worked and taught for many years in California, where he wrote and recorded a series of records that made up a cycle titled *Roots and Folklore: Episodes in the Development of American Folk Music.* Written for octet, full orchestra, and vocalists, the music moves easily across styles and genres in an assured, fearless sweep of American music. His subject was nothing less than an impressionistic history of African Americans, and as such it compares favorably—perhaps more than favorably—with Duke Ellington's *Black, Brown, and Beige*. (But is it jazz, some have worried? Was *Black, Brown, and Beige* jazz?)

These three composers have never received the attention they deserve, and most of their records have long been out of print. But the fault is not theirs, for this is music that can stand among some of the best ever composed and played in the history of jazz.

In 1991, the *New York Times Magazine* ran a fashion spread using as models five musicians then all approaching mid-career: Leroy Jenkins, Chico Freeman, Vincent Chancey, Craig Harris, and Butch Morris. Ironically, all five played new types of jazz that had come of age in the 1970s, and all five were regularly ignored by *Times* reviewers. Worse, the *Times* had only a year before run an article about young musicians who would save jazz, by unifying its scattered styles, and returning it to its essence by learning and honoring the jazz tradition. A straw man was being constructed in the *Times* and elsewhere in the press, a myth of the imminent death of jazz which ignored the continuing life of earlier jazz styles, since new mainstream players—like Scott Hamilton, Ken Peplowski, Warren Vaché, Dan Barrett, or Howard Alden—or traditionalists, such as Ted Des Plantes, James Dapogny, and Vince Giodano, had continued to appear since the '60s and '70s. New jazz musicians were still being bred in places like Dallas, San Francisco, Seattle, Cleveland, New Orleans, Brooklyn, and Downtown, in New York City. Even the avant-garde of the '60s and '70s was respectful of the jazz tradition, and regularly performed homages to the past masters of jazz—especially Ellington. But many jazz writers had missed them, or willfully ignored them while berating jazz-rock musicians or free players.

Wynton Marsalis

The image of the jazz musician has shown remarkable adaptability in the semiotic warfare of the late twentieth century. Its survival has been more a matter of diversification than specialization, and the image stretches from the weathered cool and manly poise of a Sonny Rollins or a Max Roach to the Budweiser optimism of a Branford Marsalis; from the haute couture of a Joshua Redman to the contentiousness of Cecil Taylor; and from the intellectual-as-madman of Monk to the Egyptology of Sun Ra. But no one had seen anyone like trumpeter Wynton Marsalis in jazz before. When he first emerged in the music as a professional, he came with impeccable credentials: born in a strong New Orleans musical family, he had gone on to Juilliard, Tanglewood, and a tour with Art Blakey's Jazz Messengers. He was a jazz musician with an uncommonly beautiful sound and elegant ideas, as well as a classical musician with exceptional taste and ability. But he also had the fire of the reformer in him: he was a defender of tradition with the will, energy, and intelligence to reaffirm the values associated with what he saw as a music (and a society) that had been corrupted by charlatans over the last forty years. Sometimes he seemed to be attempting to lift a mighty race again, by creating another Harlem Renaissance; at other times his voice seemed to be that of a Matthew Arnold, calling for the best that had ever been thought and played to be honored and savored. Or again, his task seemed to be the scholarly one of rewriting American cultural history, or even the lay preacher's role of strengthening the moral fiber of the entire country. In any case, once he was appointed artistic director for the new program of Jazz at Lincoln Center in New York City, he was in a unique position to shape the direction of the most powerful effort ever made to turn jazz into an institution.

From the outset in the early 1980s, Marsalis was controversial. At one time or another he has suggested that jazz developed on a different plane from European music, and that in its musical world, innovation is not a mark of progress, since the earliest jazz has never become dated; indeed, it may even be more modern than today's. He has claimed that jazz performances are so long that they bore audiences, that the highest of all jazz achievements, the improvised solo, might need to yield to ensemble playing as it did in early jazz; he has said that there are no true jazz styles, but rather only master musicians whose individual developments show us the progress of the music; or that the seriousness of the jazz project must be reinforced to drive out the dehumanizing forces of popular culture (which long ago surrendered to base instincts and the avant-garde, the dark side of Europe).

No one can deny the seriousness of Marsalis's project. His own playing and composing have evolved as his thought has developed, from his earliest days when he played in a style similar to that carved out by Miles Davis in the mid-'60s, to a more distinctive voice revealed in 1985 and 1986 through recordings such as *Black Codes (From the Underground)* and

Live at Blues Alley. He investigated the blues on recordings made between 1988 and 1992 such as *Levee Low Moan*; worked through the ballad in recordings of 1986 to 1990 like *Standard Time: Volume 2—Intimacy Calling*; and went on to write extended compositions such as *Citi Movement*, *In the House, On this Morning*, and *Blood On the Fields*, the latter having received the Pulitzer Prize for music in 1998. Finally, as the twentieth century closed, he released a great flurry of new recordings, many of which appeared under the Columbia/Sony Classical logo.

Marsalis's development as a musician and as a thinker has been fascinating to watch and is more compelling cultural theater than anything we are likely to see for a long time. Yet in his attempts to restore respect and seriousness to jazz he sometimes crosses the line into a combativeness that wounds other struggling musicians and threatens to bring the jazz house down. He is certainly not alone in feeling the sting of collapsing authority within the confusion of competing cultures at the end of the twentieth century, and when this loss of authority happens to also be African American in origin, the point is all the more poignant.

EVEN AS we note that Marsalis is unique to jazz at the end of its first century, there are others who share at least some of his values but who have taken the music in quite different directions.

Consider Dave Douglas. An inventive trumpet player possessed of a pure sound and a wide range of sonic effects, Douglas began with Horace Silver and Don Byron's klezmer band, and from there went on to explore Eastern European musics with the Tiny Bell Trio (Songlines SGL 1504) in 1993. In the same year his own *Parallel Worlds* (Soul Note 121226) appeared, including works by Kurt Weill, Stravinsky, Webern, and Ellington. As a sideman, he was at the same time becoming a key figure in John Zorn's and Myra Melford's various projects. Few musicians have a the capacity to accommodate such a range of music.

Similar to Marsalis, Douglas began his own explorations of the jazz tradition: Booker Little (*In Our Lifetime*, New World/Countercurrents 80471), Wayne Shorter (*Stargazer*, Arabesque AJ 0132), and Mary Lou Williams (*Soul on Soul*, RCA 09026 63603). But unlike Marsalis, Douglas has also explored and updated the music of the late '60s and early '70s (*Sanctuary*, Avant AVAN 066). And again as a sideman with Uri Caine, he has been part of projects such as the 1996 recording *Urlicht / Primal Light* (Winter & Winter 910 004), which merged Mahler's classical music, jazz, and Jewish tradition.

Or consider Don Byron, a fascinating case of a younger musician coming out of what some might think of as an unlikely scene—study at the New England Conservatory of Music and the Klezmer Conservatory Band—and playing the clarinet, an instrument that fell into disuse in jazz in the 1940s. He surprised everyone with his first record, *Tuskegee Experiments* in 1992. It was remarkably eclectic, with compositions that range from the political ("Tuskegee Experiments") to the romantic ("Waltz for Ellen"), and from Ellington's "Mainstem" to Schuman's "Auf einer Burg." Yet, the gaps are bridged by Byron's strong voice and the seriousness of the enterprise. All the more surprising, then, that the next record would revive the Borscht Belt comedy of Mickey Katz (*Don Byron Plays the Music of Mickey Katz*). Then came others, including a rap poetry record (*NuBlaxploitation*), the music of Duke Ellington, Raymond Scott, and John Kirby (*Bug Music*), and *Romance with the Unseen*, with compositions by Herbie Hancock, Lennon-McCartney, and Ellington, along with his own pieces. His eclecticism is the real thing.

There are others, dozens in fact, who are reexamining the jazz tradition at the same time as they transform it. There is drummer Jerry Granelli, whose various little groups have created powerful sonic portraits of Buddy Bolden (*I Thought I Heard Buddy Sing*, ITM Pacific 970066), the Badlands (*Enter the Dragon*, Songlines 1521), as well as of the history of Native Americans (*Broken Circle*, Songlines/Tonefield INY 3501). Or tenor saxophonist Joe Lovano who has almost single-handedly refined the meaning of "mainstream" with a tribute to Frank Sinatra (*Celebrating Sinatra*, Blue Note 837718), a third-stream outing (*Rush Hour*, Blue Note 829269), and a classic jazz quartet recital (*Quartets*, Blue Note 829125). Alto saxophonist Greg Osby, who emerged from Steve Coleman's M-Base collective's efforts to refine black urban music into a new level of jazz, has himself since wrestled with funk and hip hop (*3-D Lifestyles*, Blue Note 798635, from 1992) and moved on to a series of dazzling recordings that explore new and more complex ways of joining rhythm and melody (*Banned in New York*, Blue Note 96860, and his record with Joe Lovano, *Friendly Fire*, Blue Note 99125). Most recently, his work with the New Directions band reexamines some of the classic Blue Note recordings of the 1960s (*New Directions*, Blue Note 22978), and a recording with Andrew Hill and Jim Hall (*The Invisible Hand*, Blue Note 20134) locates him more precisely as extending and refining the 1960s aesthetic.

29 Europe

It may seem strange to introduce jazz from Europe this late in the story, for jazz had spread across the world within the first twenty years of its existence, affecting music of every type, everywhere, helping shape the distinctive sound of the twentieth century. But it is only in the last thirty years that American jazz musicians and audiences have become at all aware of the role the music has played elsewhere and of the original music that has developed. What has been accomplished abroad makes a separate entry for it more than a little embarrassing.

Europe was aware of jazz from the very beginning, having heard the music even before it was recorded through the sheet music of cakewalks and rags, concerts given by James Reese Europe during World War I, performances after the war in musical halls in Paris and London by African-

American musicians such as the Seven Spades and Louis Mitchell's Jazz Kings, the music that accompanied the dance crazes that swept Paris around Josephine Baker's appearances in La Revue Nègre in the 1920s, or the tours across Europe in 1925–1926 by Sam Wooding's Chocolate Kiddies. After World War I, record distribution assured the most famous jazz musicians a wide audience. By 1919 there were European jazz bands recording in Stockholm and Berlin. The first and most important writing on jazz (magazines, discographies, and books) was done by Europeans, especially by Belgian and French artists and art critics who were swept up by jazz and who saw in it a musical manifestation of the painting styles of futurism and fauvism. It was in part because of the critical success that jazz had in Europe that Americans became as aware of it as a cultural phenomenon as much as they did.

The first European musician to receive serious recognition from Americans was Django Reinhardt, the Gypsy guitarist who appeared in the 1930s and whose brilliance on the instrument forced Americans to think again about who owned the future of jazz. What was perhaps most striking about his music was his ability to play in an essentially alien style and yet make it sound comfortably like jazz. But it was not until after World War II that Europe began to make considerable contributions to jazz, and also developed its own national tastes and styles. Sweden, for instance, showed an early affinity for bebop, inviting American musicians there to perform and record with local musicians, and Charlie Parker, Dizzy Gillespie, and Stan Getz made some of their best recordings in Sweden. But some of their own—baritone saxophonist Lars Gullin, clarinetist Stan Hasselgard, alto saxophonist Arne Domnérus, and pianist Bengt Hallberg—quickly developed into musicians of the highest level by any measure.

After Django Reinhardt, the little-known Jamaican-born, U.K. alto saxophonist Joe Harriott was probably the next most innovative figure in Europe. In his short lifetime (1928–1973), he played with a wide range of musical groups, including African high-life groups and Chris Barber's Dixieland band. He recorded bebop, ballads with string accompaniment, created a double quartet with Indian musicians and formed a quartet in which he anticipated Ornette Coleman's free-tonal innovations by at least a year or two.

But it was in the last thirty-five years that Europe really came into its own. First, there was a revival of big bands. In the Netherlands, Willem Breuker turned his group into a mixture of free jazz, cabaret, and theater (sometimes comedy, sometime political). In Denmark guitarist Pierre Dørge created a series of bands who played free jazz, incorporated South African music, then early Ellington, until they were known as the New Jungle Orchestra. In Austria the Vienna Art Orchestra worked their way through perhaps the largest repertoire any orchestra had ever attempted, including Monk, Ellington, Satie, Brahms, Cocteau, and Gershwin. In Britain there were varioius bands led by Kenny Wheeler (a Canadian by birth), Mike Westbrook, and Barry Guy (London Jazz Composers Orchestra). In Germany, Alexander von Schlippenbach's Globe Unity Orchestra was made up of an international body of musicians.

These big bands not only sounded different from one another, each was organized differently. Some were city- or nation-based, others were international; a few were traditionally-led by a single individual, but most of them were collectives. Each of them had a different way of presenting themselves in performance, reflecting these varying notions of social and musical order: Mike Westbrook's band looked like a street band in a concert hall, and he often took them out into the streets like buskers; the Globe Unity Orchestra sometimes stood or sat in a circle; and once Chris McGregor's Brotherhood of Breath moved from South Africa to Europe, they formed a straight line across the stage.

In the last part of the twentieth century musicians such as the German saxophonist Peter Brötzmann, Netherlands drummer Han Bennink, and British musicians like saxophonist Evan Parker, drummer Tony Oxley, and guitarist Derek Bailey broke with some aspects of American improvisational practice to create what has been called European improvisational music, or spontaneous music. This is music that is rooted less in a tradition than in individual interests and abilities, especially the ability to improvise with minimal regard for existing forms or styles like the blues or the pop song, and with firm disregard for grooves or swing. It draws on newer forms of musicianship, such as the use of multiphonics and circular breathing, and does indeed seem to owe little to jazz. Yet, paradoxically, this is often intensely collective music, far more so than its American counterparts. If there are "groups," they are given either obscure and semi-anonymous names, like AMM, or names that reflect pure collectivity, like Company or the Spontaneous Music Ensemble. European improvised music announced its presence with Peter Brötzmann's *Machine Gun* (FMP 24), a howling screed of a piece, a Euro-answer (whether intended or not) to Albert Ayler's *New York Ear and Eye Control*,

Ornette Coleman's *Free Jazz*, and John Coltrane's *Ascension*. Saxophonists Brötzmann, Evan Parker, and Willem Breuker sustained a collective barrage over piano, two basses, and drummers Han Bennink and Sven Ake Johansson that added up to the most accurate aural testament to the spirit of 1968 in Europe. The break with American jazz was real enough, but it is hard to dismiss the influence of American free jazz, especially as played by the Art Ensemble of Chicago, Sun Ra, Anthony Braxton, Steve Lacy, Leo Smith, and Cecil Taylor.

European improvised music is as good a name as any for a music which has pushed the idea of improvisation to its furthest extremes, for we still have no language for talking about music which seeks this degree of freedom.

Further Listening:

Various Artists, *Freedom Blues: South African Jazz Under Apartheid*. Music Club 50095.

World Music, *To Hear the World in a Grain of Sand: World Music Live at the Donauescingen Festival*. Soul Note 1128.

Various Artists, *An Anthology of Swedish Jazz Piano, Vol. 1*. Dragon DRCD 179.

Joe Harriott, *Free Form*. Redial 538184.

Pierre Dørge, *Music from the Danish Jungle*. Dacapo DCCD 9423.

Vienna Art Orchestra, *The Minimalism of Erik Satie*. Hat ART 6024.

Derek Bailey, *Figuring*. Incus CD05.

Evan Parker, *Towards the Margins*. ECM 1612.

30 Acid Jazz, Drum 'n' Bass, Neo-Swing

Wynton Marsalis could have warned you that when many musicians of the 1960s and 1970s began to disavow the word *jazz,* that all sorts of people would be more than happy to claim it for their own—the word has a curious cachet all over the world, and has been applied to pop musics in places like Haiti, the Congo, and India, where the idea of jazz is an exotic and sexy concept. No surprise, then, that we now have techno jazz or acid jazz, since the gap between jazz and popular music has increased so much over the last fifty years that jazz now appears strangely fascinating to many younger listeners at home.

But there's more to it than that. A few jazz musicians in the early 1970s correctly divined a point of entry for jazz into pop music, but they were too early. Which is another way of saying that the record companies and the press were not able to

Panthalasa: The Music of Miles Davis 1969–1974. Columbia CK 67909.

Having made a career out of crossing most of the lines still left intact in music as producer or musician, Bill Laswell found his way into fusion, hip hop, reggae, psychedelia, free jazz, noise music, and world music. As a producer he not only took on *On the Corner*, but also portions of Davis's *In a Silent Way* and *Get Up With It*, reworking, remixing, revising, reconfiguring, or—as he would say—reinterpreting and translating them into a new form for Columbia Records as *Panthalasa: The Music of Miles Davis 1969–1974* (1999). The results are an edition of Davis's music that anthologizes parts of his records while bringing the rhythm up front, clarifying and expanding the sonics, and fine-tuning its attitude.

It was a big step to take, even if it's one technology and the times demanded, since *version* is a red flag for jazz purists. But this may yet be recognized as one of the signal moments in the history of jazz, for it calls attention to the fact that since around 1969, or even before, most jazz records have been recorded on multiple tape tracks and are then mixed together to create a "record." The musicians on the records may or may not be involved in the mixing and editing (Miles Davis was not), and the record that results may or may not reflect their intentions. Even if the

see the connection they were making. The way was made clear by the thick electronic/acoustic texture of Herbie Hancock's *Sextant* (more than "Rockit"), Miles Davis's "Rated X" on *Get Up with It*, where a looped organ track from another composition was edited into the piece; and most of all Miles Davis's 1972 *On the Corner* (Columbia / Legacy CK 53579), where the coming of house music, techno, jungle, trance, trip-hop and all the many permutations and hyphenations of repetitive musics were anticipated by Davis. But of all the post-1969 Davis recordings, this one was the most reviled. Issued without notes or even a list of the musicians involved, with Davis buried in the mix, no one knew what to do with it then. It's hardly a surprise that these recordings would resurface at the end of the century, now remixed by Bill Laswell.

record reflected the artist's intention, does that mean that the music—which exists in parts on tapes—cannot ever be reconfigured? Even revered classics like Davis's *Kind of Blue* have been remixed numerous times. The pitch has been corrected (it was originally recorded at the wrong speed), the rhythm section has been brought forward in the mix to approximate modern tastes, the horns realigned with each other, and all, apparently, without serious complaint from fans and critics.

The names of the genres of these musics are vague, the music hard to distinguish, the artists semi-anonymous, the records drift across the DJs' turntables and through the store bins and are gone before you've heard of them, but many of the dance musics that came after hip hop owe at least a part of their existence to jazz. Early on in the 1980s there were those who saw the connections to jazz: the turntablists were like improvisers, building new tunes on old ones with new rhythms like beboppers, their samples something like jazz quotations. Before long, you could hear X-Clan's "Raise the Flag" (with samples from Roy Ayers) and Stettsonic's "Talking About All that Jazz" (Lonnie Liston Smith sampled on organ). Digable Planets were borrowing from Miles Davis, Eddie Harris, Dizzy Gillespie, Sonny Rollins, and Art Blakey, and Gang Starr's "Jazzmatazz" used jazz horns. The X-Men now use eight DJs and create collective improvising. DJs like Funki Porcini and Amon Tobin have made albums of sampled jazz licks and drum solos, and DJ Krush has recorded with free jazz trumpeter, Toshinori Kondo.

Acid jazz was initially a British phenomenon, borrowing its name from acid house, a British variation on Detroit's house music for dance clubs, and was often merely a matter of mixing into hop hop rhythms sampled from '60s jazz records or, in the subgenre called rare groove, mixing in rare funk tracks from minor record companies. As the concept spread, some, like New York's Groove Collective or Giant Steps or Japan's United Future Organization, began to incorporate live musicians. In fact, some groups—like Medeski, Martin, and Wood or the James Taylor Quartet—have from time to time performed live as if they were mixing. And others have had their jazz records remixed (trumpeter Nils Petter Molvaer's *Khmer* on ECM comes packaged with a second CD of remixed performances).

Us3, "Cantaloop," *Hand On the Torch.* Blue Note 80883.

Us3 had the extraordinary blessings of Blue Note Records, which gave them permission to sample bop and hard bop recordings and even interviews. The samples were then restructured and mixed with new rhythms, horns, and hip hop vocals. Their reworking of Herbie Hancock's 1964 "Cantaloupe Island" is typical: the harmonic and rhythmic structure of the original is retained by sampling the piano, bass, and drums, but new skittering, shuffling drum rhythms more appropriate to hip hop are laid on top, the original bass line is boosted; a new trumpet part is added along with some accented ensemble horn lines, some Latin percussive elements are introduced to thicken the rhythmic mix, a rap vocal is added, and the structure of the piece is opened up by weakening the recurring harmonic cycles that originally signaled the starts and stops of Hancock's melodies.

Drum 'n' bass is another English phenomenon, this one built on the love for the raw interplay of acoustic rhythm instruments in jazz rhythm sections and Jamaican dub music's many manifestations in the U.K. The long stretches of unadorned rhythm drum 'n' bass are reminiscent of the way in which Count Basie regularly exposed his rhythm section for the sheer rush of its sound. But the surprise with drum 'n' bass has been that some of its proponents have moved closer to a jazz *sound* than one might have imagined when this music first appeared. *Parallel Universe* (994) by 4 Hero (the team of Dego McFarlane and Mark Clair) uses antique electronic instruments to reconnect to jazz psychedelia of the 1970s played by Herbie Hancock, Pharoah Sanders, and Alice Coltrane. Likewise, Spring Hill Jack's (John Coxon and Ashley Wales) *68 Million Shades* from 1996 mixes muted trumpet in with mountains of samples to evoke '70s Miles Davis. Almost dreamlike allusions to Sun Ra abound in this music, in CDs like UNKLE's (James Lavelle and Tim Goldsworthy) 1994 *The Time Has Come* or Carl Craig's Innerzone Orchestra. At least one jazz musician, trumpeter Tim Hagens, has been inspired enough by drum 'n' bass to try it himself, with some very interesting results on *Animation-Imagination* (Blue Note 95198).

Further Listening:

Various Artists, *The New Groove: The Blue Note Remix Project, Vol. 1*, Blue Note 36594.
Various Artists, *This is Acid Jazz: After Hours*. Instinct EX-298.
Various Artists, *Do Androids Dream of Techno Jazz?* Irma 494029.
Various Artists, *Totally Wired: A Collection of Acid Jazz Records*. Acid Jazz 13.
Various Artists, *This is Acid Jazz: A Sampler*. Instinct INS-094.
Various Artists, *Freedom Principle: Acid Jazz and Other Illicit Grooves*. Verve 837925.

AMID THE reactive boredom of the 1970s there were some punks who donned pork-pie hats and dark glasses, got tattooed, wore pegged high-top pants and wing-tipped shoes, and took up acoustic instruments: the Lounge Lizards, for example, who played a stiff-legged, awkwardly articulated version of jazz classics sprinkled with the enrichment of scratchy guitar. "Fake jazz," they called it then, reveling in the irony of it all. It was a conceptual joke, thrown out in the spirit of John Lennon's remark that "jazz never does anything." (It was also a music—one of many of that moment—that detached itself from African-American influences, something which always augurs danger in American culture.) Before another decade passed we were to hear many other less-than-ironic musicians assume a similar attitude.

Neo-swing, the swing movement, or "swing" is a case in point; a West Coast initiative, part fashion statement, part mini-dance craze, and a campy flashback during the end-of-century decade to a past decade's phenomenon, which owes as much to the existence of the Xerox machine as it does to CD reissues. "Swing" in this manifestation is not swing music, but something closer to the early 1940s rhythm and blues bands, or jump bands as they were known then. Much of it sounds like the music of Louis Jordan played by Will Bradley's Orchestra (a 1940s big band) with a touch of western swing, rockabilly, and ska (from U.K. bands like Madness) tossed in. (Joe Jackson had tried it earlier with his record *Jumpin' Jive.*) Bands like Royal Crown Revue, Big Bad Voodoo Daddy, and Cherry Poppin' Daddies are cheerful tributes to an era (albeit white and mostly male tributes, with overlays of hard-boiled detectives and mobsters), who play to an audience that enjoys role-playing.

31 What's Next?

It's a fair question to ask, now that almost a century's history of jazz is behind us. Yet given the twists and turns that jazz has taken throughout its short life, only a fool would try to predict its future. Still, perhaps it's possible to look at the directions being taken at the present time as clues to at least the range of possibilities the future might see.

The irascible Philip Larkin once asked if studios can kill jazz. At the time, the question seemed rhetorical. But now, faced with samplers and the nostalgia they traffic in, and the massive CD reissue programs that seem close to making everything ever recorded available again, Larkin's question becomes more serious. The weight of jazz tradition sometimes seems oppressive—its heroes beyond reach, their accomplishments suffocatingly exalted, the golden age of jazz retreating rapidly. How *do* you play jazz in an age in which its social underpinnings are almost dead, yet its aesthetic is still imposingly alive through recordings? How do you perform melodies that invidiously evoke their own eras? How is it possible to not live in a world of remakes and tributes?

One possible answer is the postmodern one of making these musics seem hard-bought, freshly earned by a new generation. You can hear this in some sampler- or electronics-based groups, as well as among some young jazz musicians when they approach older compositions: the original melodies are retained in skeletal form, their harmonic structures reduced to a chord or two, or a few pedal tones, every note made to seem chiseled and fought for, and conventional phrases and cadences so radically repositioned that form itself is called into question. But these processes seem strangely similar to some of the procedures of Ornette Coleman, Thelonious Monk, and the more minimalist of the modal players, so some connection to the jazz tradition is still operating. But what to do about swing, a rhythmic conception forever hooked to a dead dance form? Again, the answer offered up by some of those converging on jazz from the outside is to express the tension and forward propulsion of swing by sheer repetition or staggered phrases, or other rhythm manipulations.

But there are many other possible answers. One is to go backward, to become classical, accept greatness, enshrine a pantheon, create a canon, and elevate the music. At one extreme this means playing in the "manner" of some older musicians by using their forms, their style, but in a contemporary fashion, and at the other it means playing transcriptions of great works. To some degree, both methods have been used since the advent of recording: musicians have transcribed, or written out, the solos of the most famous jazz musicians for study, practice, and performance. Sometimes these transcriptions are published in the form of "licks" books, where the characteristic motives and clichés of great players are made available for others to insert into their own solos; or, in other cases, an entire solo is written out for a group to play in unison or in harmony, as when the McKinny's Cotton Pickers' trumpet section duplicated a Louis Armstrong solo, or when Supersax, a California band, recorded Charlie Parker's solos in harmonized form. What's more surprising is a current trend toward performing transcriptions of James P. Johnson, Duke Ellington, Fats Waller, Art Tatum, Bill Evans, and others note-for-note as part of classical piano recitals.

Another possibility is to go pop, surrender many of the traditions and standards of the past, learn new songs, look contemporary, maybe go electronic. Or go ethnic, using the materials and methods of musics from the Bronx, as Kip Hanrahan did with *Desire Develops an Edge*; or as Randy Weston did with North African music played in Brooklyn neighborhoods; or David Murray with music of the French West Indies on *Creole*; or Sidney Bechet with music of Haiti. In other words, go back to the matrix of musical elements. Yet another possibility is to go forward, do something new, break rules, innovate. Or maybe dig in where you are and never change.

The point is, of course, that jazz has always done all of

these things. Max Harrison once remarked that jazz can neither repeat its past, nor escape it: it constantly adds, and thereby modifies, everything that has gone before. Such a music cheerfully escapes definition and prognostication alike. And such a music is always scandalous.

Appendix 1: Jazz Singing

Since the most important contributions to jazz have been made by instrumentalists, and since it is quintessentially an instrumental music, jazz singing would seem to be something of an afterthought, or a concession to popular taste. And it has often been treated as such. Ever since pop singers took the spotlights away from the bands at the end of the swing era, and pop tunes became less important to jazz, there has been something of a tension between singing and playing. On the other hand, a handful of extremely important singers have emerged over the years, some of whom changed the way the music is played and even became models for a certain type of player. (Miles Davis, for example, was influenced early in his career by Blossom Dearie, Teri Moran, Jeri Southern, Billie Holiday,

Shirley Horn, and Helen Merrill, all of whom he considered masters of understatement.)

And there is no reason why the voice should not be an important part of jazz. As Robert O'Meally says in the notes to the Smithsonian's CD collection, *The Jazz Singers,* jazz has many of its roots in vocal music: work songs, the blues, spirituals, game songs, all sorts of American vernacular music, but it also has links to Africa's tonal languages, which allowed instruments to serve as substitutes for human voices when it was desirable to communicate by other means. Musicians across the world also convey music to one another by singing the parts, whether melodies, bass lines, or drum rhythms. And many musicians—notably pianists such as Erroll Garner, Bud Powell, Myra Melford, and Keith Jarrett—subvocalize along with their own playing, sometimes to the delight or distraction of an audience. Guitarists like George Benson and bassists like Slam Stewart sing along with their instruments, doubling their melody lines, and horn players may vary their sound with mutes, hats, or toilet plungers to sound like voices. Others (like flutist Rahsan Roland Kirk and trombonist Albert Manglesdorff) hum in harmony along with their played lines. More to the point, many jazz musicians conceive their solos in narrative terms, as "telling stories," and some say they hear the words in their heads as they improvise.

Jazz musicians seek their own sound, a distinctive quality, a recognizable character, a *voice*, with much the same meaning as that given to it by poets. So it's not surprising that jazz musicians can sing, and perhaps more surprising that more do not. Louis Armstrong's influence is arguably as great as a singer as as an instrumentalist, though he was very similar in both roles. The fact that some singers are also good pianists is understandable, since they often accompany themselves: Nat Cole, Sarah Vaughan, Carmen McRae, Mose Allison, and Dinah Washington come to mind. But singing players of other instruments—Woody Herman, Benny Goodman, Ray McKinley, and Jack Teagarden, for instance—exist, and their singing often rivals their playing for public recognition. But who or what a jazz singer is is a difficult question, and not just because "jazz" is hard to define. Given jazz's links to pop music and the blues, mutual borrowing between them blurs whatever distinctions might be more easily made in instrumental music.

The first problem that singers face in singing jazz is the lyrics of popular songs. If singers work with these songs and stick close to the original words, they are limited in what they can do with both melody and rhythm. If they go to the other extreme and abandon the words to existing songs by scatting (using syllables with no meaning along with any tone or rhythmic value they choose) or by vocalese (setting words to existing instrumental jazz variations of a song), they lose the recognizability and drama of the original song. If they instead sing songs without words or improvise without words, they move into an area in which instrumentalists are already dominant. It is a tension that never quite vanishes from even the best singer's work, and ultimately demands a compromise.

Those singers who choose to retain the original words to a song work within a more nuanced area, where small variations are everything. Frank Sinatra (a favorite among many older jazz musicians) sang with great concern for clarity and precision in pronunciation, and felt free to alter the melodic rhythm by adding or subtracting words (which sometimes sabotaged the song). When Sinatra first appeared in the 1940s he followed a number of tenors with light, colorless voices, and he used his rich baritone to phrase in a more rhythmic tradition than even Bing Crosby. (Crosby was one of the first white singers to display profound African-American influence, first in a minstrelized, limited way, and later by retaining a feel for blue notes, a certain syncopation, and a selective pronunciation.) Billy Eckstine, on the other hand, stuck even closer to the words than Sinatra, but used greater variations in pitch and vibrato. Both of them were much beloved of jazz fans and musicians alike for their ability to tell a story through phrasing, breath control, and articulation (it was not unusual, for example, for people in the audience to weep when Billy Eckstine sang "Sophisticated Lady"). These are singers who clearly overlapped with the pop song tradition.

A few singers form a small tradition of their own, one closer to jazz than to pop. Among them are Sarah Vaughan, who in her extreme use of range and vibrato, departed so far from the melody that her songs could take on a free, almost abstract quality; and Betty Carter, whose altered phrasing and rhythm led her to strip even the most saccharine song of its pop sensibilities.

At the other extreme from Vaughan and Carter is Billie Holiday, who had a small voice and seldom strayed from a single octave's range. While others elaborated the original melody with grand gestures, Holiday often narrowed the melody, even as she broadened its dramatic charge by a series of small but effective devices.

In between the extremes of Vaughan/Carter and Holiday

are many singers who establish a middle ground by finding new meaning in well-known songs, who elaborate or simplify, who sing with extreme vibrato or none at all. Ella Fitzgerald (the early, non-scatting Ella), Helen Forrest, Dick Haymes, and many of the singers who graced the front of bandstands in the 1930s and 1940s found this middle ground, which as the big bands fell from favor, became the favored style of pop singers.

Then there are those who make songs from language sounds (but not words) or put words to instrumental solos. The principle behind scat singing is not in and of itself exclusively a part of jazz tradition, for musicians and singers from many parts of the world imitate instruments by singing either for teaching or performance purposes. Scatting is common in Brazilian, Cuban, and Caribbean music, and has long functioned in pop music (from the "boop-boop a-doop" of the 1920s to the "shoop-shoop" of doo-wop), persisting in the "human beat box" of hip hop. But when this method is used for improvisation, something new is present. (The his-

Billie Holiday, "Foolin' Myself" *Quintessential Billie Holiday, Vol. 4.* Columbia/Legacy 44252.

Preceded by first-rate musicians taking solos, Billie Holiday has only one chorus left to sing when they finish. Her variations at first are minimal, though she announces her entry by immediately falling behind the beat. By the time she reaches the bridge, she is so extraordinarily behind the beat that the song seems about to fall apart. She had a sense of time that seems closer to what Mozart and Chopin called *tempo rubato,* the ability to stray far from a strict accompaniment while still managing to return to finish in time. Add to this her taste for stressing every syllable, giving her words a weight and a declamatory quality that captures the listener, even when the grain of her voice doesn't.

tory of scat has not yet been written, but suffice it to say that Louis Armstrong's claim to have discovered it by accident—when he dropped his sheet music while recording "Heebie Jeebies" in 1926—is not the way it happened.) Scat in jazz operates in a variety of modes, ranging from a kind of modernist poetry—the faux Chinese in Cab Calloway's 1934 "Chinese Rhythm," the mock Arabic-Hebrew-Spanish of many of Slim Gaillard's recordings in the 1940s and 1950s, or the eccentric private language used on Jimmie Noone's 1928 "Let's Sow a Wild Oat"—to the vocal imitation of solo instruments, such as Leo Watson's 1939 "Ja-da," or even entire orchestras (the Mills Brothers' early recordings are uncannily accurate imitations of swing bands of the time). The most creative scat singers, however, are those who use their voices to go beyond imitation to make creative statements. Louis Armstrong is of course the master, if only because his voice is the perfect analogue of his instrumental creativity. During the early years of bebop, Billy Eckstine, Ella Fitzgerald, and Joe Carroll each made original vocal contributions to that music.

Some jazz fans and critics have derided vocalese as a distraction from jazz (the introduction of words into an existing instrumental realm is seen as grounding an otherwise "pure" form in prosaic, unimprovised meaning). But the great users of vocalese—Eddie Jefferson, King Pleasure, and Jon Hendricks—are poets as well as singers, adding new dimensions of meaning to wordless solos, and making them into songs. They bring something new to the solos they imitate, introducing a narrative flow which often clarifies or even strengthens the instrumental originals. Hendricks's singing (and the lyrics he wrote for the songs) on Lambert,

Hendricks and Ross's *Sing a Song of Basie* punches up the rhythmic impact of the various tenor saxophonists he is imitating. By the ease with which they add words to instrumental improvisations, vocalese poets remind us that the jazz musicians they are imitating were also great songwriters.

Further Listening:

The Jazz Singers: A Smithsonian Collection. Smithsonian Records RD 113 A5–28978.

Anthology of Scat Singing, Vols. 1, 2, & 3. Masters of Jazz MJCD 801, 802, 803.

The abilities required to succeed in these various forms of singing are not all of equal magnitude, and very few singers are accomplished at more than one form. (Because Duke Ellington wrote for different kinds of singing, at one point in his career he used four different singers: Joya Sherrill for fast songs, Al Hibbler for the blues and his own features, Kay Davis for pop songs, and Marie Ellington to sing the wordless, floating songs like "Creole Love Song.")

Appendix 2: A Guide to the Record Guides

With more recordings in existence than any human can live long enough to hear (much less afford to own), advice on what to hear becomes essential. For years anyone with a sizable record collection was free to pontificate on jazz history. But today no collector—or critic, for that matter—no matter how rich or knowledgeable, can claim to know it all. With eighty-some years of recordings behind us, only fools or charlatans would even dare to say they'd heard even half of the known records.

Ironically, we know just how much we don't know because of the excellent work done by jazz discographers. The number of jazz recordings passed the capacity for human recall years ago; for example, Tom Lord's *Jazz Discography* is up to 13,000 pages and still coming. With little or no help available at most record stores, a guide is needed to know what was recorded, to know if it is still available, and to place recorded works in some kind of qualitative and historical context: what to hear and how to listen to it.

The first guides to jazz recordings were produced by record companies in Europe and Latin America to promote their own products (Leonard Hibbs's *A Short Survey of Modern Rhythm on Brunswick Records* from 1934 is typical). But the first serious attempt at a comprehensive and critical guide was *The Jazz Record Book*, produced in the United States by Charles Edward Smith and Frederic Ramsey, Jr. in 1942. Modeled on David Hull's classical music guide, *The Record Book*, it was a combination of historical essays and brief discussions of recordings. In 1948 the French critic and historian Hughes Pannasié produced *Discographie critique des meilleurs disques de jazz*, but it failed to advance the cause because it was severely limited by a scattershot approach and the author's restricted vision of what constituted jazz. Following the development of the long-playing record in the early 1950s and the subsequent rush to reissue older records in the new format, Frederic Ramsey Jr. brought out *Guide to Longplay Jazz Records* in 1954. But since it covered the music only up to the beginnings of the swing era, it essentially repeated *The Jazz Record Book* in terms of the LP. In 1958 the English writers Rex Harris and Brian Rust published *Recorded Jazz: A Critical Guide*, which again failed to go beyond the earliest years and limited itself to records released in the United Kingdom.

John S. Wilson was the first jazz writer to produce a guide that took account of the massive changes that began to occur in jazz following World War II. *The Collector's Jazz:*

Traditional and Swing (1958) and *The Collector's Guide: Modern* (1959) were valiant attempts at comprehensiveness, constrained only by the small format of the books and the biases of a single author. But it was the British authors Charles Fox, Peter Gammond, and Alun Morgan who set the standard for modern guides with *Jazz On Record: A Critical Guide* in 1960, an attempt to offer an assessment of all the major musicians' recordings in the form of an encyclopedia. An even more extensive effort along the same lines was attempted by another British author, Stanley Dance, in 1961. Along with seven coauthors he published *Jazz Era: The Forties*, which was intended to be the first of a four-volume set covering each decade of jazz through the 1950s. No other volumes ever appeared, however, and instead *Jazz on Record* was extensively revised and expanded in 1968 by Albert McCarthy and nineteen other writers as *Jazz on Record: A Critical Guide to the First 50 Years 1917–1968.* This time the encyclopedia approach was combined with a few essays on various styles, periods, and sites of musical development.

Yet another combination of these same British critics (Max Harrison et al.) attempted a comprehensive account (though it limited itself to 200 records) of jazz after 1944 in *Modern Jazz: 1945–1970 The Essential Records*. In 1984 some of these authors recombined for Max Harrison et al., *The Essential Jazz Records, Vol. 1: Ragtime to Swing*, an attempt to again mix essays with encyclopedic entries from the beginning to 1940. (The second volume, *The Essential Jazz Records, Vol. 2: Modernism to Postmodernism* has just been published in the U.K., and covers 1941 to the 1990s.)

Most of these early guides are out of date, of course, but they have not outlived their usefulness. Their discussion of the first twenty years of jazz is fuller and often better than what the more recent books offer. And there is something to be said for seeing how particular records were received when they were new or only a few years old. The newer guides suffer from the sheer enormity of recordings made in this century, the difficulty of making sense of a huge variety of styles, and even the problem of defining what the limits of jazz might be. But the good news is that a number of new guides are in print, more are on the way, and the more we have, the better.

The Penguin Guide to Jazz on CD by Richard Cook and Brian Morton is the oldest and biggest of the current batch, and the most reliable, if for no other reason than it is the most inclusive and comprehensive. Coverage of American jazz CDs is reasonably thorough, though the authors rule out limited editions from companies like Blue Note and Mosaic, and their discussions of recordings are almost always judicious, readable, and sometimes even eloquent. The grasp they have of CDs from Europe is unparalleled, as well as humbling to those of us who think the sun never sets on American jazz. You ignore their recommendations of foreign recordings at your peril, for there are rich jazz traditions developing abroad, some of which already have affected our own musicians. Here you can find treasures such as the brilliantly eccentric Dutch pianist Guus Janssen; Keith Nichols's wonderful repertory band from the U.K.; hard-to-find Vienna Art Orchestra CDs; and any number of fine Swedish musicians—swing clarinetist Putte Wickman, the neo-free Abash trio, and the inspired compositions of Jan Wallgren. (None of these records, incidentally, are listed in any of the other guides.)

But such inclusiveness does not come easy and is more than a matter of having big ears. Knowing of a record's existence is one problem, hearing it is another. These authors have listened long and far; and having gone through four editions since 1992, have had ample opportunity to revise judgments and correct errors.

This is not to say that Penguin is the only record guide you need. Each of the others has its virtues. *MusicHound Jazz*, for example, edited by Steve Holtje and Nancy Lee (with entries of variable quality written by over eighty contributors), also includes a helpful list of books, magazines, newsletters, Web sites, record labels, radio stations, and music festivals, with suggestions on what to buy first, recommendations of out-of-print records, and elaborate indices. (These extras, however, come at the expense of hundreds of musicians being excluded.)

The *All Music Guide to Jazz*, edited by Michael Erlewine and a host of other editors and contributors (the key one of whom is Scott Yanow), is now in its third edition. This is the most ambitious of all the guides, and with its lists, indices, flow charts, and short essays, it comes close to being a textbook. There are some errors, omissions, and some overreaching in the essays, but there's also much to be learned within its nearly 1,400 pages.

The Blackwell Guide to Recorded Jazz (second edition, 1995), edited by Barry Kernfeld, is structured as a beginning buyer's guide with a tilt toward a history of the music, and includes chapters by five other writers (the editor wrote or co-wrote over half the book). Most of the major figures are here, but only 250 records are discussed, presented as a kind of essential collection.

But if it's shorter, more selective guides you're looking for, either Neil Tesser's *The Playboy Guide to Jazz* and Tom Piazza's *The Guide to Classic Jazz* are it. Both offer their choices of CDs within readable histories of jazz (though the "classic" in Piazza's title should put you on alert: he leaves out the last thirty years of the music, as well as much that came before when it doesn't fit his taste). Still, there's something to be said for the consistency of the single author, even when you sometimes find yourself grumbling in disagreement.

Appendix 3: Jazz on the Internet

By now everyone knows that the Internet has become a huge part of the future of jazz. But even the most technologically committed may not yet know that it is rapidly turning into the best source of information on jazz that we are likely ever to have. Granted, the books, magazines and record collections of the best libraries are not yet available on the Web, but what's up already is astonishingly rich, easy to use, and is showing signs of outpacing the few libraries devoted to jazz. What follows is merely one fan's notes of some things to be found on the Internet (aside from Net radio locations and retail outlets, subjects big enough to warrant their own surveys), and though everything available is not listed here, if you look for these resources, many of the rest are guaranteed to turn up in the process. (Bear in mind, however, that addresses do change and Web sites disappear from time to time.)

Many people first experienced Internet jazz information on commercial sites, with the belief that with money behind them, they would be the most reliable and easy to use. But now that the flashy, much-touted, and slow-moving Jazz Central Station Web site has gone down (taking with it the Miles Davis page, the Leonard Feather scrapbooks, and Dan Morgenstern's history of jazz), we know better. Where to begin, then? If you're new at this sort of thing you might well start with Northwestern University's WNUR-FM's site (http://www.nwu.edu/wnur/jazz), which offers musicians' biographies, information on retail outlets on the Web, lists of festivals, essays, etc. But if you have a fair knowledge of jazz, or at least a real passion for it, you'll appreciate Michael Fitzgerald's voracious site (www.eclipse.net/~fitzgera) which includes a lot of everything: a number of musicians' discographies, lists of labels, essays—on the legendary Lennox School of Jazz, for example—and research tools such as lists of musicians' pseudonyms and Muslim names. His links to other jazz sites is an excellent place to begin looking to see what's out there. To find still other links, try Jazz Links (http://www.pk.edu.pl/~pmj/jazzlinks/artists.html#c) or Jazz Line (http://www.jazzonline.com); The Mining Company (http://jazz.miningco.com); Yahoo (http://dir.yahoo.com/Entertainment/Music/Genres/Jazz or http://dir.yahoo.com/Entertainment/Music/Artists/By_Genre/Jazz); and Webcrawler (http://webcrawler.com), which seems to promise some 12,000 links if you search for "jazz." For singers' links, try Jazz Singers (http://www.jazzsingers.com/RelatedLinks).

Some of the most interesting sites are those devoted to particular cities. The Jazz Institute of Chicago (http://www.jazzinstituteofchicago.com), for one, has an online newsletter that offers essays, biographies, book reviews, obituaries, and more. The June, 1999 issue, for example, had some interesting memoirs about Charlie Parker in Chicago, an account of the integration of the Chicago white and black musicians' unions locals in the '60s, and an interview with film composer/song writer David Raksin. Be sure to also look for the interesting sites for Detroit (http://www.ipl.org/exhibit/detjazz) and Philadelphia (http:www.jazzchricles.com). A few cities already have performance schedules posted for them, and Margaret Davis's Art Attack (http:/www.users.interport.net/~eye/jazznyc.html) in New York City is a model for such ventures. Many clubs also have Web pages, some of them quite spectacular, such as the Blue Note in New York City (http://bluenote.net), with its performance calendar, gift shop, and an audio and video archive of past performances; or the Knitting Factory (http://www.knitmedia.com), which sometimes broadcasts performances live.

For the jazz scene in France try Le Jazz (http://lejazz.simplenet.com/english) with recent articles, gigs in France and elsewhere, and interviews; or Jazz France (http://jazzfrance.com/en), which also includes retail sources for French CDs. Both sites are available in English. Not in English, but still essential, is the page of the great French magazine *Jazz* (http://www.jazzmagazine.com), where you can search the current year's issues. For Italy there is Italian Jazz Musicians (http://www.ijm.it/enhtm), in Italian only, but there are lists of musicians, samples of musical scores, new Italian CDs, and the best Italian recordings as chosen over the years by the writers of the magazine *Musica Jazz*.

If you want to connect with other fans, musicians, even industry people, there are Internet discussion and mailing lists where you will encounter some of the most erudite, humorous, and interesting people you'll ever run into (along with a few of the silliest, angriest, and most self-important). Start with discussion lists like rec.music.bluenote, which has a useful FAQ (frequently asked questions) list, or maybe mailing lists like Jazz-L (write listserv@brownvm.brown.edu). Or you might specialize a bit with alt.music.big-band; rec.music.collecting.vinyl; rec.music.collecting.cd; or mailing lists like Dixieland (http://www.islandnet.com/~djml); Swing (e-mail request@hepcat.com); Avant-Garde (http:www.onelist.com/subscribe.cgi/Avant-Garde); and Free Jazz (www.freejazz.org). Smooth jazz can be found at Contemporary Jazz (http://www.contemporaryjazz.com). Smooth Jazz Page (http://smoothvibes.com/jazzpage.html) and Jazz Trax (http:www.jazztrax.com) offer links in every direction.

There are also mailing lists on all sorts of subjects, such as Eric Dolphy (http://farcry.neurobio.pitt.edu/Eric.html); Miles Davis (http://www.wam.umd.edu/~losinp/music/md_sites.html#listserv); John Coltrane (http://www.nextaxs.com/~jgreshes/lists/coltrane-l.html); Thelonious Monk (http://www.onelist.com/subscribe.cge/tmonk); Duke Ellington (e-mail majordomo@concordia.ca with the message: subscribe duke-lym); Sun Ra (e-mail listserv@nic.surfnet.nl with the message: subscribe saturn <your e-mail address>); Stan Kenton (e-mail jazz-kenton-subscribe@merchant.book.uci.edu); or John Zorn and Downtown music (e-mail majordomo@lists.xmission.com with the message: subscribe zorn-list). (If you have trouble getting on these lists or want to reach them in digest form, you might try http://www.deja.com to sample what's on them.

For earlier forms of jazz, there's Early Jazz Websites (http://www.jass.com/links.html), which will lead you to things like "The History of Jazz Drumming," "The Jazz Age in Paris, 1914–1940," "Old Sheet Music," and "Traditional Jazz." Or try The Red Hot Jazz Archive (http://www.redhotjazz.com) for the history of jazz before 1930, with photos, essays, discographies, and even some early films to view on your computer. Then go on to Red Hot and Cool Jazz (http://members.aol.com/Jlackritz/jazz/index.html) which provides samples of recordings and links on the history of jazz. And at http://vintage-recordings.com you can hear recorded samples and order tapes and CDs of early jazz and pre-jazz artists available nowhere else.

If you're willing to go beyond the narrow boundaries of jazz, there's a passionate defense at Acid Jazz (http://www.cmd.uu.se/AcidJazz); or try the site "Provisionally Entitled the Clue Stick of Sound" (http://pages.prodigy.net/ecran21/cluestick), which provides eye-opening links and music samples of what it calls "unpopular music."

There are hundreds of musicians' own home pages, such as Steve Coleman's (http://www.m-base.com) or Dave Holland's (http://www.daveholland.com), and even more pages created by others on particular musicians (Bill Evans, for example (http://www.selu.edu/34skid/body_index.htl); Billie Holiday (http://shrike.depaul.edu/~kchoi/index.html or http://members.xoom.com/_XOOM/ng_varela/billieholiday.htm); for Miles Davis see Miles Ahead (http://www.wam.umd.edu/~losinp/music/ahead.html) or

Milestones (http://miles.rtvf.nwu.edu/miles/milestones.html). At Albert Ayler (http://www.utexas.edu/~jeffs/ayler.html), there is a book-length treatment of one of the saints of free jazz. Thelonious Monk can be found on (http://www.achilles.net/~howardm/tsmonk.htm) or (http://www.maison-orangina.org/grangina/assocs/jazz/monk). Gene Krupa is at (http://www.crash.simplenet.com); and Cecil Taylor is represented by Matthew Goodheart's thesis on him (http://users.lanminds.com/~mgheart/thesis/title.html).

If you want to know what records exist, you can try All Music Guide (http://www.allmusic.com) with its massive discography, lists, maps, statistics, and glossary. Even though it's not complete and has many uncorrected errors, it's a beginning. Need to know what books and videos are out there? You can go to Amazon.com and Barnes & Noble (bn.com)—the latter especially for sources of out of print books. But the place to really find out what's available is Norbert Ruecker's site (http://www.jazzrecords.com/jazzbooks/catalog.htm). His list, which is larger and more complete than you'll find in *any* library, makes a fine bibliography of jazz and blues books and videos in print. If you can't wait for what's *not* here yet, there are lists of new and forthcoming CDs on Jazzmatazz (http://home.att.net/~lankina/jazz/upcomingcds.html) and Ice (http://www.icemagazine.com).

Of the many 'zines and online mags, there are All About Jazz (http://www.allaboutjazz.com) with its own chat group and recorded samples; Jazz Corner (http://www.jazzcorner.com) with links to 100-something musicians' and organizations' home pages. Interjazz (http://interjazz.com) has musicians' Web sites and live and archived interviews.

The Wire (http://www.defuse.com/the-wire) links to a number of unusual sites and has an archive of articles from recent years. Jazzine (http://www.jazzine.com/jazzy.html) offers lists, interviews, concert listings, photos, etc. The Jazz Review (http://www.visionx.com/jazz) has reviews, interviews, photos, and a useful time line of jazz history, which can also be accessed directly (http://www.visionx.com/jazz/timeline.html). One of my favorites is Perfect Sound Forever (http://www.furious.com/perfect), an endlessly fascinating collection of interviews, essays, commentaries, and links, put together with care and love.

A few sites feature specific writers and critics, such as Mike Zwerin on Culturekiosque (http://www.culturekiosque.com/jazz/index.htm) or Bret Primack's prickly, and always engaging Bird Lives! (http://www.birdlives.com). Photographers, too, are appearing on the Internet, and you might start with Herman Leonard's (http://leonardjazz.com/portfolio), and go on to Michael Wilderman's, William Gottlieb's, William Claxton's, or Ray Avery's sites. The Jazz Journalists Association (http://www.jazzhouse.org) also provides a wide variety of material from its members in the form of articles, reviews, historical photos, interviews, and discussions, which are open to questions from the public.

Finally, here's a sample of some things you're not going to find anywhere else but the Internet. To discover the literature and poetry of jazz there is Epistrophy—The Jazz Literature Site (http://www.ualberta.ca/~mborshuk/jazz.html) with bibliography, samples of poems, novels, author's biographies, and helpful introductory essays on jazz and its relation to literature. The Pantheon of Jazz Trombonists (http://geocities.com/~5by5/) offers essays (thus far) on

Jimmy Cleveland, Benny Green, Al Grey, Frank Rehack, and Bill Harris. The Guide to Classical Indian/Jazz Fusion (http://www.nitehawk.com/alleycat/indyjazz.html) discusses the ties between jazz and classical Indian music, with lists of musicians and recordings that show the influence of Indian musical ideas; 137 Documents on Jazz Improvisation (http://www.hccq.ohio.gov/Kellysworld/7181.htm) is a big collection of Internet writings on improvisation. If you're looking to be overwhelmed, try the International Archives for the Jazz Organ (http://www.lwolf.com/iago/iago1.htm), where you can peruse or download a 140-plus page discography of jazz organ recordings; or Harry's Blues Lyrics (http://tinpan.fortunecity.com/kowalski/112), where Harry has approximately 2,000 blues lyrics up, along with his essays and indices by singer, topic, etc.

Appendix 4: Jazz at the Movies

The following are movies in which jazz is represented in a variety of ways—stereotypically, respectfully, disrespectfully, etc. But, in many cases, they are the only motion picture record we have of these musicians.

All the Fine Young Cannibals (1960)
All Night Long (1961)
Almost Blue (1993)
American Blue Note (a.k.a. Fakebook) (1989)
And There Was Jazz (1981)
Angel (a.k.a. Danny Boy) (1982)
Beat the Band (1947)
Beautiful But Broke (1944)
The Benny Goodman Story (1955)
Best Foot Forward (1943)
The Big Broadcast (1932)
Bird (1988)
Birth of the Blues (1941)
Bix (1981)
Blue Ice (1992)
Blues (L'Inspecteur Connait la Musique) (1955)
Blues for a Jacman (1962)

Blues in the Night (1941)
Broken Strings (1940)
Bye Bye Blues (1989)
Cabin in the Sky (1942)
Carolina Blues (1944)
C'est la Vie, Ma Chere (1993)
The Connection (1961)
The Cotton Club (1984)
Dingo (1991)
The Fabulous Dorseys (1947)
The Five Pennies (1959)
Follow the Band (1943)
French Quarter (1978)
The Gangs All Here (1943)
The Gene Krupa Story (1959)
The Gig (1985)
Girl Crazy (1943)
The Glenn Miller Story (1954)
Glory Alley (1952)
Here Comes the Band (1935)
I'll Get By (1950)
It's Trad, Dad (1962)
The Jazz Singer (1927)
Jitterbugs (1943)
Jivin' in Be-bop (1946)
Juke Joint (1947)
Kansas City (1996)
King of Jazz (1930)
Lady Sings the Blues (1972)
Legend of 1900 (1999)
Look Out Sister (1947)
Love With the Proper Stranger (1963)
Lush Life (1993)
Malcolm X (1992)
A Man Called Adam (1966)
The Man With the Golden Arm (1955)
Mo' Better Blues (1990)
The Nat "King" Cole Musical Story (1955)
New York, New York (1977)
Nightmare (1956)
Orchestra Wives (1942)
Paradise in Harlem (1939)
Paris Blues (1961)
Pennies From Heaven (1936)
Pete Kelly's Blues (1955)
Pretty Baby (1977)
Reveille for Beverly (1943)
Rhapsody in Blue (1945)
Rhythm on the River (1940)
'Round Midnight (1986)
St. Louis Blues (1958)
Scott Joplin (1976)
Second Chorus (1940)
Shadows (1959)
The Sky's the Limit (1943)
Some Call It Loving (1973)
Some Like It Hot (1959)
A Song Is Born (1948)
Space Is the Place (1974)

Stormy Monday (1987)
Stormy Weather (1943)
Strike Up the Band (1940)
The Strip (1951)
The Subterraneans (1960)
Sun Valley Serenade (1941)
Sven Klang's Combo (1976)
Sweet and Lowdown (a.k.a. Moment For Music) (1944)
Sweet and Lowdown (1999)
Sweet Love, Bitter (1967)
Sweet Smell of Success (1957)
Swing High, Swing Low (1937)
Swing Kids (1993)
Syncopation (1942)
The Tic Code (1998)
Too Late Blues (1961)
Uncle Joe Shannon (1978)
Winter in Lisbon (1990)
Young Man With a Horn (1950)
Zachariah (1970)

Musicians' Cameo Appearances

Bells Are Ringing (1960)
Blazing Saddles (1974)
The Cincinnati Kid (1965)
Crossfire (1947)
Hallelujah (1941)
Hellzapoppin' (1941)
Lord Shango (1975)
Repulsion (1965)

Jazz Film Scores

Alfie—Sonny Rollins (1966)
Anatomy of a Murder—Ellington (1959)
Ascensuer pour l'echafaud [a.k.a. Frantic]—Miles Davis (1957)
Asphalt Jungle—Ellington (1959)
The Color of Money—Gil Evans (1986)
The Criminal—John Dankworth and Cleo Laine (1960)
Des Femmes Disparaissant—Art Blakey
I Want to Live—Johnny Mandel (1958)
Les Liaisons Dangereuse—Art Blakey, Duke Jordan (1959)
Mickey One—Stan Getz (1965)

New Kind of Love—
Erroll Garner (1963)
Odds Against Tomorrow—
Modern Jazz Quartet (1959)
Once a Thief
—Lalo Schifrin (1965)
The Pink Panther—Henry
Mancini (1964)
Sait-On Jamais (a.k.a. One Never Knows)
—John Lewis (1957)
Un Temoin dans la Ville
—Kenny Dorham
Walk on the Wild Side
—Elmer Bernstein (1965)
The Wild One—
Shorty Rogers, Leith
Stevens (1953)

Musicals

Absolute Beginners (1986)
Atlantic City (1944)
Bathing Beauty (1944)
Carmen Jones (1954)
Check and Double Check (1930)
Disc Jockey Jamboree (1957)
Going Places (1938)
High Society (1956)
Hollywood Hotel (1937)
Killer Diller (1948)
Kitten on the Keys (1946)
Make Believe Ballroom (1949)
Make Mine Music (1945)
New Orleans (1947)
Rhythm Inn (1951)
Small Town Girl (1953)
Stage Door Canteen (1943)
Swing Fever (1943)
Thousands Cheer (1943)

Appendix 5: Select Bibliography

General

Adorno, Theodor. "On Jazz." *Discourse* 12, no. 1 (Fall–Winter 1989–1990) [1936], 45–69.

Adorno, Theodor. "Perennial Fashion—Jazz." *Prisms*. Cambridge, MA, 1981.

Belgrade, Daniel. *The Culture of Spontaneity: Improvisation and the Arts in Postwar America*. Chicago, 1998.

Brown, Lee B. "The Theory of Jazz Music: 'It Don't Mean a Thing.' " *The Journal of Aesthetics and Art Criticism* 49, no. 2 (Spring 1991), 115–27.

Carr, Ian, Digby Fairweather, Brian Priestley. *Jazz: The Rough Guide*. London, 1995.

Carr, Roy. *A Century of Jazz*. New York, 1997.

Carr, Roy, Brian Case, and Fred Dellar. *The Hip: Hipsters, Jazz and the Beat Generation*. London, 1986.

Feather, Leonard, and Ira Gitler, eds. *The Bibliographical Encyclopedia of Jazz*. New York, 1999.

Gabbard, Krin. *Jazz Among the Discourses*. Durham, NC, 1995.

Gabbard, Krin, ed. *Representing Jazz*. Durham, NC, 1995.

Gioia, Ted. *The Imperfect Art: Reflections on Jazz and Modern Culture*. New York, 1988.

Jasen, Davis A., and Gene Jones. *Spreadin' Rhythm Around: Black Popular Songwriters, 1850–1930*. New York, 1998.

Johnson, Bruce. "Hear Me Talkin' to Ya: Problems of Jazz Discourse." *Popular Music* 12, no. 1 (1993), 1–12.

Lock, Graham. *Blutopia: Visions of the Future and Revisions of the Past in the Work of Sun Ra, Duke Ellington, and Anthony Braxton*. Durham, NC, 1999.

Mandel, Howard. *Future Jazz*. New York, 1999.

Murray, Albert. *Conversations with Albert Murray*. Roberta S. Maguire, ed. Jackson, MS, 1997.

The New Grove Dictionary of Jazz. London, 1988.

Tate, Greg. *Flyboy in the Buttermilk*. New York, 1992.

Young, Bob, and Al Stankus. *Jazz Cooks: Portraits and Recipes of the Greats*. New York, 1992.

Zwerin, Mike. *Close Enough for Jazz*. London, 1983.

Anthologies

Gottlieb, Robert, ed. *Reading Jazz: A Gathering of Autobiography, Reportage, and Criticism from 1919 to Now*. New York, 1996.

Meltzer, David., ed. *Reading Jazz*. San Francisco, 1993.
Piazza, Tom. *Setting the Tempo: Fifty Years of Great Jazz Liner Notes*. New York, 1996.

Jazz Histories/Textbooks

Berendt, Joachim E. *The Jazz Book*. Brooklyn, 1992.
Blesh, Rudi. *Shining Trumpets: A History of Jazz*. 2d rev. ed., New York, 1958.
Collier, James Lincoln. *The Making of Jazz*. New York, 1978.
DeVeaux, Scott. *The Birth of Bebop: A Social and Musical History*. Los Angeles, 1997.
Finkelstein, Sidney. *Jazz: A People's Music*. New York, 1948.
Gioia, Ted. *The History of Jazz*. New York, 1997.
Gridley, Mark C. *Jazz Styles: History and Analysis*. 5th ed. Englewood Cliffs, NJ, 1994.
Hennessey, Thomas J. *From Jazz to Swing: African-American Musicians and Their Music, 1890–1935*. Detroit, 1994.
Hobsbawm, Eric. *The Jazz Scene*. New York, 1993.
Hobson, Wilder. *American Jazz Music*. New York, 1939.
Hodier, André. *Jazz: Its Evolution and Essence*. Rev. ed. New York, 1979.
Kernfeld, Barry. *What to Listen for in Jazz*. New Haven, 1995.
Nicholson, Stuart. *Jazz-Rock: A History*. New York, 1998.
Panassie, Hugues. *Hot Jazz: The Guide to Swing Music*. New York, 1936.
Porter, Lewis, and Michael Ullman. *Jazz From Its Origins to the Present*. Englewood Cliffs, 1993.
Sargeant, Winthrop. *Jazz: A History*. (Original title: *Jazz: Hot and Hybrid*.). New York, 1946.

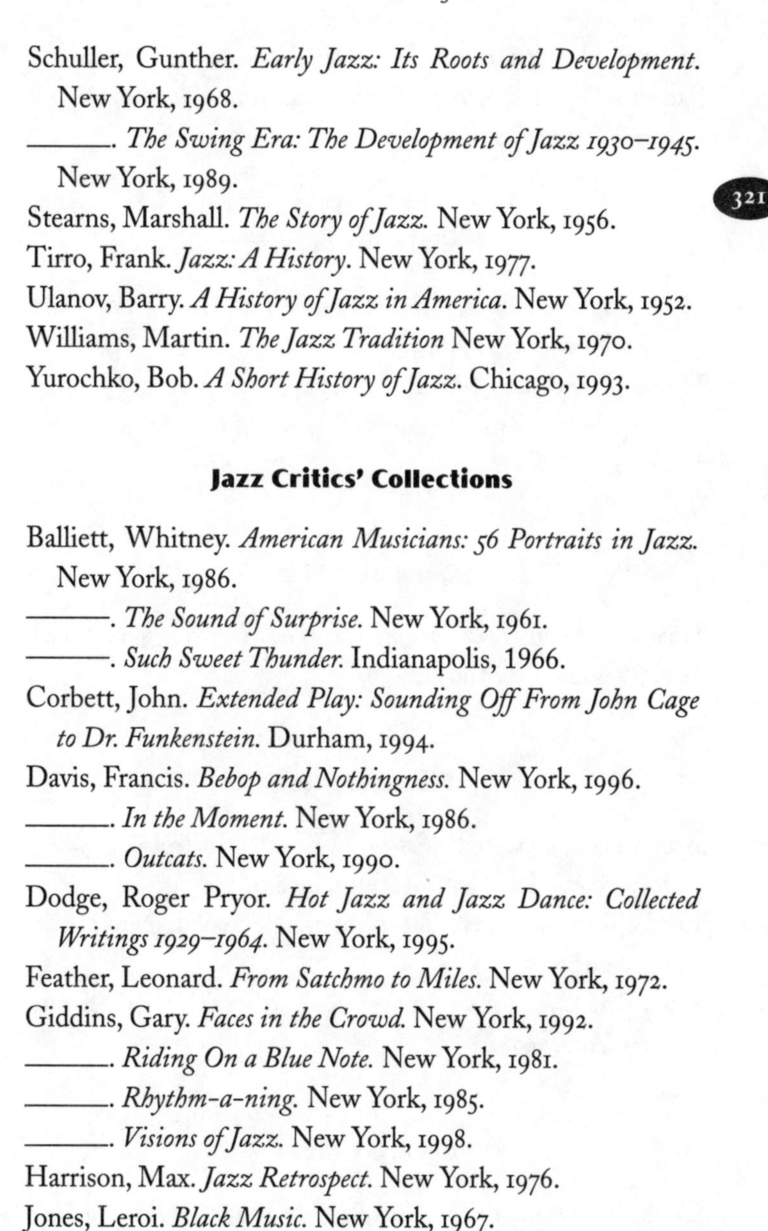

Schuller, Gunther. *Early Jazz: Its Roots and Development.* New York, 1968.

———. *The Swing Era: The Development of Jazz 1930–1945.* New York, 1989.

Stearns, Marshall. *The Story of Jazz.* New York, 1956.

Tirro, Frank. *Jazz: A History.* New York, 1977.

Ulanov, Barry. *A History of Jazz in America.* New York, 1952.

Williams, Martin. *The Jazz Tradition* New York, 1970.

Yurochko, Bob. *A Short History of Jazz.* Chicago, 1993.

Jazz Critics' Collections

Balliett, Whitney. *American Musicians: 56 Portraits in Jazz.* New York, 1986.

———. *The Sound of Surprise.* New York, 1961.

———. *Such Sweet Thunder.* Indianapolis, 1966.

Corbett, John. *Extended Play: Sounding Off From John Cage to Dr. Funkenstein.* Durham, 1994.

Davis, Francis. *Bebop and Nothingness.* New York, 1996.

———. *In the Moment.* New York, 1986.

———. *Outcats.* New York, 1990.

Dodge, Roger Pryor. *Hot Jazz and Jazz Dance: Collected Writings 1929–1964.* New York, 1995.

Feather, Leonard. *From Satchmo to Miles.* New York, 1972.

Giddins, Gary. *Faces in the Crowd.* New York, 1992.

———. *Riding On a Blue Note.* New York, 1981.

———. *Rhythm-a-ning.* New York, 1985.

———. *Visions of Jazz.* New York, 1998.

Harrison, Max. *Jazz Retrospect.* New York, 1976.

Jones, Leroi. *Black Music.* New York, 1967.

Jones, Max. *Talking Jazz.* New York, 1988.

Mandel, Howard. *Future Jazz.* New York, 1999.
Santoro, Gene. *Dancing in Your Head: Jazz, Blues, Rock, and Beyond.* New York, 1994.

Definitions of Jazz

Harrison, Max. "Jazz," in *The New Grove Gospel, Blues and Jazz.* New York, 1986, 223–35.
Hunt, David C. "Speech-Inflected Jazz/Rhythm-Dominated Jazz + Other Influences." *Jazz & Pop*, August 1970, 32–34.

Demographics

DeVeaux, Scott. *Jazz in America: Who's Listening?* National Endowment for the Arts, 1995.

Discographies

Bruyninckx, Walter. *Seventy Years of Recorded Jazz, 1917–1987.* Mechelen, Belgium, 1978–1990.
Lord, Tom. *The Jazz Discography.* Redwood, New York, 1993–2000.
Rust, Brian. *Jazz Records: 1987–1942.* 4th ed. New Rochelle, New York, 1978.

Record Guides

Cook, Rich, and Brian Morton. *The Penguin Guide to Jazz on CD.* 4th ed. New York, 1999.

Harrison, Max, Charles Fox, and Eric Thacker. *The Essential Jazz Records: Ragtime to Swing, Vol. 1*. Westport, CT, 1984.

Harrison, Max, Eric Thacker and Stuart Nicholson. *The Essential Jazz Records: Modernism to Postmodernism, Vol. 2*. London, 2000.

Kernfeld, Barry. *The Blackwell Guide to Recorded Jazz*. 2d ed. Cambridge, MA, 1995.

McCarthy, Albert, Alun Morgan, Paul Oliver, and Max Harrison. *Jazz on Record. A Critical Guide to the First 50 Years: 1917–1967*. London, 1968.

Piazza, Tom. *The Guide to Classic Recorded Jazz*. Iowa City, 1995.

Shadwick, Keith, ed. *The Gramophone Jazz Good CD Guide*. Harrow, Middlesex, U.K., 1997.

The Language of Jazz

Gold, Robert S. *Jazz Talk* (originally, *A Jazz Lexicon*). New York, 1964.

Lee, Bill. *Bill Lee's Jazz Dictionary*. New York Shattinger International Music, 1979.

Major, Clarence. *Juba to Jive: A Dictionary of African-American Slang*. New York, 1994.

The Origins of Jazz

Badger, R. Reid. "James Reese Europe and the Prehistory of Jazz." *American Music* 7 (Spring, 1989), 48–67.

Borneman, Ernest. "Jazz and the Creole Tradition." *Jazzforsching/Jazz Research* 1 (1969), 99–112.

Dodge, Roger Pryor. *Hot Jazz and Jazz Dance: Collected Writings 1929–1964*. New York, 1995.

Fiehrer, Thomas. "From Quadrille to Stomp: the Creole Origins of Jazz." *Popular Music* 10, no. 1 (1991), 21–38.

Martin, Denis-Constant. "Filiation or Innovation?: Some Hypotheses to Overcome the Dilemma of Afro-American Music's Origins." *Black Music Research Journal* 11, no. 1 (Spring 1991), 19–38.

Oliver, Paul. "That Certain Feeling: Blues and Jazz . . . in 1890?" *Popular Music* 10, no. 1 (1991), 11–19.

Szwed, John F., and Morton Marks. "The Afro-American Transformation of European Set Dances and Dance Suites." *Dance Research Journal* 20, no. 1 (Summer 1988), 29–36.

Tagg, Philip. " 'Black Music,' 'Afro-American Music' and 'European Music.' " *Popular Music* 8 no. 3 (October 1989), 258–98.

van der Merwe, Peter. *Origins of the Popular Style: The Antecedents of Twentieth-Century Popular Music*. New York, 1989.

Race and Music

Gubar, Susan. *Racechanges: White Skin, Black Face in American Culture*. New York, 1997.

Jones, LeRoi. *Blues People: Negro Music in White America*. New York, 1963.

Monson, Ingrid. *Saying Something: Jazz Improvisation and Interaction*. Chicago, 1996.

Rogin, Michael. *Blackface, White Noise: Jewish Immigrants in the Hollywood Melting Pot*. Berkeley, CA, 1996.

Ross, Andrew. "Hip, and the Long Front of Color," in *No Respect: Intellectuals & Popular Culture*. New York, 1989.

Szwed, John F. "Race and the Embodiment of Culture." *Ethnicity* 2, no. 1 (1975), 19–33. Reprinted in *The Body as a Medium of Expression*, J. Benthall and T. R. Polhemus, eds. London and New York, 1975.

Gender and Music

Dahl, Linda. *Stormy Weather: The Music and Lives of a Century of Jazzwomen*. New York, 1984.

Gill, John. *Queer Noises: Male and Female Homosexuality in Twentieth-Century Music*. Minneapolis, 1995.

Gourse, Leslie. *Madame Jazz*. New York, 1997..

Wilmer, Val. *Mama Said There'd be Days Like This: My Life in the Jazz World*. London, 1989.

Improvisation

Alperson, Philip. "On Musical Improvisation." *The Journal of Aesthetics and Art Criticism* 43, no. 1 (Fall 1984), 17–29.

Bailey, Derek. *Improvisation: Its Nature and Practice in Music*. London, 1992.

Berliner, Paul F. *Thinking in Jazz: The Infinite Art of Improvisation*. Chicago, 1994.

The Reception of Jazz in the United States

Broyard, Anatole. " 'Keep Cool, Man': The Negro Rejection of Jazz." *Commentary* 2, no. 4 (April 1951), 359–62.

Collier, James Lincoln. "The Faking of Jazz." *The New Republic*, 18 November 1985, 33–40.

DeVeaux, Scott. "The Emergence of the Jazz Concert, 1935–1945." *American Music*, 7 (1989), 6–29.

Douglas, Ann. *Terrible Honesty: Mongrel Manhattan in the 1920s*. New York, 1995, 387–433.

Dupree, Mary Herron. " 'Jazz,' the Critics, and American Art Music in the 1920s." *American Music* 4, no. 3 (Fall 1986), 287–301.

Gendron, Bernard. "A Short Stay in the Sun: The Reception of Bebop." *Library Chronicle* 24, no. 1 (1994), 137–59.

Leonard, Neil. *Jazz and the White Americans*. Chicago, 1962.

Levine, Lawrence W. "Jazz and American Culture," in *The Unpredictable Past*. New York, 1993.

Moore, Mcdonald Smith. *Yankee Blues: Musical Culture and American Identity*. Bloomington, 1985.

Ostransky, Leroy. *Jazz City: The Impact of Our Cities on the Development of Jazz*. Englewood Cliffs, NJ, 1978.

Peretti, Burton. *The Creation of Jazz*. Urbana, IL, 1992.

———. *Jazz in American Culture*. Chicago, 1997.

Radano, Ronald. "Hot Fantasies: American Modernism and the Idea of Black Rhythm." *Music and the Racial Imagination*, Philip Bohlman and Ronald Radano, eds. Chicago, 1997.

Stowe, David W. *Swing Changes: Big-Band Jazz in New Deal America*. Cambridge, MA, 1994.

The Reception of Jazz Abroad

Collier, James Lincoln. *The Reception of Jazz in America: A New View*. Brooklyn, 1988.

———. "La France Decouvre le Jazz," special issue of *Jazz Magazine* (Paris) 325 (January 1984).

Gendron, Bernard. "Jamming at Le Boeuf: Jazz and the Paris Avant-Garde." *Discourse* 12, no. 1 (Fall–Winter 1989–1990), 3–27.

Godbolt, Jim. *A History of Jazz in Britain 1919–50*. London, 1984.

———. *A History of Jazz in Britain 1950–70*. London, 1989.

Goddard, Chris. *Jazz Away from Home*. London, 1979.

Kator, Michael H. *Different Drummers: Jazz in the Culture of Nazi Germany*. New York, 1992.

Kenney, William H., III. "Le Hot: The Assimilation of American Jazz in France, 1917–1940." *American Studies* 25, no. 1 (1984), 5–24.

Leiris, Michel. "Jazz." *Sulfur* 15 (1986), 97–104.

Rye, Howard. "Fearsome Means of Discord: Early Encounters with Black Jazz." *Black Music in Britain*, Paul Oliver, ed. Philadelphia, 1990.

Starr, S. Frederick. *Red & Hot: The Fate of Jazz in the Soviet Union*. New York, 1983.

Szwed, John F. "Afro Blue: Improvising Under Apartheid." *Village Voice*. 25 August 1987, Jazz Special Section, 11–12.

———. "World Views Collide: The History of Jazz and Hot Dance." *Village Voice*, 25 February 1986, 73–4.

Zwerin, Mike. *La Tristesse de Saint Louis: Swing Under the Nazis*. London, 1985.

Jazz and Dance

Banes, Sally, and John F. Szwed. "From 'Messin' Around' to 'Funky Western Civilization': The Rise and Fall of Dance

Instruction Songs." *New Formations* 27 (Winter 1995–96), 59–79.

Dodge, Roger Pryor. *Hot Jazz and Jazz Dance: Collected Writings 1929–1964*. New York, 1995.

Emery, Lynne Fauley. *Black Dance from 1619 to Today*. Princeton, NJ, 1988.

Hazzard-Gordon, Katrina. *Jookin': The Rise of Social Dance Formations in American Culture*. Philadelphia, 1990.

Kurath, Gertrude P., and Nadia Chilkovsky. " Jazz Choreology." *Men and Culture*, Anthony Wallace, ed., 152–59.

Malone, Jacqui. *Steppin' on the Blues: The Visible Rhythms of African American Dance*. Urbana, IL, 1996.

Stearns, Marshall and Jean. *Jazz Dance*. New York, 1968.

Szwed, John F., and Morton Marks. "The Afro-American Transformation of European Set Dances and Dance Suites." *Dance Research Journal* 20, no. 1 (Summer 1988), 29–36.

Thompson, Robert Farris. "Dance and Culture, an Aesthetic of the Cool: West African Dance." *African Forum* 2, no. 2 (Fall 1966).

Jazz and the Visual Arts

Appel, Alfred, Jr. *The Art of Celebration: Twentieth-Century Painting, Literature, Sculpture, Photography, and Jazz*. New York, 1992.

Cassidy, Donna M. *Painting the Musical City: Jazz and Cultural Identity in American Art, 1910–1940*. Washington, DC, 1997.

Mandeles, Chad. "Jackson Pollack and Jazz: Structural Parallels." *Arts Magazine* (October 1981), 138–41.

Powell, Richard J. "Art History and Black Memory: Toward a 'Blues Aesthetic.' " In *History and Memory in African-American Culture*, Genevive Fabre and Robert G. O'Meally, eds. New York, 1994.
———. *Black Art and Culture in the 20th Century*. London, 1997.
———. *The Blues Aesthetic: Black Culture and Modernism*. Washington, DC, 1989.
Tower, Beeke Sell. "Jungle Music and Song of Machines: Jazz and American Dance in Weimar Culture." in *Envisioning America: Prints, Drawings, and Photographs by George Grosz and his Contemporaries, 1913–1933*. Cambridge, MA, 1990.

Jazz Photography

Abe, K., et al. *Jazz Giants*. New York, 1986.
Berendt, Joachim. Jazz: A Photo History. New York, 1978.
Brask, Ole, and Dan Morgenstern. *Jazz People*. New York, 1976.
Carner, Gary. "Jazz Photography: A Conversation with Herb Snitzer." *Black American Literature Forum* 25, no. 3 (Fall 1991), 561–92.
Claxton, William. *Jazz*. San Francisco, 1996 [1987].
Roy DeCarava: A Retrospective. Peter Galassi, ed. New York, 1996.
Gottlieb, William P. *The Golden Age of Jazz*. New York, 1987.
Hinton, Milt, and David G. Berger. *Bass Line: The Stories and Photos of Milt Hinton*. Philadelphia, 1988.
Keepnews, Orrin, and Bill Grauer. *A Pictorial History of Jazz*. New York, 1955.

Leonard, Herman. *Jazz Memories*. Paris, 1996.

Reiff, Carole. *Nights in Birdland 1954–1960*. New York, 1987.

Salaam, Kalamu ya. "Herman Leonard: Making Music with Light." *African American Review* 29, no. 2 (Summer 1995), 241–46.

Stewart, Charles, and Paul Carter Harrison. *Chuck Stewart's Jazz Files*. London, 1985.

Wilmer, Valerie. *The Face of Black Music*. New York, 1976.

Album Cover Art

ECM. *Sleeves of Desire: A Cover Story*. Baden, Switzerland, 1966.

Gachter, Sven. "Kleine semiotik des covers," *Du* no. 8 (August 1989), 68–69 (Miles Davis covers).

Ochs, Michael. *1000 Record Covers*. Köln, 1996.

O'Meally, Robert. "Jazz Albums as Art: Some Reflections." *International Review of African American Art* 14, no. 3 (1997), 39–47.

Thorgerson, Storm, and Roger Dean, eds. *Album Cover Album*. Surrey, U.K., 1977.

Jazz and Film

Carby, Hazel V. "In Body and Spirit: Representing Black Women Musicians." *Black Music Research Journal* 11, no. 2 (1991), 177–92.

Gabbard, Krin. *Jammin' at the Margins: Jazz and the American Cinema*. Chicago, 1996.

Klotman, Phyllis. *Frame by Frame: A Black Filmography*. Bloomington, IN, 1979.

Klotman, Phyllis, and Gloria J. Gibson. *Frame by Frame II: A Filmography of the African American Image, 1978–1994*. Bloomington, IN, 1997.

Meeker, David. *Jazz in the Movies*. Enlarged ed. New York, 1981.

Rogin, Michael. *Blackface, White Noise: Jewish Immigrants in the Hollywood Melting Pot*. Berkeley, CA, 1996, 73–120.

Jazz Autobiography, Biography and Oral History

Daniels, Douglas Henry. "Oral History, Masks, and Protocol in the Jazz Community." *Oral History Review* 15 (1987), 143–64.

Kenny, William H., III. "Negotiating the Color Line: Louis Armstrong's Autobiographies." *Jazz in Mind*, Reginald T. Buckner and Steve Weiland, eds. Detroit, 1991, 38–59.

Ogren, Kathy. " 'Jazz Isn't Just Me': Jazz Autobiographies as Performance Personas." *Jazz in Mind*, Reginald T. Buckner and Steve Weiland, eds. Detroit, 1991, 112–27.

Stone, Albert E. "Two Recreate One: The Act of Collaboration in Recent Black Autobiography." *REAL* 1, no. 1 (1982), 227–66.

Sudhalter, Richard. "What's Your Story, Mornin' Glory?: Reflections on Some Jazz Autobiography." *Annual Review of Jazz Studies* 5 (1991), 210–16.

Tomlinson, Gary. "Cultural Dialogics and Jazz: A White Historian Signifies." *Black Music Research Journal* 11, no. 2 (1991), 229–63.

Wilburn, Ron. "Toward Theory and Method with the Oral History Project." *Black Music Research Journal* (1986), 79–95.

Jazz Autobiographies and Biographies: A Sampling

Armstrong, Louis. *Satchmo*. New York, 1954.

Baker, Chet. *As Though I Had Wings*. New York, 1997.

Bechet, Sidney. *Treat It Gentle*. New York, 1960.

Bergreen, Lawrence. *Louis Armstrong*. New York, 1997.

Bernhardt, Clyde. *I Remember*. Philadelphia, 1986.

Berrett, Joshua, and Louis G. Bourgois III. *The Musical World of J.J. Johnson*. Lanham, MD, 1999.

Berton, Ralph. *Remembering Bix*. New Rochelle, NY, 1974.

Carr, Ian. *Keith Jarrett: The Man and his Music*. New York, 1991.

———. *Miles Davis: The Definitive Biography*. London, 1999.

Catalano, Nick. *Clifford Brown: The Life and Art of the Legendary Jazz Trumpeter*. New York, 2000.

Chambers, Jack. *Milestones*. Rev. ed. 1998.

Chilton, John. *Billie's Blues*. New York, 1975.

———. *Sidney Bechet*. New York, 1987.

———. *Song of the Hawk* [Coleman Hawkins], 1990.

Clarke, Donald. *Wishing On the Moon* (Billie Holiday). New York, 1994.

Collier, James Lincoln. *Benny Goodman and the Swing Era*. New York, 1989.

———. *Duke Ellington*. New York, 1982.

———. *Louis Armstrong: An American Genius*. New York, 1983.

Davis, Miles, with Quincy Troupe. *Miles Davis: The Autobiography*. New York, 1989.

Giddins, Gary. *Satchmo*. New York, 1988.

Gillespie, Dizzy, and Al Frazier. *To Be or Not to Bop*. New York, 1979.

Gourse, Leslie. *Straight No Chaser* (Monk). New York, 1997.

Hajdu, Davis. *Lush Life* (Billy Strayhorn). New York, 1996.

Holiday, Billie, and William Duffy. *Lady Sings the Blues*. New York, 1956.

Irwin, Lew. *The Importance of Being Eric Dolphy*. Tunbridge Wells, UK, 1989.

Kruth, John. *Bright Moments: The Life & Legacy of Rahsaan Roland Kirk*. New York, 2000.

Levinson, Peter J. *Trumpet Blues: The Life of Harry James*. New York, 1999.

Litweiler, John. *Ornette Coleman: The Harmolodic Life*. New York, 1992.

Lomax, Alan. *Mr. Jelly Roll*. New York, 1952.

McPartland, Marian. *All in Good Time*. New York, 1987.

Milkowski, Bill. *Jaco*. New York, 1995.

Mingus, Charles. *Beneath the Underdog*. New York, 1971.

Nicholson, Stuart. *Billie Holiday*. Boston, 1995.

O'Meally, Robert. *The Many Faces of Billie Holiday*. New York, 1991.

Pepper, Art. *Straight Life*. New York, 1979.

Porter, Lewis. *John Coltrane*. 1998.

Russell, William, ed. *"Oh, Mister Jelly": A Jelly Roll Morton Scrapbook*. Copenhagen, 1999.

Shipton, Alyn. *Groovin' High: The Life of Dizzy Gillespie*. New York, 1999.

Stewart, Rex. *Boy Meets Horn*. New York, 1991.

Szwed, John F. *Space Is the Place: The Lives and Times of Sun Ra*. New York, 1997.

Jazz and Poetry: Anthologies

Algarin, Miguel, and Bob Holman, eds. *Aloud: Voices from the Nuyorican Poets Cafe.* New York, 1994.

Feinstein, Sascha, and Yusef Komunyakaa, eds. *The Jazz Poetry Anthology.* Bloomington, IN, 1991.

———. *The Jazz Poetry Anthology, The Second Set, Vol. 2.* Bloomington, IN, 1996.

Lange, Art, and Nathaniel Mackey, eds. *Moments' Notice: Jazz in Poetry and Prose.* Minneapolis, 1993.

Parker, Chris, ed. *B Flat, Bebop, Scat.* London, 1986.

Jazz and Poetry: Criticism

Adams, Hazzard, and Bruce R. Park. "The State of the Jazz Lyric." *Chicago Review* 10, no. 3 (1956), 5–20.

Creeley, Robert. *The Collected Essays of Robert Creeley.* Berkeley, CA, 1989.

Feinstein, Sascha. *A Bibliographic Guide to Jazz Poetry.* Westport, CT, 1998.

"A Forum on the Prosody of Thelonious Monk." *Caliban* 4 (1988), 35–79.

Freedman, Morris. "Jazz Rhythm and T.S. Eliot." *South Atlantic Quarterly* 51 (1952), 419–35.

Ginsberg, Allen. *Composed on the Tongue.* San Francisco, 1980.

———. *Howl: Original Draft Facsimile.* New York, 1986.

Harris, William J. *The Poetry and Poetics of Amiri Baraka: The Jazz Aesthetic.* Columbia, MO, 1983.

Hartman, Charles O. *Jazz Text: Voice and Improvisation in Poetry, Jazz, and Song.* Princeton, 1991.

Henderson, Stephen, ed. *Understanding the New Black Poetry*. New York, 1973.

Johnson, Charles S. "Jazz Poetry and Blues." *Carolina Magazine* (May 1928), 16–20.

Komunyakaa, Yusef, and William Matthews. "Jazz & Poetry: A Conversation." *Georgia Review* 146, no. 4 (1992), 645–61.

Lenz, Günter H. "The Politics of Black Music and the Tradition of Poetry: Amiri Baraka and John Coltrane." *Jazzforshung/Jazz Research* 18 (1986), 193–231.

Mackey, Nathaniel. "The Changing Same: Black Music in the Poetry of Amiri Baraka." *Boundary* 2, no. 6 (1978), 355–86.

"Michael Harper and John Coltrane." *History and Tradition in Afro-American Culture*, Günter H. Lenz, ed. Frankfurt, 1984, 277–326.

Nielsen, Aldon Lynn. *Black Chant: Languages of African-American Modernism*. Cambridge, MA, 1997.

Smith, D. Newton. "The Influence of Music on the Black Mountain Poets: I." *St. Andrews Review* 3, no. 1 (1974), 99–115.

Thomas, Lorenzo. " 'Communicating By Horns': Jazz and Redemption in the Poetry of the Beats and the Black Arts Movement." *African American Review* 26 (1992), 291–98.

Tracy, Steven C. *Langston Hughes and the Blues*. Urbana, IL, 1988.

Wallerstein, Barry. "Poetry and Jazz: A Twentieth-Century Wedding." *Black American Literature Forum* 25, no. 3 (1991), 595–620.

———. "Jazz Poetry/jazz-poetry/'jazz poetry' " *African American Review* 27, no. 4 (1993), 665–71.

Jazz Drama and Fiction: Anthologies and Bibliographies

Albert, Richard N. *An Annotated Bibliography of Jazz Fiction and Jazz Fiction Criticism.* Westport, CT, 1996.

Albert, Richard N., ed. *From Blues to Bop: A Collection of Jazz Fiction.* Baton Rouge, 1990.

Breton, Marcela, ed. *Hot and Cool: Jazz Short Stories.* New York, 1990.

Lange, Art, and Nathaniel Mackey, eds. *Moment's Notice: Jazz in Poetry and Prose.* Minneapolis, 1993.

Parker, Chris, ed. *B Flat, Bebop, Scat.* London, 1986.

Jazz Drama and Fiction: Criticism

Albert, Richard N. *An Annotated Bibliography of Jazz Fiction and Jazz Fiction Criticism.* Westport, CT, 1996.

Berry, Jason. "Jazz Literature." *Southern Exposure* 6, no. 3 (Fall 1968), 40–49.

Burns, Jim. "Kerouac and Jazz." *The Review of Contemporary Fiction* 3, no. 2 (Summer 1983), 33–41.

Cataliotti, Robert H. *The Music in African American Fiction.* New York, 1995.

Mansell, Darrel. "The Jazz History of the World in The Great Gatsby." *English Language Notes* 25, no. 2 (December 1987), 57–62.

Meisel, Perry. *The Cowboy and the Dandy: Crossing Over from Romanticism to Rock and Roll.* New York, 1998.

Neal, Larry. "Ellison's Zoot Suit." *Black World*, 20, no. 2 (December 1970), 31–50. Reprinted *in Ralph Ellison: A*

Collection of Critical Essays, John Hersey, ed. Englewood Cliffs, NJ, 1974.

Panish, Jon. *The Color of Jazz: Race and Representation in Postwar American Culture.* Jackson, MS, 1997.

Szwed, John F. "Josef Škvorecký and the Tradition of Jazz Literature." *World Literature Today* 54 (1980), 586–90.

Tallman, Warren. "Kerouac's Sound." *Evergreen Review* (Jan–Feb 1960), 153–69. Reprinted in *A Casebook on the Beats*, Thomas Parkinson, ed., New York, 1961.

Weinstein, Regina. *The Spontaneous Poetics of Jack Kerouac.* Carbondale, IL, 1987.

Werner, Craig Hansen. *Playing the Changes: From Afro-Modernism to the Jazz Impulse.* Urbana, IL, 1994.

Wilkerson, Margaret B. "Music as Metaphor: New Plays of Black Women" in *Making a Spectacle: Feminist Essays on Contemporary Woman's Theatre*, Lynda Hunt, ed. Ann Arbor, MI, 1989.

Young, Al, Larry Kart, Michael S. Harper. "Jazz and Letters: A Colloquy." *Tri-Quarterly*, no. 68 (Winter 1987), 118–58.

Appendix 6: Records by Mail

Most chain record stores at best carry only a small fraction of the jazz available on record in the United States. On top of this, European and Japanese record companies now rival American companies in the production of jazz records, but not all of them are distributed here. All of this to say that the Internet and mail order have assumed new importance in jazz.

Mail Order

Cadence Records
Cadence Building
Redwood, NY 13679-9612
A principal source for jazz. Their catalog is printed every month in *Cadence* magazine.

Mosaic Records
35 Melrose Place
Stanford, CT 06902
(203) 327-7111
For reissues of records not available elsewhere.

Smithsonian Performing Arts
1-800-863-9943 or www.si.edu/youandsi/products
Sells the Smithsonian Collection of Classic Jazz, the best overall overview of jazz available on record LP, CD or cassette, with book.

Roots and Rhythm
6921 Stockton Ave.
El Cerrito, CA 94530
(510) 614-5353
Outstanding source for blues, country, early rock, and some jazz.

Fantasy
2600 10th St.
Berkeley, CA 94710-9887
(510) 549-2500
Contemporary, Fantasy, Landmark, Milestone, Pablo, Prestige, Riverside, and Galaxy labels; keeps LPs in print.

Auction

Leon Leavitt
P.O. Box 38395
Los Angeles, CA 90038

G's Jazz Inc.
P.O. Box 259164
Madison, WI 53725-9164

Mole Jazz
311 Gray's Inn Road
WC1X 8PX
London, England
or www.molejazz.co.uk

Appendix 7: Current Reading

Some Jazz Magazines in English

Down Beat
Coda (Canada)
The Wire (UK)
Jazz Journal International (UK)
Cadence
Jazziz
JazzTimes

Jazz Reviews

Reviews or even mentions of jazz recordings and musicians are almost completely absent from American newspapers and magazines, but the daily and Sunday *New York Times* usually have something, and *The Nation*, *Village Voice*, and *Atlantic Monthly* run occasional columns.

Index